# New International

## A MAGAZINE OF MARXIST POLITICS AND THEORY

**NUMBER 7, 1991**

W9-BWR-262

# *Contents*

EDITOR Mary-Alice Waters

MANAGING EDITOR Steve Clark

PRODUCTION MANAGER Michael Baumann

BUSINESS MANAGER Cindy Jaquith

CONTRIBUTING EDITORS Jack Barnes, Sigurlaug Gunnlaugsdóttir,
Carl-Erik Isacsson, Russell Johnson, Nat London,
Steve Penner, Ron Poulsen, Samad Sharif,
Jonathan Silberman, James Mac Warren


**New International** is edited in collaboration with
**Nouvelle Internationale**, Michel Prairie, editor, and
**Nueva Internacional**, Luis Madrid, editor.
*Many of the articles that appear here in English are also available in
French and Spanish. All three publications are available from
New International, 410 West St., New York, NY 10014.*

Cover photograph: J. Langevin/Sygma
Cover and design by Toni Gorton

*New International* is distributed internationally by Pathfinder Press:
Australia (and Asia and the Pacific):
   Pathfinder, 19 Terry St., Surry Hills, Sydney, NSW 2010
Britain (and Europe, Africa, and the Middle East):
   Pathfinder, 47 The Cut, London, SE1 8LL
Canada:
   Pathfinder, 6566, boul. St-Laurent, Montréal, Québec, H2S 3C6
Iceland:
   Pathfinder, Klapparstíg 26, 2d floor, 121 Reykjavík
New Zealand:
   Pathfinder, 157a Symonds Street, Auckland
Sweden:
   Pathfinder, Vikingagatan 10, S-113 42, Stockholm
United States (and Caribbean and Latin America):
   Pathfinder, 410 West Street, New York, NY 10014

# IN THIS ISSUE

THE SIX-WEEK BOMBARDMENT and one-hundred-hour invasion of Iraq by Washington and its allies devastated the country and its peoples. In a land that had been semi-industrialized, the assault left millions homeless, hungry, and vulnerable to disease. It was one of the most massive, cold-blooded slaughters in modern history. Economic dislocation now stalks Turkey as well as Kuwait and Jordan, coming down hardest on the toilers. Environmental catastrophe has been spread even further. In addition, the strangulation of Iraq through economic blockade, now entering its tenth month, prevents even medicine, foodstuffs, and agricultural implements from being imported. Acute malnutrition, along with cholera and other epidemic horrors, are beginning to threaten the region.

Washington launched its war drive in early August 1990 with an air, sea, and ground blockade. The initial ships and aircraft as well as the first troops and war matériel were dispatched to the Arabian Peninsula and surrounding waters. In a little more than six months, these became a half-million-strong mechanized and armored invasion force. The U.S. rulers' goal was to impose a virtual protectorate in Baghdad, a reliable regime subservient to U.S. imperialism; secure greater control over oil reserves in the Gulf; shift the relationship of forces against the region's toilers, especially the Palestinian people whose *intifada* and internationalist dignity remain the biggest thorn in Washington's side; and in the process stabilize and strengthen pro-U.S. regimes in the region. In pursuing these aims, the U.S. capitalist class sought to use its military might to deal economic and political blows to its imperialist rivals in Europe and Japan.

Far from the stunning war victory proclaimed by President

George Bush on February 27, however, the massive U.S. armored invasion force did not fight a war at all. Instead, allied imperialist forces on the land and from the air and sea conducted a militarized slaughter of tens of thousands of individual Iraqis—workers and peasants in tattered uniforms—attempting to flee Kuwait and return to Iraq. The Saddam Hussein regime had abandoned them in foxholes and trenches without air cover, stripped of all but a skeletal command structure, with minimal communications and few provisions. Despite its grab to control oil, land, and waterways in Kuwait, Baghdad never intended to fight a war against U.S. imperialism.

Nor has Washington achieved its political aims in the region. The capitalist regimes and imperialist order in the Gulf and Mideast are more unstable today than before August 1990. The imposition of a "solution" to the Palestinian "question" short of justice for the Palestinians continues to evade the imperialists. Far from becoming closer and warmer, the U.S. and Israeli rulers continue to diverge in their policy interests. Washington has failed so far to oust Saddam Hussein and impose a regime more to its liking. Growing numbers of working people in the United States are questioning the purpose of a war that, as they are now learning, destroyed the Iraqi people's modern means of life support and culminated in two massacres: one in late February against defenseless Iraqi soldiers fleeing Kuwait—carried out by Washington and its allies, with the complicity of Baghdad; the other, in March, against the Kurds and Shiites in northern and southern Iraq—carried out by Baghdad with the complicity of Washington.

The U.S. government stands guilty before the world for making refugees of some two million Kurds and others who fled Baghdad's murderous assault. But Washington and its allies have refused to open their borders to the Kurds and other refugees seeking asylum.

Having won a military "victory," U.S. imperialism is breaking its teeth in the attempt to achieve its political goals. This outcome has opened wide tactical divisions within U.S. ruling circles over the Bush administration's policy decisions in the Gulf. The "Vietnam syndrome" has been reinforced, not pushed back as Bush initially boasted at the end of February. It will be slightly harder, not easier, for the U.S. rulers to mobilize public support

for their next military adventure. It will be slightly more difficult for union bureaucrats and other misleaders, echoing the
wishes of the government and corporations, to get away with
demanding that working people and the oppressed accept sacrifices, defer strikes, or postpone protest actions for patriotic
reasons. More political space can be taken—right now—by
working-class opponents of imperialism and war.

The war and its immediate consequences did not resolve, but
rather exacerbated the economic and political contradictions in
the United States and worldwide that increasingly drove Washington to use its military might in the first place. The war
accelerated the rivalry between Washington and other imperialist powers and increased the likelihood of sharpening conflicts
among them. Neither the German nor Japanese imperialist
ruling classes were politically able to send units to participate in
the allied assault. For the first time since the buildup to World
War II, however, the war in the Gulf put Bonn and Tokyo on an
accelerated course toward using their military forces abroad to
advance their respective state interests.

WORKING PEOPLE around the world today face an unstable
prewar situation, not a stabilized postwar period. Washington's
assault on Iraq was the first of the wars that will mark the
segment of the historic curve of capitalist development announced by the October 1987 crash of stock markets from New
York to Tokyo, from Bonn to Hong Kong. Capitalism today is
marching not only toward more wars but at the same time
stumbling toward a depression and world social crisis. We will
see deepening capitalist economic dislocation within which a
partial shock or breakdown—a collapse of the banking system,
a steep recession in a major industrial country, an inflationary
explosion, a massive crop failure—could trigger a collapse of
world industrial production.

With no end in sight, fear is growing that the recession in
North America, Britain, France, New Zealand, and Australia
could become both as deep as the 1981-82 downturn (or
deeper) and worldwide in scope, as happened in 1974-75. It is
precipitating the kind of pressures on capitalist profits that

further intensify interimperialist competition. As a result, the employers will try to take more out of the hides of the hundreds of millions of debt slaves in the semicolonial world. They will drive harder at home to lower living standards and step up the pace and intensity of production inside mines, mills, and factories. They will extend their efforts to chip away at rights and democratic liberties and seek to weaken and restrict the space open to the working class and its organizations for independent political action.

Washington's war against Iraq was thus an announcement, a loud and clear one, of the conflicts that lie ahead as the imperialist rulers follow the historic logic of their declining world system of exploitation and oppression—a line of march that, willy-nilly, moves toward World War III.

For working people the world over, for vanguard working-class fighters, and for that section of the working-class vanguard who are communists, these political assessments are decisive in charting a course to advance the historic line of march of *our* class. The future of humanity depends on the independent political organization of the world's toilers to resist the devastation the rulers seek to impose on us. It depends on our capacity to fight, to win revolutionary battles, and to take war-making powers out of the hands of the exploiters and oppressors by establishing governments of the workers and farmers. Whether or not the unthinkable horrors of a third imperialist world slaughter are unleashed will be decided by mighty class battles and their outcome in the coming years. It is in our hands, the hands of the workers of the world, to prevent the calamities that imperialism is marching, and stumbling, toward. We will have our chance.

These, in brief, are the central political conclusions of the two opening articles in this issue of *New International*.

WASHINGTON'S Mideast war tested all those who call themselves socialists and claim to speak in the interests of the working class and its allies. It tested all those who claim to act, unconditionally and unflinchingly, against the horrors of imperialist war.

In 1990, as the logical culmination of Washington's war drive became inescapable, the Socialist Workers Party—its elected leadership bodies, party branches, fractions of members in industrial unions, and its supporters—began *campaigning* against imperialism and war. Members and supporters of the SWP—together with those of its sister Communist Leagues in Australia, Britain, Canada, France, Iceland, New Zealand, and Sweden—campaigned to get out the truth to co-workers, strikers and other unionists, high school and college students, GIs and reservists, farmers, and others about why we should oppose the assault on Iraq by Washington and its allies. They collaborated with members of the Young Socialist Alliance to rebut the U.S. rulers' lies and pretexts and to explain the imperialist roots and goals of the war drive. They joined with others to build antiwar street actions, as well as teach-ins and other forums to discuss the war and the stakes for working people. They sold thousands of copies of *U.S. Hands Off the Mideast! Cuba Speaks Out at the United Nations.* This book, published by Pathfinder Press in English and Spanish, documents each step of the calculated escalation of Washington's war preparations and refutes imperialism's lies.

The first two articles in this issue—"The Opening Guns of World War III" and "The Working-Class Campaign against Imperialism and War"—are based on talks presented by SWP national secretary Jack Barnes as part of this campaign. The public forums at which Barnes spoke were held in connection with national meetings of party members and supporters who are members of one of ten industrial unions: the Amalgamated Clothing and Textile Workers Union; International Association of Machinists; International Ladies' Garment Workers' Union; International Union of Electronic Workers; Oil, Chemical and Atomic Workers; United Auto Workers; United Food and Commercial Workers; United Mine Workers; United Steelworkers; and the United Transportation Union.

The first article is based on a speech given at a fund-raising meeting for *New International,* hosted by the Militant Labor Forum in Cleveland, Ohio, in March 1991, following the cessation of offensive operations by the Bush administration. In editing it for publication, political developments in the month following have been incorporated by the author.

The second article is drawn from talks given in late November and early December at meetings hosted by the Militant Labor Forum in Washington, D.C., and in New York City. It was initially published in December 1990 by the *Militant* newsweekly in its *International Socialist Review* supplement. Thousands of copies of that supplement have been sold since, together with subscriptions and single issues of the *Militant*. The article by Barnes is reprinted here without revision or political updating. Notes have been added by *New International*.

Both articles incorporate material from the discussion periods at each forum, free-speech exchanges where workers, students, socialist candidates for public office, and other participants advanced their points of view and asked questions about the U.S. rulers' justifications for the war drive and the broader conjuncture in world politics. Both articles were also discussed, and their general line adopted, at meetings of the party's National Committee, trade union leadership, and international co-thinkers.

The second section of this issue, "Communists Don't Have a Revolutionary Policy in Peacetime and a Peace Policy in Wartime," documents the political evaluation and tactical response by the vanguard of the working class to Washington's three militarization drives over the past fifty years—the drive from 1937 through the end of World War II; the drive from 1947 to the defeat of U.S. imperialism in the Vietnam War; and the opening of the drive that began in the early 1980s during the administration of James Carter. The section contains "Washington's Third Militarization Drive," by SWP leader and *New International* editor Mary-Alice Waters, excerpts of a resolution on the fight against the Vietnam War adopted by the 1969 convention of the SWP, and an article by Waters, "1945: When U.S. Troops Said 'No!'" that tells the hidden history of the mass protests by GIs overseas at the end of World War II demanding to be brought home.

The third section is entitled "Communism, the Working

Class, and Anti-Imperialist Struggle: Lessons from the Iran-Iraq War." The August 2, 1990, invasion of Kuwait by Saddam Hussein's military forces flowed from the same trajectory that previously had impelled the Baghdad Baathist regime to launch a bloody eight-year-long war against Iran. The toilers of Iraq had no communist vanguard that voiced their class interests and pointed the way forward in solidarity with their brothers and sisters in Iran. The nucleus of an internationalist, communist leadership did exist in Iran, however, at the time Baghdad launched its counterrevolutionary war in the early 1980s. Resolutions of this communist organization in 1980 and 1982, reprinted here with an introduction by Samad Sharif, who helped lead this work in Iran, are of lasting political value to revolutionists, anti-imperialist fighters, and communists everywhere.

❖

PUBLISHED simultaneously with this special issue on campaigning against imperialism and war, *New International* no. 8 is devoted to articles on "Che Guevara, Cuba, and the Road to Socialism." *New International* no. 9, scheduled for publication in the fall of 1991, will focus on the foundations of the world political and economic situation and the tasks of building proletarian parties. It will contain the fundamental documents on world politics and political economy that have been discussed and adopted by conventions and leadership bodies of the Socialist Workers Party and other communist organizations around the world since 1988.[1]

The first three issues of the Spanish-language magazine *Nueva Internacional,* scheduled for publication this year, will have the same contents as these three 1991 issues of *New International.* Issue nos. 4 and 5 of *Nouvelle Internationale,* containing much of the same material in French translation, will also be published in 1991.

Issue nos. 1-6 of *New International,* which appeared between

*ENDNOTES FOR THIS ARTICLE BEGIN ON PAGE 14.*

1983 and 1987, were published under the editorial direction of leaders of the two communist organizations in North America—the Socialist Workers Party in the United States and the Communist League (formerly Revolutionary Workers League) in Canada. Leaders of these two organizations have also taken editorial responsibility for *New International*'s French-language sister publication, *Nouvelle Internationale*, three issues of which have appeared since its launching in August 1985.

THE CONTRIBUTING editors for this seventh issue of the magazine register the broadening editorial participation and support for *New International*. Since 1987 revolutionary workers' organizations in several countries have made substantial advances in organized political collaboration on common work to prepare an international communist movement. These organizations include Communist Leagues in Australia, Britain, Canada, Iceland, New Zealand, and Sweden; the Communist Organizing Committee of France; and the Socialist Workers Party of the United States.

Beginning with this issue, officers and central leaders of these organizations make up the contributing editors of *New International*. They are: Jack Barnes, Sigurlaug Gunnlaugsdóttir, Carl-Erik Isacsson, Russell Johnson, Nat London, Steve Penner, Ron Poulsen, Samad Sharif, Jonathan Silberman, and James Mac Warren. These individuals are also contributing editors to *Nouvelle Internationale* and *Nueva Internacional*.

At the time *New International* was launched in 1983, the members of its editorial board belonged to communist parties that were affiliated to the Fourth International and had considered themselves Trotskyist. The Socialist Workers Party had fraternal ties to the Fourth International, and the Communist League was the statutory section in Canada. Both parties had been associated with the Fourth International since it was founded under the guidance of Leon Trotsky in 1938 to regroup revolutionists who were continuing the communist policies of the Bolshevik Party and Communist International under the leadership of V.I. Lenin. The communist forces that made up the Fourth International had refused to capitulate to the counterrevolutionary politics and police-state terrorism that, by the opening years of the 1930s, had become consolidated in the Stalinized government and party in the Soviet Union and in the Communist International. Trotsky was assassinated by an agent of Stalin's murder machine in 1940 at the opening of the second world imperialist slaughter.

Following World War II, the Socialist Workers Party and its proletarian traditions soon became a minority current within the Fourth International. For more than three decades, public differences were numerous and profound, documented in the pages of the *Militant, International Socialist Review,* and the international newsweekly *Intercontinental Press,* which ceased publication in 1986. From 1979 on, however, accelerating divergences marked the course and character, on the one hand, of the SWP, the Communist League in Canada, and others, and, on the other hand, the leadership bodies of the Fourth International. These differences centered above all on a political assessment of the revolutionary victories in Grenada and Nicaragua, and the character of the workers' and farmers' governments established through those victories; the historical importance and weight of the communist leadership in Cuba and its political trajectory; and the necessity for communist forces the world over to decisively turn toward building parties that are proletarian in composition and leadership as well as program and perspectives.

At the end of the 1980s the Socialist Workers Party and the Communist Leagues in Australia, Britain, Canada, Iceland, New Zealand, and Sweden each decided to terminate their affiliation, whether fraternal or statutory, to the Fourth International. Through their political work, internationalist collaboration, and place within communist continuity and tradition, these parties had in reality for some time already become communist organizations that no longer considered themselves Trotskyist and were separate from the world Trotskyist movement and its various competing parties and international groupings. Leaders of these organizations recognized that any course other than formalizing this political fact could only falsely imply some parochial organizational maneuver and become an obstacle to normal relations of solidarity and collaboration among parties in the working-class movement.

The contents of the first nine issues of *New International,* beginning with its inaugural issue in the fall of 1983 featuring an article by Jack Barnes entitled "Their Trotsky and Ours: Communist Continuity Today," are the best single guide to the programmatic foundations and political trajectory of the communist organizations whose leaders now assume editorial responsibility for the *New International, Nouvelle Internationale,* and *Nueva Internacional.*[2]

In addition to the common board of contributing editors of these sister publications, the editors directly responsible for each of the magazines in the three languages collaborate closely in their editorial preparation. Mary-Alice Waters is the editor of *New International* and Steve Clark is its managing editor. Michel Prairie is the editor of *Nouvelle Internationale.* Luis Madrid is the editor of *Nueva Internacional.* The extensive translation work involved in the trilingual publication effort is done by an international team of volunteer translators, typists, proofreaders and copy editors, most of whom are employed as full-time garment workers, machinists, rail workers, packinghouse workers, miners, and in similar occupations.

Members and supporters of communist organizations around the world participate in internationally coordinated sales campaigns to sell *New International, Nouvelle Internationale,* and *Nueva Internacional* as widely as possible, together with subscriptions to the *Militant* newsweekly, the monthly Spanish-language *Perspectiva Mundial,* and the quarterly French-language *L'internationaliste.* They are also conducting a $75,000 international fund drive to make possible the publication of *New International, Nouvelle Internationale,* and *Nueva Internacional* in 1991. This work is organized by the director of business and promotions of the three publications, Cindy Jaquith. We urge our readers to contribute to this collective effort, both by volunteering your time and abilities as part of the translation team, and by giving your financial support. Your political comments on the issues raised in the pages of the magazine are more than welcome; they are solicited and encouraged.

Correspondence and contributions should be addressed to New International, 410 West St., New York, NY 10014.

❖

Numbers 7 and 8 of *New International*, issues against imperialism and war and on the political contributions of Ernesto Che Guevara, are dedicated to the men and women who, in unflinching opposition to the war drive of Washington and its allies, produced a vast arsenal of political weapons—publications that tell the truth about imperialism and war and why the interests of working people the world over are irreconcilable with those of the exploiting classes. Workers from a dozen countries translated, copyedited, designed, typeset, indexed, proofread, stripped up, printed, reprinted, cut, collated, bound, shipped, promoted, and distributed these political weapons needed by working-class fighters. At the same time, they joined in raising the money to buy the machinery, organized to maintain the computers and other machinery, and set about reconstructing the school, offices, headquarters, bookstores, and production plant—without which a working-class campaign against imperialism and war would not be sustainable.

These issues are also dedicated to the worker-bolsheviks in ten industrial unions in North America—and those like them in similar workplaces and unions from Stockholm to Paris to Christchurch, from Reykjavík to Manchester to Sydney—who took this arsenal and transformed their capacity as thinking workers to oppose imperialist war and to join with others in fights, on and off the job, against exploitation and oppression at home and abroad. They became better worker-correspondents, financed their own meetings, and began transforming the financial base of the day-to-day work of their parties. In the process, these communist workers changed themselves, their fractions, and their parties into more political, more tempered, more combat-ready, more self-confident, more disciplined, and thus a more trustworthy component of the world revolutionary movement.

May 1, 1991

# NOTES

1. *New International* no. 9 will feature documents adopted by the 1988 and 1990 conventions of the Socialist Workers Party. The two major resolutions can be obtained in draft form by writing: Socialist Workers Party National Office, 406 West St., New York, NY 10014. Please enclose $2.50 for the 1988 resolution, which concentrates on the world economic crisis; and $10.00 for the 1990 resolution, which analyzes the interplay of world politics as it unfolded at the end of the decade, taking particular note of the disintegration of Stalinist parties and regimes throughout Eastern Europe and the deepening crisis of the privileged caste in the Soviet Union. Add $2.50 for shipping and handling.

2. In addition to the articles from *New International* nos. 7-9 that will appear in French- and Spanish-language translation in forthcoming issues of *Nouvelle Internationale* and *Nueva Internacional,* a substantial number of the articles from *New International* nos. 1-6 have appeared in *Nouvelle Internationale* nos. 1-3. For information on ordering these issues of *Nouvelle Internationale,* see the advertisement elsewhere in this issue. Several of these articles have also been published in Spanish translation in the monthly *Perspectiva Mundial* and will be reprinted in more permanent form in forthcoming special issues of *Nueva Internacional.* For information on the material currently available in Spanish, write Perspectiva Mundial, 410 West St., New York, NY 10014.

# MIDDLE EAST

| COUNTRY | POPULATION (MILLIONS) | COMPOSITION | PER CAPITA GNP |
|---|---|---|---|
| BAHRAIN | 0.5 | 73% Arab (including 10% immigrants), 13% Asian, 8% Iranian, 6% other | $ 7,550 |
| EGYPT | 54.7 | Nearly all Arab | 700 |
| IRAN | 55.6 | 51% Persian, 25% Azerbaijani, 9% Kurdish, 1% Arab, 14% other | 1,800 |
| IRAQ | 18.8 | 75-80% Arab, 15-20% Kurdish, 5% other | 1,940 |
| ISRAEL | 4.6 (6.3 including occupied territories) | 82% Jewish, 17% Arab (60% Jewish, 40% Arab including occupied territories) | 8,700 (not including occupied territories) |
| JORDAN | 3.1 | Nearly all Arab (more than half Palestinian) | 1,760 |
| KUWAIT | 2.1 | 75% Arab (including 35% Palestinian), 20% Iranian, Indian; two-thirds of population are not Kuwaiti citizens | 10,500 |
| LEBANON | 3.3 | 93% Arab, 7% Armenian, other | 700 |
| OMAN | 1.5 | Nearly all Arab | 6,000 |
| QATAR | 0.5 | 40% Arab, 36% South Asian, 10% Iranian, 14% other | 17,070 |
| SAUDI ARABIA | Estimates: 10 to 17 million (incl. 4 million immigrant workers) | Nearly all Arab | Estimates: 4,700 to 7,300 |
| SYRIA | 12.5 | 90% Arab, 10% Kurdish, other | 1,540 |
| TURKEY | 56.7 | 85% Turkish, 12% Kurdish, 3% other | 1,350 |
| UNITED ARAB EMIRATES | 2.3 | 42% Arab (more than half immigrants), 50% South Asian, 8% other | 11,680 |
| YEMEN | 9.7 | Almost all Arab | 690 |

Sources: 1990 World Fact Book, New York Times

# OPENING GUNS OF WORLD WAR III

WASHINGTON'S ASSAULT ON IRAQ

Aftermath of U.S. bombing of road from Kuwait city to Basra, February 1991. "That was the killing zone. You couldn't move down the road, up the road, or off the road. The allied forces simply kept bombing and firing—at every person, jeep, truck, car, and bicycle. This slaughter ranks among the great atrocities of modern warfare."

# THE OPENING GUNS OF WORLD WAR III

*by Jack Barnes*

## I. DEVASTATION OF IRAQ

THE U.S.-organized carnage against the Iraqi people is among the most monstrous in the history of modern warfare. "*Is*" not "was." Death and dislocation continue today, as does the imperialists' culpability for them.

We may never know the actual numbers of toilers killed in Iraq and Kuwait during the six weeks of incessant allied air and sea bombardment and the murderous one-hundred-hour invasion launched by Washington February 24, 1991. But the one common media estimate that as many as 150,000 human beings were slaughtered is conservative, if anything. Just think about the impact of a massacre of that magnitude on the less than 19 million people of Iraq. Compare the blow of this number of deaths, and many additional maimings, and the relatively short period over which they mounted, with the impact many of you can remember in the United States, a country of 250 million, of the 47,000 U.S. combat deaths during Washington's nearly ten-year—not ten-week—war to prevent Vietnam's reunification.

The most concentrated single bloodletting was organized by the U.S. command in the final forty-eight hours of the invasion, as Iraqi soldiers fled Kuwait along the roads to Basra. While publicly denying that Iraqi forces were withdrawing from Kuwait, Washington ordered that tens of thousands of fleeing Iraqi soldiers be targeted for wave after wave of bombing, strafing,

---

*This article is based on a talk given in Cleveland, Ohio, on March 30, 1991. It has been edited for publication by the author in light of political developments over the subsequent five weeks. Jack Barnes is national secretary of the Socialist Workers Party.*

and shelling. These were people who were putting up no resistance, many with no weapons, others with rifles packed in bedrolls, leaving in cars, trucks, carts, and on foot. Many civilians from Iraq, Kuwait, and immigrant workers from other countries were killed at the same time as they tried to flee.

The U.S. armed forces bombed one end of the main highway from Kuwait city to Basra, sealing it off. They bombed the other end of the highway and sealed it off. They positioned mechanized artillery units on the hills overlooking it. And then, from the air and from the land they simply massacred every living thing on the road. Fighter bombers, helicopter gunships, and armored battalions poured merciless firepower on traffic jams backed up for as much as twenty miles. When the traffic became gridlocked, the B-52s were sent in for carpet bombing.

That was the killing zone. You couldn't move down the road. You couldn't move up the road. You couldn't move off the road. You couldn't surrender, wave a white flag, or give yourself up. The allied forces simply kept bombing and firing—at every person, jeep, truck, car, and bicycle. One allied air force officer called it a "turkey shoot." Others called it the biggest of the "cockroach hunts." That's the American way—carpet bombed, and shot in the back.

This slaughter, along with similar unreported operations during Bush's heroic hundred hours, ranks among the great atrocities of modern warfare. It was the Guernica, the Hiroshima, the Dresden, the My Lai of the U.S. war against Iraq.[1]

The imperialist coalition and the Baghdad regime both have their own reasons for covering up the truth about the bloodbath. As a result, we'll never know how many people died in the massacre. In late March Gen. Colin Powell, chairman of the Joint Chiefs of Staff, was asked by a reporter to provide an estimate of the number of Iraqis killed as a result of combined allied bombing and ground operations. Showing a little of the true face of imperial arrogance and racism, Powell replied: "It's really not a number I'm terribly interested in."

Neither has Baghdad made any attempt to give an accounting to the families of the workers and peasants in uniform slaugh-

*ENDNOTES FOR THIS ARTICLE BEGIN ON PAGE 126.*

tered in the trenches, in the foxholes, in the open desert, and on the highways in Kuwait and southern Iraq. As during the Saddam Hussein regime's 1980-88 war against Iran, tens of thousands of families in Iraq had their sons, brothers, nephews, and husbands sent off to war and then never saw them again or heard of their fate.

The U.S. government slaughter was not an operation with any military purpose per se. The victims were not part of military units or of an organized retreat. They had become individual human beings simply trying to get away from the war. It was a mass rout. By established "rules" of modern warfare they were not soldiers fighting; they were refugees fleeing. Even during the massive slaughter of World War II, both the Allied and German officer corps sometimes allowed soldiers fleeing down roads from battle to get away without this kind of murderous bombardment. But not the bipartisan killing machine organized by U.S. secretary of defense Richard Cheney (Republican), Gen. Colin Powell (Independent), and Gen. Norman Schwarzkopf (Democrat), commander of the U.S. forces in the Gulf.

W E CAN BE sure that this massacre had a devastating impact on many of the U.S. soldiers who were on the scene those days or saw its horrible results afterwards. Some GIs have already begun to talk publicly about these horrors they witnessed and raise questions about the seemingly pointless inhumanity of what was done. They will play an important role in bringing these war crimes by Washington to light and into U.S. politics in the months ahead.

What's more, the deaths and destruction during the U.S. invasion account for only a portion of those who were killed as a result of the military blockade of Iraq that began in the first days of August 1990 and the six-week-long air war launched January 16, 1991. Some of the horrendous damage is detailed in the March 20 report drafted by United Nations under-secretary-general Martti Ahtisaari of Finland, following a trip by a UN fact-finding commission to Iraq. To the credit of the *Militant* newsweekly—showing what it means to publish a paper in the interests of working people worldwide—the UN report was printed immediately and widely distributed for all to read. I know of no other newspaper that did so.

"It should . . . be said at once that nothing that we had seen or read had quite prepared us for the particular form of devastation which has now befallen the country," Ahtisaari wrote. The people of Iraq face an "imminent catastrophe" due to the war's destruction of an "economic infrastructure of what had been, until January 1991, a rather highly urbanized and mechanized society. Now, most means of modern life support have been destroyed or rendered tenuous."

THE EMBARGO continues to deprive millions of toilers in Iraq of food, potable water, medicines, seed and agricultural supplies, and other vital necessities. Washington and its allies, contrary to their "carefulness" in bombing Baghdad, unleashed round-the-clock grid bombardment against other cities, small towns, highways, "reinforced structures," and troop concentrations. The allied bombers destroyed factories, bridges, electrical generation plants, irrigation works, water purification facilities, and everything nearby them. Altogether 109,876 sorties were carried out by U.S., British, French, Canadian, Saudi, and other planes, dropping 88,500 tons of bombs.

An article in the April 28 issue of the *New York Times*—headlined "Hussein's Ouster Is U.S. Goal, But at What Cost to the Iraqis?"—summarized what it called "the first full assessment of war damage in Iraq" by the "United States intelligence community," that is, by the CIA, armed forces intelligence outfits, and the like. Due to lack of clean water, the article points out, cholera has reappeared in Iraq, and UN and other relief officials fear its spread. But water purification plants crippled or damaged as a result of the U.S. bombardment won't be repaired for months. Other diseases associated with impure water and malnutrition have reappeared in Iraq for the first time in more than a decade, taking a heavy toll on children in particular; for example, cases of kwashiorkor ("swollen belly" disease) are rising rapidly. The article reports that there are massive shortages of medicines, chlorine, and grain; that livestock herds have been depleted; and that it will take five years—under optimum conditions—merely to restore the country's electrical grid. The *Times* reporter called U.S. government policy "strangulation of Iraq's economy." It is. Most of all, it strangles tens of thousands more toilers living in Iraq.

This onslaught against Iraq was a modern "total war," in the true and terrible sense that term has taken on since the last year of the U.S. Civil War, when Union general William Sherman led his forces through Georgia on his "march to the sea."[2] Sherman's troops demolished warehouses, stores, crops, wagons, livestock, horses, silos, farmhouses—and anyone who got in their way as they did so. The aim was to put the torch to anything that could conceivably aid the Confederate army and to send the secessionist regime a message that the entire population would suffer the consequences of the refusal by the Confederate States of America to surrender.

That was the objective of the allied bombardment of Iraq. But with modern weapons technology, and the massive firepower brought to bear on Iraq under the banner of Washington's moral mission, the results of the annihilation from the air were far more devastating than Sherman could have even imagined in 1864. The allied targets were the total industrial, agricultural, transportation, and communications support system of the country—what the Ahtisaari UN report calls "means of modern life support," anything that could permit Iraq to continue quasi-normal social functioning. Some cities, like Basra in southern Iraq, were pounded with special ferocity.

As the editors of the *Wall Street Journal* described Washington's "military doctrine": "When force must be used it should be used overwhelmingly." In carrying out this "doctrine," the allied forces inevitably killed and maimed Iraqi civilians by the tens of thousands. The top U.S. officer corps was completely conscious of this fact. They both tried to cover up this death and devastation as well as use the euphemism "collateral damage" to describe it, hoping in that way to turn the Iraqi people into faceless nonhumans. And in this cover-up effort, the generals had the craven complicity of the owners of the big-business media.

The death toll of Iraqis was cold-bloodedly discounted by the White House and Pentagon before the slaughter began. Their stress on the "precision" of the bombing and "smartness" of the bombs was damage control from day one—pure, cynical public relations. It was later reported that only some 7 percent of the bombs dropped were "smart" bombs, and of the total tonnage dropped on Iraq some 70 percent missed their "military" targets. What's more, Washington planned on the "collateral damage" done by the bombing outside Baghdad being qualitatively worse than in the capital city itself. The hope was to keep it off television and out of the way of eyewitness reports.

Capturing this imperial disregard for the massive maiming and murdering of Iraqis, General Schwarzkopf told interviewer David Frost in late March about the initial report from U.S. divisions approaching the Euphrates River valley deep inside Iraq after the first day of the allied invasion. At the time, only one U.S. soldier had been reported as wounded in action. "So, you could imagine how that made me feel," said Schwarzkopf with his usual maudlin catch in his throat, "that here we were not only winning this war, but we were routing the enemy—absolutely routing the enemy—and yet, our casualties were practically . . . nonexistent. You know, that kind of made you feel that God was on your side." God as imperialism's angel of death against colonial peoples.

Recently *Harper's* magazine published a figure pointing to the great disparity between the number of Vietnamese killed during the U.S. war against the people of that country and the number of U.S. soldiers who died there—some 58,000 GIs (47,000 in action). *Harper's* posed the question: How many walls the size of the Vietnam Memorial, with the same type size per name, would be needed to list all the Vietnamese who were killed as a result of the war? (The Vietnam Memorial in Washington, D.C., is a large slab of black granite on which the names of the U.S. armed forces deaths are inscribed.) Their answer is about seventy such walls, *seventy* walls. Some of us can remember what an enormous political impact the mounting death toll of U.S. soldiers had in the United States. A sense of loss spread throughout the U.S. population, helping propel organized opposition to the war. But then just think about what *seventy times* that number of deaths means—in a country with only some one-quarter of the U.S. population!

That got me to wondering: What if you took all the names of U.S. GIs killed in action during the war in the Arab-Persian Gulf—140 during the air war and invasion, and that includes those killed by "friendly fire" (we will never know the accurate percentage of "friendly fire" deaths)—and listed them on a wall the same size as the Vietnam Memorial. Then do the same for the Iraqis who were killed, again with the same size inscription per name. How many walls would that take? Even using the very conservative 100,000 figure for Iraqi casualties estimated unofficially by U.S. military officers at the time, the answer would be: 714 such walls.

Just imagine, if you can, the one "American" wall—with 70 more the size of the Vietnam Memorial stretching in one direction listing the victims of U.S. imperialism's war against the Vietnamese people. And then another "American" wall—with 714 walls heading off at an angle with the names of the victims of Washington's war against the peoples of Iraq. That gives you just a bit of a mental picture of the price toiling humanity pays for living under the imperialist system.

So far in this century some 100 million people have been killed in imperialist wars. Relative to U.S. war deaths over that same ninety years, a comparable line of walls listing those victims would disappear into the Atlantic Ocean. And that doesn't take account of the multimillioned deaths from other forms of political violence, famine, preventable diseases, and other consequences of imperialism. It's almost unimaginable.

AFTER FLEEING the killing fields in Kuwait, some units of Baghdad's defeated army went into open rebellion against the Iraqi regime. They were fed up with the disastrous consequences for Iraqi soldiers and civilians alike of Saddam Hussein's expansionist adventure in Kuwait and treacherous refusal to organize its troops to fight. These soldiers joined in revolts by working people who took up arms against the regime in cities, towns, and villages across southern and northern Iraq. Much of the population in the south, although far from all, is from the Shiite Islamic majority and face discrimination from Iraq's predominantly Sunni Islamic ruling clique. In the north most are members of the oppressed Kurdish nationality who rose up, as they have done repeatedly in this century, to press for autonomy and national self-determination.

Throughout March 1991 Saddam Hussein used the troops of the elite Republican Guards—as well as helicopter gunships and heavy armor he had held in reserve and refused to commit during the allied invasion—to drown these rebellions in blood. Cities in southern Iraq such as Basra, Najaf, and Karbala were savagely bombed and shelled. As a result of this brutal suppression, tens of thousands of Shiite and other Iraqis in the south, and more than two million Kurds and others in northern Iraq, have been uprooted and turned into desperate refugees.

Hundreds of thousands of Kurds fled into neighboring Iran and Turkey; hundreds of thousands more are massed along their borders, living in wretched conditions with little food, shelter, or medical care. According to a United Nations report in late April, some 2,000 are dying each day from the cold, disease, and malnutrition; other reports from early May indicate there may already have been 20,000 to 30,000 deaths. The spread of contagious disease threatens to push these numbers even higher.

The U.S. and Western European imperialist rulers—themselves responsible throughout this century for repeated sabotage of efforts to establish a sovereign Kurdistan—are today cynically exploiting Baghdad's repression of the Kurds to enhance their own rival economic, political, and military interests in the Gulf region. They are organizing to drive the Kurds back into Iraq, and turning emergency relief for them over to the United Nations, with a piddling budget. Not one of the imperialist governments in North America, Europe, Japan, New Zealand, or Australia—all supporters of the imperialist slaughter—has offered to throw open its borders to these or other refugees from Baghdad's attacks and provide them with jobs and housing. Nor have the Gorbachev regime or other U.S. "allies" in the war opened their borders to the refugees. All of them merit some variant of the title they so freely gave to Saddam Hussein—the "Butcher of Baghdad."

WITH THE END of the Iraqi occupation of Kuwait, soldiers and rightist vigilantes backing the al-Sabah monarchy—its "legitimate rights" restored by the Pentagon—have rounded up, beaten, tortured, and frequently killed Palestinians who remained in Kuwait or returned after the end of the fighting. Immigrant workers from many parts of the world who have lived and worked in Kuwait, sometimes for several generations—many in desperate need of food, clothing, and medical attention—have been turned back at the border when they sought to reenter the country following the reimposition of the al-Sabah family dynasty.

Thus, the aftermath of Washington's devastation of Iraq has produced an even more criminal replay of the massive uprooting of populations that followed Baghdad's occupation of Kuwait August 2, 1990, and the subsequent launching of the U.S. war drive in the Gulf. At that time, as you remember, the Saddam Hussein regime pushed tens of thousands of immigrant workers out of Iraq and Kuwait—Palestinians, Egyptians and other North Africans, Filipinos, Pakistanis, and others. The Saudi regime expelled some 900,000 Yemeni workers, as well as many Palestinians and Jordanians, because the governments of Yemen and Jordan and the Palestine Liberation Organization refused to join in the U.S.-organized war alliance against Iraq.

These immigrants produced the wealth, provided the services, staffed the professions, refined and transported the oil, and cared for the children of the rich and the middle class in these countries. (In 1989, 25 percent of the population of Kuwait were listed as domestic servants!) The lives and livelihoods of workers and their families were devastated. They were left without income or personal property. While the imperialist powers devoted billions of dollars to the war buildup, only token funds were doled out to feed and shelter—"corral" is a more accurate word—these refugees, or to transport and resettle them in the countries of their choice.

Hundreds of thousands slaughtered and maimed; millions homeless, hungry, diseased, or displaced throughout the region: this is the fruit of Washington's war drive and military "victory" in the Gulf war. Inscribe the names of *all* these victims on granite slabs, and the memorial walls stretch so far in the distance they pass beyond what the unaided eye could see. That's the real U.S. war memorial.

## II.  RESULTS OF WASHINGTON'S WAR REINFORCE 'VIETNAM SYNDROME'

**T**HE IMMEDIATE goal of the Republican/Democratic bipartisan war drive and assault on Iraq was to use Washington's military might to bolster U.S. dominance in the Arab-Persian Gulf region, which has some 65 percent of the world's known oil reserves. To accomplish this aim, the U.S. rulers sought to pursue the war drive in such a way as to guarantee the establishment of a regime in Baghdad that for all practical purposes would be an imperialist protectorate, politically subservient to the U.S. government. They hoped the political momentum of such a blow would enable them to shift the class and state relationship of forces in the Gulf more to their favor, as well as advance their interests vis-à-vis their imperialist competitors. That was the purpose of the U.S. government's war drive against Iraq—not to liberate Kuwait or restore its national sovereignty, let alone bring democracy to the Arabian Peninsula.

In pursuing these objectives, the U.S. rulers sought to emerge with a victory that would at least substantially weaken the "Vietnam syndrome," if not put it behind them altogether. Bush and his bipartisan supporters openly proclaimed this goal during the war drive. The stakes were big ones, and they remain so. Accomplishing that goal would open the door to pushing back the lasting gains registered by the U.S. working class through the Black rights struggles that mounted through the late 1950s and into the 1960s, and of the subsequent anti–Vietnam War movement and fights for women's rights. It would be an aid to them in attempting to shove the labor movement toward the fringes of politics in the United States and push the relationship of class forces further to the advantage of the employing class. This would in turn open up new possibilities of using strategic military power in their interests around the world.

The Bush administration's decision to halt offensive operations in southern Iraq at midnight February 27 also registered an assessment that the decisive allied military victory, *won with such few U.S. casualties,* had laid the basis for accomplishing U.S. imperialism's goals both in the Gulf region and at home. The rulers concluded that the results of the embargo, bombard-

ment, and invasion meant that a post–Saddam Hussein protectorate could be put in place in a matter of weeks if not days:
some Iraqi officers (Baathist thugs, just like Hussein himself)
willing to organize the kind of regime Washington had in mind
would soon knock off Saddam Hussein. U.S. imperialism would
be at a new pinnacle of power abroad. And the war party—that
is, the bipartisan patriotic gang led by the Bush administration
supporting the war effort—would be in a new position of
strength at home.

When Washington claimed its military "victory" over the Iraqi
armed forces at the end of February, the U.S. rulers initially
acted as if they had taken a giant step toward furthering these
objectives. On March 1 President George Bush gloated: "By
God"—he meant by hook or by crook—"we've kicked the Vietnam syndrome once and for all!"

It's important to remember that from the standpoint of the
ruling capitalist families in the United States, getting rid of the
so-called Vietnam syndrome involves a number of elements.

One central ruling-class goal over the past fifteen years has
been to restore the self-confidence of the U.S. officer caste, as
well as broader esteem for the brass in the eyes of bourgeois
public opinion (including within the ranks of the armed
forces). The aim is to restore the image of a command structure
whose members are "military professionals"; who carry out
stated government policy and are seen as neither politicized
apologists nor antagonists of the administration; who don't
sacrifice the lives of soldiers in battle—or "enemy" civilians or
villages—unnecessarily; who don't lie to the troops and the
public about "body counts" on either side; and who fight for
goals, established and clearly enunciated by the White House
and Congress, that are for "all Americans," for "us," for "our"
interests, "our" needs and values. Thus, when "we" have to fight,
we do so reluctantly but decisively, thus maximizing the speed of
the victory and minimizing losses of "our boys."

The problem confronting the ruling class since the Vietnam
War was underlined by General Schwarzkopf during a fawning
television interview conducted by Barbara Walters in mid-
March. Acknowledging that U.S. officers routinely lied to the
public during the Vietnam War about the numbers of Vietnamese casualties and their implications, Schwarzkopf said: "There

was a terrible erosion in integrity in the armed forces during Vietnam. I don't think that many of us came out of Vietnam and could hold our heads up and say, 'My sense of integrity is still lily-white and pure,' because we all know that we had lied about body count. We all knew that there had been a lot of other lies and it did bad things to the officer corps." Things got so bad, Schwarzkopf added in his self-dramatizing, bathetic style, that he had even considered leaving the military following Vietnam, but decided to stay since "there were a lot of things that needed to be fixed."

Of course, the point of Schwarzkopf's "moving frankness" was to reassure the viewers that everything was different now; that the U.S. command in the Gulf told the truth, the whole truth, and nothing but the truth. "It's a different officer corps today," he told Walters. "It's an officer corps that has learned from that experience, but when we went into this thing, I was bound and determined that we were going to tell it like it was, absolutely tell it like it was."

Chairman of the Joint Chiefs of Staff Colin Powell had the same goal of reassurance, and the same mock humility, in mind as he stood before maps and photographs at a televised press conference January 23 during the war and demanded: "Trust me, trust me."

In order to give this appearance of "telling it like it is," however, the Pentagon found it necessary to impose the most severe press restrictions and censorship of war news in this century. Done under the guise of military necessity to protect "our boys," reportage was limited to press pools (handpicked, arranged, and chaperoned by the military) and sterile Pentagon press briefings. All news reports from the war zone itself—99 percent of the action received *no coverage at all*—had to be sent through military censors. The big-business media went along with these undemocratic restrictions and engaged in massive self-censorship of facts about the war drive and protests at home. And so it was that the generals' claims of astounding accuracy in bombing raids, minimal "collateral damage," and virtual perfection in Patriot missile intercepts all became "facts" for the duration.

A second ruling-class objective in pushing back the "Vietnam syndrome" is restoring public confidence in the government's direction of foreign and military policy. The capitalist rulers still

suffer the effects of the exposures and consequences of government actions throughout the Vietnam War and its aftermath:
the Pentagon Papers, the post-Watergate revelations of CIA
assassination plots abroad and—more damaging—of FBI "dirty
tricks" at home. The rulers aim to convince broad layers of the
U.S. population that the *stated goals* of government policies are
the *real goals*. And, more importantly, to convince working people that these goals are not those of just one social class or layer
in this country, but are instead "our goals," the goals of "the
nation," goals that are in "our interests"—all of us, employers
and workers, rich and poor, exploited and exploiter alike. The
bipartisan capitalist politicians must reinforce the patriotic
myth that "we" are "all Americans," and thus all have common
interests. It's our oil, our emirs, our jobs. The rulers must try to
prevent us from identifying our interests with our fellow working people worldwide instead. If there is to be popular support
for deploying imperialist military forces abroad—and Washington will be driven to deploy them time and again in coming
years, as the capitalists seek to maintain their declining social
system—then the U.S. ruling class must have this patriotic consensus in place; they must institutionalize class collaboration
under the flag or the yellow ribbon.

Third, the employing class is determined to push back the
acceptability of any far-reaching public discussion and debate of
their policies during wartime or other "national emergencies."
To the degree such discussion does develop, their aim is to
channel it into lobbying and passive observance of debates in
Congress; to limit discussion to tactical differences; and to keep
the kind of discussion that can lead to street protests out of
union halls and off television. They aim to roll back the potential for growing antiwar mobilizations as a factor limiting their
options at any stage of the use of U.S. military power abroad.

### Washington breaks its teeth on the war

This is what the U.S. employing class believed they had achieved
through what they initially portrayed as one of the purest, most
complete military victories in U.S. history. But it took only a few
days after the suspension of offensive operations in southern
Iraq at the end of February for the initial patriotic euphoria to
begin to turn sour. A political fiasco rapidly unfolded.

In the weeks that followed, more of the truth has come out about the "turkey shoot" and the "cockroach hunt," the broader U.S.-organized slaughter and devastation, and the consequences of the war for those who rose up in rebellion in Iraq. Questioning and revulsion have grown among working people in the United States, including returning GIs.

Apparently the officer corps and the politicians *did* lie once again about "the body count," that is, about the "collateral damage" in all its forms. It turns out the reviled Peter Arnett telecasting over CNN from Baghdad was telling a lot more of the truth than "Stormin' Norman," as Schwarzkopf is called. Or than "America's Black Eisenhower," as the ultraright *National Review* magazine glowingly dubbed Gen. Colin Powell in a front-page feature plumping him as a Republican Party candidate for president later in the '90s. "Trust me"? Yes. To try to "cut off and kill" any rebelling victim of imperialism you're ordered to—at home as well as abroad.

BAGHDAD'S MASSACRES of Shiite and Kurdish rebels and the uprooting of massive new refugee populations is shattering the illusion that Washington's war somehow contributed to the welfare of oppressed peoples anywhere in the region. Reports from Kuwait of the reinstalled al-Sabah monarchy's tyranny, opulent corruption, and gratuitous brutality—after their display of such craven physical cowardice—elicit disgust.

Responding to the political impact of the United Nations report on the devastation of the "means of modern life support" in Iraq, White House press spokesperson Marlin Fitzwater sought to defend the U.S. war and reject "the argument that somehow there is a guilt associated with the destruction of a war caused by Saddam Hussein." Notwithstanding such feeble government disavowals, fewer and fewer people in the United States are so ready today as they were in January and February to speak about "our goals" in the war and "our responsibility" for its outcome in Iraq and throughout the region.

And, to top things off, Saddam Hussein hasn't yet been assassinated, overthrown, or deposed; he hasn't been replaced by a new Baathist thug that Washington and Riyadh would be more than happy to do business with. The U.S. rulers thought they had that one "in the bag." But each day Saddam Hussein remains head of state, the less likely it is that Washington's hoped-for outcome will materialize. The longer he remains in charge in Baghdad, the more the U.S. rulers find themselves objectively working *with* the person Bush called "the new Hitler" *against* the welfare of the people of Iraq. What does that make Bush?

So, from the standpoint of the U.S. ruling class, the outcome of the war in the Gulf stands in striking contrast to that of Washington's invasions of Grenada in October 1983 and Panama in December 1989. In both those cases Washington succeeded through limited military operations in installing subservient and relatively stable capitalist regimes almost overnight. The U.S. rulers' resulting *political* victory was virtually simultaneous with the *military* victory—and at the cost of very few U.S. casualties. Neither Grenada nor Panama will remain stable forever, of course. But Washington achieved its political goals in both cases.

From the beginning, however, a military victory for Washington in its war against Iraq had different implications. Such a victory could not simultaneously secure the political goals for which the war was launched. The changes U.S. imperialism sought, *because it needs them,* were too far-reaching. In fact, far from achieving these political goals, the war's outcome has done the opposite: it has exacerbated political turmoil, instability, and national, class, and state conflicts throughout the region. As we said from the beginning of Washington's bipartisan war drive, whatever happened militarily, the U.S. rulers would break their teeth on this effort to impose imperialist order and stability in the Gulf by unleashing a massive war against Iraq.

Washington's war has actually created new problems for American imperialism in the Gulf region. It has set in motion unforeseen and uncontrollable social forces. It has opened up new conflicts and struggles. It has set off new flows of displaced populations. All this was virtually inevitable, since world capitalism at its current stage of crisis and decline is incapable of bringing economic development—and thus meaningful national independence, sovereignty, or social stability—to these or other countries and peoples in the semicolonial world.

This post-cease-fire reality set off sharp tactical divisions—more accurately, *recriminations*—in the U.S. capitalist class, as its spokespeople second-guessed the Bush administration's recent policy decisions in the Gulf. The administration's ruling-class detractors charge that by deciding to halt offensive operations at the end of February, lift some sanctions, agree to a cease-fire, and allow Baghdad to smash internal rebellions, Bush dropped the ball in the high-stakes drive to accomplish more of U.S. imperialism's political goals in the region. (Few of them, however, say what alternative course should, or could, have been pursued by the administration.)

IN THE EARLY months of Washington's war drive, the main tactical "concerns" over the direction of Bush administration policy came from those bourgeois politicians and spokespersons, mainly in the Democratic Party, who advocated trying to find some way of achieving U.S. imperialism's goals in the Gulf short of taking the political risks—both in the region, and at home—of launching a ground war against Iraq. The character and narrow limits of the differences expressed by this "bourgeois peace party" are detailed in the talk printed last December in the *International Socialist Review*,[3] which communists campaigning against imperialism and war have circulated by the thousands to working people and students in the United States and other countries. When the shooting war commenced with the U.S. bombardment of Iraq in mid-January, the Democratic and Republican party politicians closed ranks and rallied around the flag and "commander in chief"—just as they've done at the opening of every U.S. war in this century, with or without a UN blessing.

Since Bush declared the unilateral "pause" in hostilities on February 27, however, the debate has shifted to whether that decision and the subsequent course of the U.S. military forces in the region has somehow snatched defeat for the rulers from the jaws of victory. Initially this new sniping at the Bush administration came primarily from the right wing of the Republican Party, but Democratic and Republican party liberals soon joined in. At the same time, handwringing is increasing among bourgeois politicians who continue to defend Bush's policy decisions in the Gulf but now feel it expedient to take their distance from responsibility for the "turkey shoot," devastation of Iraq, growing threats of epidemics, and horrors of the new mass refugee flight.

A couple of weeks after the pause in the fighting, the *Wall Street Journal* ran a lead editorial warning that "the Euphrates may prove to be George Bush's Elbe." The editorial refers to Iraq's Euphrates River, the furthermost point of advance by the allied forces into Iraq, to echo the charges by the U.S. right wing following World War II that by halting the advance of U.S. troops at the Elbe River in central Germany the Democratic administration "handed over Eastern Europe to the Communists."

*New York Times* columnist A.M. Rosenthal beat the drums urging the White House to use Baghdad's massacre of the Kurds as a pretext to relaunch military action to directly topple Saddam Hussein, regardless of the costs. "America at the Vistula" was the headline of one column; Rosenthal harks back to the Warsaw people's uprising of August 1944 against the Nazi-imposed regime in Poland, when the Soviet government led by Joseph Stalin condemned the revolt to bloody defeat by refusing to come to the aid of the rebels—despite the Soviet army's presence in the city just across the Vistula River.

Liberal *New York Times* columnist Anthony Lewis, while still maintaining that the war itself "was worse than unwise," condemned the decision of the Bush administration "to sit by passively while Iraqi helicopter gunships, warplanes, spray napalm and acid at the [Kurdish] rebels." And some days later the headline of the lead article in "The Week in Review" section of the Sunday *New York Times* proclaimed, "Iraq Is Left to the Mercy of Saddam Hussein." This was followed by the *New Republic*'s screaming front-page headline: "THE MURDER OF THE KURDS: Why Bush Let It Happen, and How He Could Stop It."

William Buckley, an editor of the *National Review*, wrote April 10: "The events of the past two weeks have been as destructive of Western morale as anything that might have been conceived of during the ecstasy of early March short of a midnight raid by Iraq's Republican Guard that carried off General Schwarzkopf and his principal aides."

The most publicized exchange was that between Bush and Schwarzkopf at the end of March. This was just weeks after the "commander in chief" and his "conquering 'almost five-star' general" were being hyped throughout the media as being closer than two peas in a pod. Unlike Vietnam, it had been said, open and clear goals were set by Bush, and Schwarzkopf devised the military plan to carry them out. But by late March, Schwarzkopf was singing a different tune over nationwide television: "Frankly, my recommendation [to Bush] had been . . . continue the march. I mean we had them in a rout and we could have continued to . . . wreak great destruction upon them. We could have completely closed the door and made it, in fact, a battle of annihilation."

(Just think about the language. With full knowledge of the murder of tens of thousands of fleeing Iraqi soldiers during the one-hundred-hour invasion, Schwarzkopf complains that the mass slaughter fell short of "annihilation"—and uses the phrase elsewhere in the interview.)

*New York Times* editorial writers, while not budging from their defense of the war, now use the word "slaughter" to refer to what happened during the hundred hours of the U.S. invasion in Iraq and Kuwait. Even the editors of the *Wall Street Journal*— among the most fervent backers of the war, and proponents of the view that the allied offensive should not have stopped short of Baghdad—sought to respond to growing revulsion against the reported devastation by suggesting that the Pentagon conduct a study of "whether military purposes were served by the destruction of Iraq's infrastructure, with civilian effects a U.N. team described as 'near apocalyptic.'"

The point is not that one or another section of the ruling class or current of bourgeois public opinion had some course that would have "worked" better than Bush's in advancing U.S. imperialist interests in the Gulf. They didn't. From at least September 1990 through the end of February, the Bush administration, representing the dominant wing of the ruling class, had a coherent and consistent course.

It was a *military* course aimed at launching an all-out assault against Iraq, and Washington followed the logic of the war drive right through to its murderous culmination. It served a double *political* purpose: to establish a post–Saddam Hussein protectorate; and to do so with minimal U.S. casualties, regardless of the total cost in human life and limb. On February 27, Bush administration officials were confident they had not only locked up the first goal but—if U.S. forces avoided battle with the best Iraqi elite units—that they could also achieve the second, and in that way reap what they assumed would be enormous political benefits at home (including setting up broader support for the next massive use of force).

It isn't turning out that way.

A COLLATERAL objective of the war drive was putting Washington in a stronger position to force a "solution" to the Palestinian national question. For the U.S. rulers, the realization of this goal—somehow eliminating the roots of the *intifada*,[4] without igniting a broader revolutionary upheaval—is intertwined with progress toward their long-standing aim of establishing stable, profitable relations with the major capitalist regimes in the region, whose populations are predominantly Arab. These regimes, which stretch from the Atlantic coast of northern Africa to the Arab-Persian Gulf, rule over populations many, many times the size of Israel's and over lands that contain strategic supplies of oil and other major sources of natural wealth. Washington aims to assert more strongly than ever its position as the predominant imperialist power in its relations with these regimes.

From the early 1960s, the U.S. government increasingly supplied Israel with modern military equipment and had to rely on it as a bastion to defend imperialist interests in the Middle East. During the mid- to late 1950s, an upswing in worker and peasant struggles for national sovereignty and land throughout the region gave rise to bourgeois regimes in a number of countries that, from the standpoint of imperialism, were too weak and unreliable to play this role. With the consolidation over the past quarter century of larger and stronger capitalist classes, and a growing middle class, however, Washington grabbed the chance to use these bourgeois governments more effectively to promote its own interests. The military defeats dealt to these regimes by Israel in wars in 1967 and 1973 induced sections of

their ruling classes to turn more sharply toward imperialism.
The Egyptian rulers have led the way in this regard, recognizing
the State of Israel following the 1978 Camp David Accords
engineered during the James Carter administration.[5]

The U.S.-organized war in the Gulf widened the divergence
between the foreign policy interests of the U.S. and Israeli
ruling classes. The Israeli rulers come out losers from U.S.
imperialism's strengthened alignment with the Egyptian, Saudi,
and Syrian regimes, which joined in the military alliance against
Baghdad. This weakens Israel's influence with Washington, its
special place in the world imperialist system, and thus its leverage in wresting ever-increasing U.S. economic and military assistance and attempting to block such U.S. aid to regimes in the
Arab countries.

This divergence between Washington and Tel Aviv is contrary
to what most of the major media portrayed during the war as a
new high point of cooperation. This is supposedly exemplified
by the Israeli government's "agreement" not to send its warplanes against targets in Iraq in response to Baghdad's Scud
missile attacks and Washington's subsequent dispatch of Patriot
antimissile missile batteries to Israel. The truth, however, is that
Tel Aviv never had any choice in the matter. The U.S. military
command simply refused to give the Israeli air force the "friend
or foe" codes that would have allowed Tel Aviv's bombers and
fighter jets to enter Iraqi airspace without being shot down
by—or shooting down—the U.S. aircraft that controlled those
skies.

IN FACT, Washington humbled Tel Aviv during the Gulf war in
order to block it from disrupting the U.S. rulers' foreign policy
and military goals. Israel relies on its proven record as a garri-
son state: that it will respond militarily to any perceived threat,
and respond tenfold to any attack on its territory. The Israeli
regime, though, was forced by the U.S. government to take the
hits from Baghdad's Scud missiles without responding. Although the Scuds are militarily insignificant, the inability to
retaliate was another political humiliation for Tel Aviv. The
bitterness and frustration in Israeli ruling circles grew even

more as it later became clear that Washington's much-touted Patriot missiles are a failure. They didn't destroy most warheads or prevent the Scuds from doing damage. The Patriots did nothing more than blow apart the highly inaccurate Scuds, scattering the warheads and other debris at random. Scud warheads came down and exploded on Israeli territory regardless, and parts of both the Scuds and Patriots did damage as well. (In fact, Israeli military evaluations insist that each Scud missile launched by Baghdad *after* the deployment of the Patriots did more damage than those beforehand.)

While Washington's interests have diverged further from Tel Aviv's, however, this has not brought the U.S. rulers any closer to a "solution" to the Palestinian question, without which their efforts to establish stable relations with bourgeois regimes in the Middle East are continually disrupted. Washington's biggest political obstacle in this regard is the irrepressible fight by the Palestinians for their national self-determination—above all the struggles of the Palestinians living inside the post-1967 borders of "Greater Israel." This remains an enormous problem for imperialism, no matter how much cooperation the U.S. government gets from Moscow, and no matter how many trips Secretary of State James Baker makes to the region, shuttling between Tel Aviv and the capital cities of Washington's allied regimes in various Arab countries.

Tel Aviv seized on Washington's war drive as cover to extend its garrison-state brutality against the Palestinian population in the West Bank, Gaza, southern Lebanon, and inside Israel itself. It imposed a round-the-clock curfew—virtual house arrest—on the Palestinian population, depriving hundreds of thousands of families of their livelihoods. Thousands of Palestinians were rounded up, beaten, and jailed. Israeli cops, troops, and rightist vigilantes murdered Palestinian fighters with greater impunity. Tel Aviv stepped up air raids on Palestinian refugee camps in Lebanon. Despite earlier pledges to Washington, the Israeli regime openly organized immigrants from the Soviet Union and other Jewish settlers to expand land takeovers in the West Bank and Gaza. If the Israelis can't fly the skies against the U.S. Air Force, they can still build settlements on stolen Arab land—for a while.

Within an imperialist framework, *there is no solution* to the

Palestinian question. The fight for the national rights of the Palestinian people is the axis of the class struggle in Israel and throughout those areas that historically constituted Palestine. The Palestinian people continue to press forward the fight against their dispossession and earn solidarity from Arab peoples and conscious fighters among the oppressed and exploited around the world. The Palestinians have not been so dispersed geographically as to lose their national identity and cohesion.

Above all, so long as the Palestinians are not expelled en masse from Israel and the occupied territories, every step forward in their struggle for national liberation is at the same time an *internal* social and political crisis for Tel Aviv. Moreover, every move by Tel Aviv to incorporate the occupied territories into a permanent "Greater Israel" guarantees intensified resistance, including among the Palestinians inside Israel itself, thereby deepening its internal crisis. In addition to some 3.5 million Jews, 2.5 million Palestinians are currently living under Israeli rule: 800,000 inside the pre-1967 borders, and 1.7 million on the West Bank and in the Gaza Strip.

Palestinian national self-determination is irreconcilable with the class interests of the Israeli ruling class. The bourgeois regimes in the surrounding Arab countries, while claiming to speak on behalf of their "brothers" the Palestinians, have repeatedly shed Palestinian blood to preserve their own class power and state privileges. Washington is pressuring more of these governments to follow in the footsteps of Cairo by establishing diplomatic relations with Israel, and some may do so. Nonetheless, these capitalist regimes must take into account the potentially destabilizing political consequences at home among the Arab and other oppressed peoples—who strongly identify with the Palestinian struggle and who, along with working people the world over, are the only reliable ally of the Palestinians.

The nearly four-year-long intifada on the West Bank and Gaza Strip has reaffirmed that the Palestinians will not stop fighting until they have won their struggle for land and national self-determination. That's why Washington is no closer after the Gulf war than it was beforehand to finding a way around this dilemma. The U.S. rulers urge Tel Aviv to trade "land for peace." But the response by the Israeli rulers in deeds outweighs any diplomatic words. Tel Aviv acts on the conviction that only the peace of the grave will still the Palestinians' struggle for land.

## Kurdish national self-determination

The U.S. rulers' military "victory" put an international spotlight on another unresolved fight for national self-determination in the region—that of the Kurdish people. Prior to the Gulf war the Kurdish struggle had largely been in retreat, having been dealt repeated defeats over the past half century by the Iraqi, Turkish, Iranian, and Syrian ruling classes, with the complicity of Washington, London, Paris, and Moscow. The consequences of the Gulf war have now posed Kurdish national self-determination more sharply than at any time since the close of World War II and the years just after the 1958 revolution that overthrew the monarchy in Iraq.

Some twenty million to thirty million Kurds are divided between southeastern Turkey, northeastern Syria, northern Iraq, and northwestern Iran, as well as a small region in the southern part of the USSR. An independent Kurdish republic came into existence in northern Iran after the establishment of a workers' and peasants' government in neighboring Azerbaijan in December 1945.[6]

Although the Kurdish republic was crushed by the Iranian monarchy a year later, the Kurds continued their struggle during the decades that followed. The U.S. rulers have alternately doled out aid with an eyedropper to Kurdish nationalist groups, and then abruptly cut off this backing, depending on Washington's shifting relations with regimes in the area, especially Baghdad and Tehran.

The Kurdish people took advantage of the weakening of the Saddam Hussein regime as a result of the war to press forward their struggle once again, holding many villages and towns—including the major city of Kirkuk—for a week or more in March. Baghdad used helicopter gunships and heavy armor to crush the Kurdish rebellion with ruthless brutality, causing two million or more Kurdish refugees to attempt to cross the Turkish and Iranian borders.

As we discuss here today, the U.S. and European imperialist powers have declared a temporary refugee "enclave" for the Kurds north of the thirty-sixth parallel in northern Iraq near the Turkish border. Washington is sending troops, Special Forces units, into northern Iraq to function as what amounts to little more than a police force for Saddam Hussein. Along with Turkish soldiers, the U.S. troops are forcing the refugees out of Turkey and off nearby mountains into ill-provisioned and barren transit camps. Washington's aim is to push the Kurds back to the towns and villages from which they fled.

At best, this enclave will be the temporary equivalent of an Indian reservation in the United States or one of the many blocked-off areas near Israel's borders containing Palestinian refugee camps. The imperialists share a common interest with the capitalist regimes in Baghdad, Ankara, Damascus, and Tehran in ensuring that such a "haven" for the Kurds is short-lived. All of them know that any more-or-less-permanent Kurdish area can only breed aspirations for more land that is justly theirs, as well as potential "intifadas" among young generations of Kurdish fighters. Bush will have nightmares about setting up a very large reservation, nightmares about a modern-day Geronimo leading a new breakout.[7]

This is another of the unresolved and uncontrollable social forces in the Gulf that has been unleashed, rather than contained, by the results of Washington's war against Iraq.

As we continue campaigning against imperialism and war today, we must call not only for "All foreign troops out of Iraq!" but also "Open the U.S. borders!"—to the Kurdish people and to all Iraqi and Kuwaiti refugees fleeing the Baghdad regime and the al-Sabah monarchy.

For the ruling class in Turkey, which joined Washington in the war against Iraq in hopes of winning trade favors and military aid and hardware, the results so far—nearly one million refugees pounding at its borders—are nothing short of a catastrophe. (The Turkish regime is also suffering major economic blows from honoring the continuing blockade, which shuts off Turkey's oil pipeline with Iraq and the resulting flow of funds into the state treasury.) These events have brought to greater world attention once again the Turkish rulers' own suppression of the Kurdish people, until recently legally denied the right even to speak their own language in Turkey— and they are still denied the right to read, write, or be educated in Kurdish.

Above all, the Kurdish people have come to the center stage in world politics as never before, not primarily as victims, but as courageous and determined fighters for national rights.

THE BRUTAL REGIMES of the royal families in Saudi Arabia and Kuwait have emerged from the war in a weakened position as well. Living off enormous oil rents, the Saudi rulers in particular had long functioned on the illusion that massive petrodollar payoffs could substitute for military power in regional and world politics. Baghdad's rapid annexation of Kuwait and clear threat to Saudi borders put an end to such illusions once and for all.

Saudi Arabia, Kuwait, and the other kingdoms in the Arabian Peninsula (the United Arab Emirates, Oman, Qatar, and Bahrain) all rest on the narrow social base of parasitic merchant, banking, and oil-rentier ruling classes, with little industrial capital. All depend to one degree or another on imported wage-workers who toil under contract-labor conditions and who—no matter how long they have lived and worked in these countries—are denied the most basic rights of citizenship. (The salaried middle classes and professionals in these countries are largely drawn from immigrants as well.)

The war in the Gulf shone a spotlight on the reactionary social structures and semifeudal foundations of the Arabian oil kingdoms and the underlying political and military weakness of the oppressive, superrich, rentier families who rule them. Conflicts will increase between the tiny handful of parasitic exploiters and the workers from throughout the region who produce the wealth that keeps these monarchies afloat. The determination of young people to win freedoms and political and intellectual space they know exist elsewhere in the world, and by women to cast off humiliating restrictions if not semislavery, has been reinforced by the upheavals in the region since August.

Far from finding themselves in a stronger position to hold the imperialist powers hostage to the flow of oil, these kingdoms have now proven to be overtly dependent for their very survival on the support of Washington and, to a lesser degree, their more semi-industrialized rival regimes of Egypt and Syria. (They feel pressure from the relatively enhanced power of Tehran in the Gulf region as well.) Washington will use its leverage to reassert greater control over the organization of world oil markets, reinforce its position relative to postwar Saudi Arabia, Kuwait, and other Gulf states, and bolster its competitive standing against other imperialist powers.

The Gulf war has also accelerated the degree to which the capitalist regimes in Syria and Iran are increasingly being pulled toward finding ways to work with Washington. They are following the trail blazed by Cairo more than a decade ago, and Egypt's capitalist rulers more and more speak as a proxy, sending up trial balloons to make it easier for other regimes in the region to advance along this path. Coming on top of the deepening economic and social crisis of the Soviet bureaucracy, the Gulf war exposed the fact that the USSR cannot arm and organize a hopeful client regime to climb above being anything more than a second-rate military power. Moscow proved that it can less and less be depended on by "friends" abroad for effective military assistance or substantial economic aid. Nor was the position of Paris, Bonn, Tokyo, or even London strengthened vis-à-vis Washington as the dominant imperialist power to be reckoned with by bourgeois regimes in the Gulf region. To the contrary.

Finally, the capitalist regimes throughout North Africa with majority Arab populations—especially Morocco and Algeria—emerged from the Gulf war chastened by the realization that they have not yet narrowed the space for political action by the toilers to the extent accomplished by Cairo, let alone Damascus and Baghdad. Leaving aside Jordan, it was in these two countries during the war that the largest and potentially most destabilizing popular mobilizations took place in solidarity with Iraq in face of the imperialist-organized onslaught. So we should be on the lookout for further reverberations of these events in the class struggle in northern Africa.

For the ruling classes throughout the Middle East today, from Morocco to Iran, the threat from the workers and peasants within their own borders is first and foremost in their political calculations, not the external pressures they feel from imperialism. Contrary to the U.S. rulers' aims, the consequences of Washington's "victory" in Iraq have to a greater or lesser degree increased the instability throughout this part of the world, from the Gulf monarchies to the regimes of the Maghreb in North Africa.

**Not a defeat like Nicaragua**

Washington's failure to shift the relationship of class forces to its favor in the Gulf region, despite its devastating use of military might, does not mean that the U.S. rulers made no initial gains as a result of the war. They did register some. They strengthened their position relative to their imperialist rivals in Bonn, Tokyo, and Paris. They demonstrated more decisively their dominance over Moscow as a strategic power. They bolstered their position as the predominant imperialist power in relation to a new alignment of semicolonial bourgeois regimes in Cairo, Damascus, and Riyadh. They paved the way for reknitting at least some initial political relations with Tehran.

The U.S. rulers, however, failed in their efforts to come out of the Gulf war with a new impulse to their more than decade-long offensive against the working class and labor movement in the United States. The devastation of Iraq and the one-hundred-hour slaughter by Washington will be totally different in its consequences for U.S. working people than the defeat of the Nicaraguan revolution during the latter half of the 1980s. That defeat dealt us a real and lasting blow.

Massive popular mobilizations by Nicaraguan workers and peasants in 1979 culminated in the smashing of the U.S.-backed Somoza dictatorship and its state apparatus, ushering in a workers' and farmers' government. It was headed by a revolutionary leadership that, whatever its weaknesses and inconsistencies, organized the toilers during the opening years of the revolution to advance their interests against imperialism and against the Nicaraguan landlords and capitalists. It reached out toward the Cuban revolution and toward revolutionary Grenada. It directly aided and politically supported rebels in El Salvador and Guatemala. Demonstrating a capacity to learn from and correct initial errors, it advanced the fight of the indigenous peoples and for Afro-Latin unity in the Americas and the Caribbean. It stood as an example that communist workers in the United States and other countries could point to in our discussions and common struggles with militant workers, farmers, and youth.

The workers' and farmers' government in Nicaragua was defeated without the U.S. rulers having to commit U.S. troops to attempt to smash the revolution in what would have been a bloody Central American war. In fact, by the end of 1987 the Nicaraguan toilers had defeated the U.S.-organized and -financed contra war, a grinding conflict that resulted in almost 60,000 dead and billions of dollars in damage to the Nicaraguan economy. Despite this victory over the contras, the foundations of the revolutionary government eroded during the closing years of the 1980s as a result of the political retreat and degeneration of its leadership under the economic pressures and destabilization operations it faced on a daily basis. This process culminated in the electoral victory in 1990 of the pro-Washington coalition around presidential candidate Violeta Chamorro.[8]

The demoralizing setback in Nicaragua dealt a blow to workers and farmers not only in Central America and the Caribbean, but also here in North America and worldwide. It came little more than half a decade after the overthrow of the workers' and farmers' government in Grenada, and the assassination of the revolution's central leader, Maurice Bishop, by the Stalinist Coard faction of the New Jewel Movement.[9] The defeat in Nicaragua reinforced a retreat by revolutionary forces throughout Central America and the Caribbean, including those in El Salvador and Guatemala, who had been looked to by many people radicalized by the Grenada and Nicaraguan revolutions.

THE BAGHDAD regime's lack of will to organize a fight, and the bloody invasion and occupation of one-fifth of Iraq by U.S. forces, were altogether different in their impact on workers and farmers in the United States and elsewhere. Not only was there not a government of the workers and peasants in Iraq, but the Baathist regime was not and never has been a revolutionary regime of any variety. It came to power in Iraq through a counterrevolutionary coup in 1963, following which the new regime completed the beheading of the vanguard of the 1958 revolution that had toppled the monarchy, carried out a land reform, and implemented other democratic and anti-imperialist measures. Saddam Hussein's Baathist Party is not a degenerated revolutionary nationalist movement; it is a bourgeois party that, as expediency dictates, resorts to nationalist and anti-imperialist demagogy to rationalize its repressive and expansionist course.

The consolidation of the Baathist regime put an end to revolutionary mobilizations of the working class, peasants, and layers of the middle classes in Iraq. For almost three decades the Iraqi toilers have not been led to carry out massive struggles that could inspire other fighting workers and peasants in the region, bring closer the bonds of solidarity with working people and youth in imperialist countries, or chart a course to challenge imperialism and the rights and prerogatives of capital. In fact, Baghdad's course had been the exact opposite—from its bully-boy methods in the region to its eight-year war against the Iranian revolution; from its repression of the Kurdish people to its refusal to use Iraq's natural patrimony to the benefit of oil-dependent countries in the semicolonial world, especially those in conflict with imperialism.

Baghdad had not even come into substantial conflict with imperialism, and never intended to, until its annexation of Kuwait convinced Washington that the Saddam Hussein regime had become a destabilizing, unpredictable, and unreliable ally in the oil-rich Gulf (as well as one that impeded the U.S. rulers' interests in the region relative to those of their French rivals). Prior to August, Washington, Paris, and other imperialist regimes had cultivated their ties to Baghdad for more than a decade, especially during Saddam Hussein's bloody war against Iran. Washington was continuing to trade with Iraq and to send top-level government and congressional delegations to Baghdad up through the first half of 1990.

So, while Washington dealt murderous blows to the Iraqi toilers and other peoples throughout the region, this did not have the same kind of negative consequences for the relationship of class forces, either in the Gulf region or anywhere else in the world, as does a defeat of a revolutionary government or an advancing struggle by workers and peasants. The millions of workers and peasants—including a million in uniform—were never organized to fight. That fight is still down the road. It has not been settled.

Earlier in Schwarzkopf's career as a hired "annihilator" for

U.S. capital, he got a taste of how a people can fight back against imperialist firepower when they've had the benefit of some revolutionary leadership and preparation for battle. Schwarzkopf was the deputy task force commander of the troops that invaded Grenada in October 1983—an opportunity handed to Washington on a silver platter by the Stalinist Coard faction when it overthrew the workers' and farmers' government. Schwarzkopf recalled what the invading forces ran into during the invasion in an interview published in the March 11, 1991, *New Republic.*

What "started as a highly unconventional, surgical in nature operation went sour right away," Schwarzkopf said. "And it went sour because of the assumption that the Cubans weren't going to fight. We had 800 Cubans on the island who were well armed and damn sure *were* going to fight." (Actually, the truth is even more impressive. Not all of the 800 Cubans on the island were involved in the fighting. Only the construction workers were under orders to defend themselves against a U.S. assault on the site of the uncompleted Grenada international airport project where they were working as volunteers. Many Cubans in Grenada were diplomatic, medical, and other personnel stationed elsewhere on the island.)

Schwarzkopf added that the U.S. invading forces also anticipated that Grenadan soldiers would be poorly trained and that their antiaircraft fire would be no match for U.S. helicopter gunships. (Most Grenadan working people, in and out of uniform, had been politically demobilized and demoralized by that time as a result of the bloody coup earlier in October.) But this, too, turned out to be a misjudgment, Schwarzkopf said. Paraphrasing the general, the interviewer reported that "as the invading American forces—among them the special [forces] strike teams—soon discovered, many of the gunners had been trained in Cuba; they were brave and highly disciplined; not only did they remain at their posts in the face of withering fire from U.S. helicopter gunships, they fired back."

### Iraq was not Cuba or North Korea
In the aftermath of the Gulf war, the U.S. rulers are now in a weaker position, not a stronger one, to launch a military assault against a people who are organized and prepared for a fight.

Cuba and North Korea, for example, top the list of propaganda targets for bourgeois pundits and spokespeople who release trial balloons on behalf of the U.S. administration. But Washington is in a worse position to assault either one of them today than it was prior to August 2. In their military calculations, the U.S. rulers took into account the character of the Saddam Hussein regime. They knew that the Iraqi toilers, in and out of uniform, had not been prepared for a war, deliberately so. But Washington also knows that the story would be a different one if it chose to launch aggression against the Cuban or North Korean governments and peoples.

CUBA'S WORKERS and farmers have been armed and trained by that country's communist leadership to fight a "war of all the people" in defense of the revolution. If Schwarzkopf was sobered in Grenada by several hundred Cuban construction workers and a handful of antiaircraft gunners, then taking on ten million Cubans is something else again. And the Cuban government wouldn't send its fighter jets to Iran, hold back its helicopter gunships to later turn on the Cuban people, or ground its fighter bombers.

As President Fidel Castro told an audience of Cuban students and youth on March 13, Iraq had "a big conventional army, many tanks, many things, but not a people prepared for war, there wasn't a doctrine of the war of all the people." But "if war is imposed on us," Castro said, "we will know how to wage it very well, and we've been preparing ourselves for that for many years. . . . In a war of that kind the people won't be watching the events unfold as if it were in a stadium. . . . It would be the people actively engaged in it."[10]

Moreover, Cuba would not be isolated in the face of a Yankee assault. Washington would have to reckon on the political consequences throughout the Americas, where Cuba's principled internationalism and defense of national sovereignty against imperialism have won it the respect of millions of workers, peasants, and youth. Unlike the Baghdad regime, the Cuban government would appeal for outpourings of solidarity around the world, and it would welcome support from abroad to fight alongside the Cuban people in their resistance to aggression. The political price that Washington would have to pay for such an adventure would be qualitatively greater.

The U.S. rulers also know that launching a war against North Korea has nothing in common with the operation they carried out in the Arab-Persian Gulf, either. It's not just that any such assault would meet formidable organized resistance by a well-prepared North Korean army and civilian population determined to defend their national sovereignty and independence—that's for sure. But a U.S. effort to build up a massive invasion force in South Korea (even leaving aside the much bigger logistical difficulties for Washington of getting such a force to that part of Asia compared to the Gulf) would shake the capitalist regime in Seoul to its very foundations. Likewise, any attempt to use South Korean forces to invade the North would ignite explosions in the streets, factories, and campuses everywhere on the peninsula south of the thirty-eighth parallel. Washington's client regime in Seoul could survive only through a U.S. military effort of such dimensions that the political price the U.S. rulers would have to be willing to pay is virtually inconceivable today. Even a joint U.S.–South Korean air strike against the Yongbyon nuclear reactor or other targets in North Korea would carry enormous political risks for both Washington and Seoul—risks that are greater today in the aftermath of the U.S. rulers' Gulf fiasco than before it.

The truth is that Washington is *already* paying a big political price for its failure to accomplish its aims in the Gulf region. It is paying a political price for its failure to push back the "Vietnam syndrome" at home.

And fighting workers, trade unionists who are communists, and young people campaigning against imperialism and war in the United States are making that price a little higher by taking and using the slightly wider political space open to us as a result of the political fiasco now unfolding for Washington. We are making that price a little higher by getting out the facts and throwing ourselves into the widening discussions among working people about the U.S.-organized slaughter, the lies by the government and army brass, the economic and social devastation of Iraq, the uprooting of the Kurdish and other refugees, the bloodbath against the Shiites in the south—all the results of Washington's bloody war.

## III.   NOT A 'NEW WORLD ORDER'
## BUT INCREASING INSTABILITY OF THE OLD,
## DECLINING IMPERIALIST WORLD ORDER

THE BUSH administration presents the war against Iraq as the first triumph of the "new world order." It points to the fact that Moscow not only gave public backing to the U.S. war drive, but also voted for every U.S.-initiated motion in the United Nations Security Council, right down to the April 2 resolution rubber-stamping Washington's stranglehold cease-fire conditions that in practice suspend Iraqi sovereignty. This enabled the U.S. rulers to use the UN as a fig leaf in a more brazen manner than any time since the opening of the 1950s during its war against Korea.[11]

Washington succeeded in gaining political and diplomatic cover for each new stage of its aggression in the Gulf with the aid of all four of the Security Council's other members with veto powers: Britain, China, France, and the Soviet Union. Enlisting the collaboration of the Stalinist regimes of the Soviet and Chinese workers' states was decisive to Washington's ability to present the devastating assault on the people of Iraq as if it flowed from a mandate of an "international community."

Only the government of Cuba—currently one of ten governments serving a two-year rotating stint on the Security Council—is using its position in the UN to speak out consistently against Washington's right to intervene in the Arab-Persian Gulf, under any circumstances or with whatever rationalization. Cuba exposed the successes of Washington and its allies in using this body as cover to justify its murderous course. The record of much of that effort by the Cuban government is presented in the book published by Pathfinder in October 1990 entitled *U.S. Hands Off the Mideast! Cuba Speaks Out at the United Nations,* which contains speeches and letters by Cuba's deputy foreign minister and chief UN representative Ricardo Alarcón and by President Fidel Castro. Later speeches by Alarcón and other Cuban representatives were run in the *Militant* newsweekly.

The truth is that Washington's Gulf war and its outcome did not open up a new world order of stability and UN-overseen harmony. Instead, it was the first war since the close of World

War II that grew primarily out of the intensified competition and accelerating instability of the crises-ridden old imperialist world order. It is the increasing internal strains within this declining order that drove Washington to launch its murderous military adventure. The irremediable social and political conflicts, and consequent instability, that existed before the Gulf war and that underlay it have all been exacerbated:

• between imperialism and the toilers of the Middle East and elsewhere in the semicolonial world;

• among the rival imperialist powers;

• between the various imperialist states and the oppressed nations;

• between exploiters and exploited within these oppressed countries;

• between the toilers and the bourgeoisified leaderships who speak in their name and claim to represent their interests;

• among the bourgeois states of the Middle East and other oppressed nations;

• between Washington and the governments of the deformed and degenerated workers' states, first and foremost, the Soviet Union;

• between the U.S. imperialist rulers and the two workers' states that pose the biggest problems for them, North Korea and Cuba; and

• between Washington and the revolutionary government and communist leadership right on U.S. imperialism's very doorstep in the Americas—that of Cuba.

The war demonstrated once again that there is no "international community" under the aegis of world capitalism. Most importantly, it has driven home the fact that there *can be* a world community—if the exploited and oppressed worldwide remove the exploiters and oppressors, the war makers, from power.

### Crisis of Stalinist regimes in workers' states

Imperialism's war drive in the Gulf opened a new chapter in the desperate efforts by the privileged caste in the Soviet Union to integrate itself into the declining world capitalist system. (This is also the goal of the regimes of the grotesquely deformed workers' states in Eastern Europe and, to a lesser degree, China as well.) In hopes of ameliorating its deepening economic and social crisis, Moscow has staked its fortunes on earning—through political concessions to the citadels of world finance capital—expanding investments and massive loans, trading privileges, and entry into imperialist financial institutions such as the International Monetary Fund.

Whatever their other conflicts and rivalries, the dominant sections of the privileged Soviet bureaucracy are committed to this goal, which they pray will be their salvation; each of their decisions on how to respond to developments in the world class struggle is a tactical move subordinated to advancing this objective. Not only those directly associated with President Mikhail Gorbachev, but also those aligned with Boris Yeltsin in the Russian republic and elsewhere, and the broadest layers of the dominant elements in the officer corps of the internal "security" police (the KGB) and armed forces, are in agreement.

In craven pursuit of this goal, the Soviet government threw its support behind Washington's war drive against Iraq. Moscow's warm diplomatic ties with Baghdad cooled; the Kremlin tossed aside its extensive military agreements with the Iraqi regime. So slavish was Moscow in backing Washington's every move in the Security Council that in March the Soviet delegation voted to reject each of eighteen amendments put forward by the Cuban government to a U.S.-initiated resolution; the Cuban amendments sought to exempt food, medicine, and other vital necessities from the UN-sanctioned embargo of Iraq.[12] In effect, the Soviet government sold its votes in the Security Council in the vain hope of investment, trade, loan, and aid favors from the U.S. and other imperialist governments and international institutions. (In fact, however, Moscow is further away from gaining entry into the IMF and its other major international economic goals than prior to August 2. So much for imperialist hand-kissing—the core of Gorbachev's "new thinking"—as the royal road to financial progress.)

The same economic and political considerations lie behind other recent foreign policy moves by Moscow. These include the Soviet government's offer during Gorbachev's April 1991 trip to Tokyo to begin negotiating a return of the Kurile Islands to Japan; Moscow's course toward openly endorsing the "two Koreas" policy long advocated by the capitalist regime in Seoul and its masters in Washington to block the aspirations of the Korean people for national reunification; the Kremlin's growing diplomatic relations with Israel and trade ties with the apartheid regime in South Africa; and its steps toward rapidly implementing trade relations with Cuba at world market prices paid for in scarce hard currencies.[13]

Beijing—also a permanent member of the Security Council—followed a course fundamentally the same as Moscow's. Since the economic and social crisis of the caste is not yet as acute there as in the Soviet Union, the Chinese regime succeeded in maneuvering enough to stay in Washington's good graces while maintaining its diplomatic standing among bourgeois governments in the Middle East—those outside as well as inside the U.S.-organized coalition. The Chinese delegation voted for most of the major U.S.-initiated resolutions in the Security Council; abstained on just enough to keep up appearances; but never once obstructed the U.S. rulers' war plans by simply voting "no."

The various crisis-ridden regimes in Eastern Europe all fell in line behind Washington's war drive, as well. It is in these countries that the disintegration of the Stalinist parties and government apparatuses has gone the furthest. Powerful popular rebellions, or concessions by privileged layers to head off such uprisings, have brought an end to hated tyrannies in one country after another. In the absence of any revolutionary leadership of the workers' movement, the new governments in these workers' states all remain as petty bourgeois in composition and as thoroughly anti-working-class in political orientation as the regimes they supplanted.

The regime of the former German Democratic Republic has been dismantled and a united government dominated by German finance capital has been formed. Several other of these deformed workers' states (Poland, Czechoslovakia, and Hungary in particular) are headed by overtly procapitalist and pro-imperialist figures drawn from various middle-class and professional layers as well as remnants of the previous Stalinist regimes. The Czechoslovak, Polish, Hungarian, and Romanian regimes went so far during the Gulf war as to send medical teams to function as part of the U.S.-organized war alliance against Iraq. Their foreign and military policies, like their faltering "privatization" efforts, come down hardest on workers and farmers—at home and abroad.

As the U.S. war drive unfolded during late 1990 and early 1991, world capitalism demonstrated that it is incapable of and unwilling to deliver on the kind of major financial assistance that the regimes in the Soviet Union, China, or Eastern Europe have the illusion could reverse the economic stagnation and social crisis they face. Promised grants and loans from imperialist governments and banks have been much smaller than anticipated. Investment plans are being scaled back, since profit rates there are simply not competitive with more lucrative alternatives in the capitalist world, including in a number of semicolonial countries.

Although initially hailed by many as a gigantic boon to German capitalism, the attempt to integrate the workers' state in the east into a united Germany has turned out to be an enormous financial burden—to the tune of nearly $100 billion this year and an estimated $1 trillion in the 1990s. Together with the large outlays to Washington for the Gulf war, Bonn's expenditures to keep the east German economy afloat have put increasing pressure on the mark, driven up interest rates, and threatened to turn Germany's economic slowdown into a recession. The once-anticipated massive flow of German capital into the rest of Central and Eastern Europe has been sharply restricted.

The working class in both parts of Germany is growing more and more dubious about a new economic miracle, and these workers are increasingly willing to strike to defend their living and working conditions. Bonn fears that more German workers are being impelled toward independent political action. Greater instability, not stability, marks Germany.

WASHINGTON'S MASSIVE war mobilization in the Gulf spotlights anew the degree to which the strategic military weight of the Soviet Union has eroded relative to U.S. imperialism. It also underlines the fact that Moscow's military equipment and weaponry are inferior to Washington's, despite the much larger relative burden of the bureaucratic caste's military spending on the stagnant Soviet economy.

This decline has its roots in the deepening economic and

social crisis that the Soviet Union has been led into by successive Stalinist regimes. The living and job conditions of workers and working farmers continue to skid. Basic standards of medical care, education, housing, and other social services are deteriorating, drastically in some cases. The environment continues to be ravaged, while the poisonous legacy of past contamination persists (including the "hot" remains from the Chernobyl nuclear disaster). Workers who are women are among those hit hardest by these conditions as a result of their continued second-class status and absence of adequate birth control, child care, and other needed services. Oppressed nationalities face deepening inequality, systematic discrimination, and repression.

Decades of political tyranny over the toilers and Stalinist methods of economic planning and management have had disastrous consequences for every aspect of social life in the Soviet Union. It should come as no surprise, therefore, that these same methods cannot work miracles with regard to the organization, morale, modern provisioning, or projection abroad of the Soviet armed forces. Given a choice, no worker any of us knows would buy a car, a television set, a can opener produced in the Soviet Union. How, then, can we expect the quality of Soviet military production, over time, to match that of the most advanced weapons of the imperialist countries? In fact, especially after the war in the Gulf, many bourgeois regimes in the Middle East and Africa with traditionally close ties to Moscow are surely drawing the conclusion they are better off making a few more concessions if they can get Washington to become their quartermaster.

Moscow has little strategic capacity to use its armed forces effectively to fight a war beyond countries bordering it. (And even in that case, as the war in Afghanistan showed, there are narrower limits than many who look to the Soviet bureaucracy had anticipated.)

Moreover, the parts of the world shielded from the danger of imperialist attack under the Soviet nuclear umbrella—that is, countries that the Soviet regime considers vital to its own security, and would therefore consider nuclear retaliation if necessary to defend them—continue to shrink, perhaps limited today to the area inside the borders of the USSR itself. And the shrinkage hasn't stopped. It is doubtful that this umbrella any longer extends over Eastern Europe, where Washington assumed that it did stretch from the 1960s through the 1980s. And we know from the history of the past several decades that it did not cover the Chinese, North Korean, Vietnamese, or Cuban workers' states. Their survival in the face of imperialist military pressures or assault has been primarily the product of the efforts of the peoples and governments of those countries, supplemented by aid from the Soviet Union and the political constraints on Washington at home and abroad.

Of course, the Soviet government retains its capacity as a strategic nuclear power, with a massive modern army, to defend the territory of the USSR from imperialist attack. That would change only if Washington were to succeed in perfecting a "Star Wars"–type anti–strategic missile system that would enable it to pick off Soviet intercontinental ballistic missiles early in flight, thus giving the U.S. rulers a blackmail "first-strike" capacity without fear of devastating retaliation. That's one of the reasons the U.S. ruling class will continue to press to develop a satellite-based missile intercept system. But a strategic nuclear standoff between Moscow and Washington will continue to be the reality in world politics for the foreseeable future.

Faced with the loss of diplomatic leverage in bargaining with imperialism as a result of its relative decline as a world power, the Soviet government is increasingly prone to rhetoric advocating a "return" to the "original peacekeeping functions" of the United Nations. It points to the actions of the Security Council in response to Baghdad's annexation of Kuwait as an example. But the permanent members of the Security Council—especially Moscow and Beijing—simply acted as shills for U.S. imperialism's war drive against Iraq. The Security Council's actions had nothing to do with keeping the peace or defending national sovereignty. The so-called UN "peacekeeping" forces established along the Iraq-Kuwait border to monitor the cease-fire, or to "protect" Kurds in the north, will themselves be nothing but a surrogate for Washington's armed forces.

In fact, the United Nations is *already* functioning as it was originally structured and intended when it was founded at the close of World War II. The structure of the Security Council was consciously fashioned by Washington, London, and Paris to ensure that it could never act against the interests of the imperialist powers. That's the purpose of the veto power reserved to the U.S. government and the other four permanent members of the Security Council—veto powers held only by the five largest allied victors in World War II. What's more, when Washington is able to win the open collusion of Moscow and Beijing—as we've just witnessed during the war drive against Iraq—the Security Council can then be used by the imperialist rulers as direct, if subsidiary, political camouflage for the deadly military pursuit of their class interests and dominance.

Contrary to the illusions promoted by Washington and Moscow alike, there is no such thing as "the United Nations." There is simply a complex of buildings, a giant bureaucracy, and a General Assembly where some 150 governments occasionally read position papers on various world events and adopt resolutions that have symbolic value. Ultimately, only the five permanent members of the Security Council have a say over any action carried out in the name of the United Nations. Thus, the "history" of UN "peacekeeping" is at bottom nothing more than the history of the evolving relations among these five powers, any of which can exercise its veto.

## Acceleration of interimperialist conflict

The assault against Iraq was the first of Washington's wars since World War II in which it sought to use its military might to deal blows, indirect but palpable, to U.S. imperialism's rivals, especially in Bonn, Tokyo, and Paris. The Gulf war exacerbated the conflicts and divisions between Washington and its imperialist competitors, as well as between these rival powers themselves. While we know these sharpening conflicts already existed (every working person has been deluged by protectionist propaganda from the U.S. government, bourgeois politicians, trade union bureaucrats, and their radical hangers-on), the war brought them to the surface with greater force and accelerated them to a degree not seen in world politics for some time.

Coming out of World War II, U.S. imperialism emerged the dominant power in the world imperialist system, both economically and militarily. For a substantial period following that war the rate of profit, and for even longer the tempo of growth of the mass of profits, was rising in all the imperialist countries. As a result, competition between the imperialist powers over markets for commodities and capital and over sources of raw materials was buffered.

Since the mid-1970s, however, the combination of the declining rate of profit, halting growth in the mass of profits, and relative slowdown in economic expansion has precipitated growing, sometimes sharp rivalry among the imperialist ruling classes. The years 1974-75 saw the first *worldwide* recession since 1937, as economic interdependence among the major capitalist powers grew alongside their competition and conflict. Although the sheer size and output of the U.S. capitalist economy remains enormous, and while it remains the largest market in the world, its position as an industrial and trading power has slipped substantially in recent decades in the face of growing challenges from German, Japanese, and other rivals. U.S. strategic military power remains unchallenged, however, and is the main lever the U.S. rulers have to compensate for their relative decline.

No power other than Washington could have transported and put in place the mammoth order of battle necessary to carry a war to Iraq. While waged behind the facade of a broad "international coalition," the war was a U.S. government operation, with London's enthusiastic support and with Paris being forced to join in out of weakness. Bonn and Tokyo—still limited in their use of strategic military power abroad flowing from their defeat in World War II—took no part in the combat at all.

Through the initiation, organization, domination, and execution of this war effort, U.S. imperialism strengthened its control over Gulf oil reserves, gaining additional leverage over its rivals in Bonn, Tokyo, and Paris in the competition for world markets for commodities and capital. By throwing the biggest military forces of any other imperialist power behind Washington's war effort, the rulers in London successfully sought to guarantee themselves a privileged junior position alongside U.S. finance capital in this region, which was once largely a British protectorate but had been penetrated more and more by French trade, aid, and loans. The commitment of combat forces abroad by the Canadian ruling class for the first time since the Korean War, and Ottawa's increasingly open and unqualified backing of Washington's foreign policy moves, indicate the pressure to grab more firmly onto the skirt of U.S. imperialism. The regime in New Zealand did the same, easing conflicts with Washington that have grown up there over port visits by U.S. ships armed with nuclear weapons. The Australian ruling class, as usual, made sure it was represented in Washington's armed entourage as well.

The relationship of forces that existed prior to the Gulf war among the capitalist powers in Europe has not been altered, but the national and state conflicts between them have been exacerbated. The war underlined the limits of the European Community's modest steps toward greater "economic integration" (lowered barriers to trade, investment, and travel). The U.S.-engineered war drive exposed beyond doubt that these measures do not translate into a "common European" foreign policy, a "common European" military policy, let alone steps to build up a "common European" armed forces. Nor do they even translate into a "common European" economic policy, let alone a common currency; in fact, strides in this direction were set back.

Instead, the rival capitalist classes in the European Community (EC) were further propelled toward defending their separate state interests, whatever their common stake in a trading bloc in face of U.S. and Japanese competition.

The war set back German imperialism's goal of an integrated European Community under Bonn's domination. It battered the Bonn-led alliance of German and French imperialism in the EC. The French imperialists—who had made special ties to Baghdad one of the axes of their foreign policy in the Middle East, in hopes of regaining a stronger economic foothold in the Gulf—suffered humiliating cuffs from Washington.

Drawing on the advantage gained through its total collaboration with the U.S. war drive, London took an extra inch or two in its constant attempts to buffer the effects of British imperialism's decades-long decline relative to its chief European capitalist competitors. But growing subordination to the deutsche mark and involvement in Europe remain the central lines of development for British capital.

Japan stands to be the biggest loser from the Gulf war among the major imperialist powers. It is the most dependent of all on imported oil, with 70 percent of its supply coming from the Middle East (compared to some 15 percent for the United States and 35 percent for Germany). Japan is thus most vulnerable to Washington's use of the "oil weapon" in interimperialist conflict.

SEVERAL EXAMPLES from the outcome of the war in the Gulf illustrate what Washington was able to accomplish as a result of its military predominance.

First, U.S.-owned companies have already been awarded an estimated 70 percent of the multibillion dollar reconstruction contracts signed by Kuwait's royal oil barons. British-owned firms rank second (London finds the degree of the U.S. capitalists' greediness a little colonial, to say the least). Germany and Japan have been virtually iced out. General Motors is getting in on the act, replacing Japan as the supplier of thousands of automobiles to Kuwait for the remainder of 1991, many of which will be used to replenish the stock of cop cars damaged during the war.

Second, the U.S. rulers brought such enormous pressure on rivals to cover their "fair share" for the Gulf operation that if they actually pay up, Washington stands to make a "profit" on the war. Some $54 billion has been pledged to the U.S. government, while congressional estimates put the direct costs of the war at $40-45 billion. (Evidence is mounting, however, that the U.S. rulers' expenses are far from over.) Among the imperialist contributors to Washington, the biggest are Japan (more than $10 billion) and Germany (nearly $7 billion). And the U.S. rulers have also gotten agreement from the Saudi and Kuwaiti monarchies to pay more than $30 billion. London, too, may come out in the black, with contributions from Germany and the Gulf monarchies already totaling $2.7 billion.

Another example is the U.S. Treasury's recent unilateral actions to cancel major portions of the foreign debts of Poland and Egypt—a decision met with public protest from Tokyo bankers and their government. (These debt reductions, of course, were contingent on assurances from the Polish and Egyptian regimes that more will be taken out of the hides of toilers in both countries and that new loans will have more stringent conditions.) Since Japan is the world's largest lender, and more vulnerable as such, officials in Tokyo point out that Washington's move is a direct blow to their ability to collect on massive debts. Through that single action, the U.S. imperialists destroyed large quantities of paper wealth and put long-run pressure on the income flows that Japanese capitalists can anticipate. Unlike Tokyo, which up to now has relied on the leverage it gains in semicolonial countries from massive loans, Washington has a broader range of trade-offs flowing from its military dominance.

The U.S. war against Iraq once again emphasized the fact that for any ruling class aspiring to world power, a chasm cannot be allowed to persist between its economic power and its ability to use strategic military might abroad. A time comes when a ruling class recognizes that it has to put the checkbook away, put the gold away, and reach for the troops—or else it cannot maintain itself as a world power capable of defending its own class interests, either against workers in rebellion or competitors on the prod.

O NE CERTAIN result of the Gulf war will be efforts by the German and Japanese rulers to strengthen their armed forces and to push back political constraints—both at home and abroad—on the use of military power beyond their own borders. The German and Japanese rulers are determined they will never again be in a position of forking over billions of dollars to their chief rival to help it strengthen its strategic and competitive power. Their resolve is all the stronger after having paid for a war that strengthens Washington's domination over a vital commodity, especially one that both Germany and Japan must import. Bonn and Tokyo have just been compelled to pay through the teeth to make the cost of their access to that oil more vulnerable to manipulation by Washington and Wall Street.

Germany and Japan already have large and modern standing

armies—much more so in reality than their image in the United States would lead us to believe. Germany has the largest army in Western Europe, with 480,000 soldiers in uniform; it spends some $30 billion on its military annually. Japan has 247,000 soldiers in uniform and an annual military budget roughly the same as Bonn's. Tokyo and Bonn will now seek to transform these armies into forces capable of taking decisive action in the world.

The bourgeois press has played up the fact that the German and Japanese constitutions have provisions restricting the use of military forces abroad. But the history of the modern capitalist world proves that constitutions don't prevent ruling classes from doing what they need to do to advance their state interests: substantial agreement in the ruling class, well-prepared public opinion, a shift in the class relationship of forces, and—voilà!—a new "interpretation" of the constitution, or an amendment to it.

The German and Japanese rulers *will* start acting as military powers in their regions and in the semicolonial world. This fact alone means that the world has become more volatile and unstable. Political conflicts will sharpen between these two mighty imperialist powers and Washington, Paris, and other rivals—and between each other. Conflicts will be exacerbated between Japan, Korea, and the United States, as well as between North and South Korea. These conflicts can spark real political battles at home that the vanguard of the working-class movement can involve itself in by advancing a political course that defends working people independent of any wing of the capitalist rulers.

Bonn and Tokyo can take steps in this direction relatively rapidly without beginning to introduce strategic nuclear arms into their arsenals. That's a different question. That would be very difficult to do today without a massive political battle at home that could threaten social stability not only in Japan but also in Germany. There's no reason to change our estimate on that.

But the dominant bourgeois political forces in both Bonn and Tokyo have already begun to wage the political fight to marshal bourgeois public opinion behind the use of conventional armed forces abroad, and they are making progress. A member of no multilateral military pact, Tokyo will pay a larger domestic price for these moves, but Japan's rulers will absorb that price (while trying to minimize it) in order to strengthen their position as a world military power. In both Germany and Japan, big wings of the officialdom of the Social Democratic parties and their allied trade union bureaucracies will swing behind this "patriotic" and "world peacekeeping" effort.

Increased probes along these lines have already begun to be made by both the German and Japanese rulers in the aftermath of the Gulf war. In Germany the government of Chancellor Helmut Kohl is pressing for a constitutional amendment to permit German troops to join in international "peacekeeping" coalitions outside the framework of NATO. In backing this course, Manfred Wörner, Bonn's representative to NATO and currently its secretary general, points out: "There are cases where diplomacy, without the sword, is impotent." The Social Democratic "opposition" wants to assure that such German troop deployments abroad will only be done as part of UN Security Council efforts!

For its part, the Japanese government, in its first military deployment abroad since World War II, has sent minesweepers to the Gulf as part of the allied force.

Ultimately, this is not simply a political or a military question; it's an economic question. The rulers in Tokyo remember how the Roosevelt administration put an embargo on oil sales to Japan in 1940. (And the U.S. Navy remembers Tokyo's rejoinder: the December 7, 1941, bombing of Pearl Harbor.) There is a good reason why the Gulf region was one of the most contested prizes in both the first and second world wars. Oil is vital in the modern world, and the Gulf today supplies more than 20 percent of the world oil market. No capitalist ruling class can with impunity allow itself to become vulnerable to oil blackmail by its rivals.

## Opening guns of World War III

The Gulf war revealed that important changes have occurred in what appeared to be the continuing pattern of world politics coming out of the initial consequences of World War II.

Washington was the chief victor in that war. It emerged as imperialism's predominant economic and strategic military power, and the only one nuclear-armed to boot. The Soviet toilers, at the sacrifice of tens of millions of workers and peasants, had repelled the onslaught by German imperialism. By the beginning of the 1950s capitalist property relations had been overturned throughout much of Eastern and Central Europe, even if under Stalinist-led regimes. By the latter half of the 1950s the USSR had its own nuclear arsenal (although not effective parity with Washington in weaponry and delivery systems until late in the 1960s).

Struggles for national independence and self-determination gained powerful momentum throughout the colonial and semicolonial world during World War II and its aftermath. During the decade and a half following 1945, victorious national liberation struggles in Azerbaijan, Yugoslavia, Albania, China, North Korea, Vietnam, and Cuba grew over into deep-going anticapitalist revolutions; brought to power workers' and peasants' governments; and (except for Azerbaijan) culminated in the expropriation of the landlords and capitalists and the establishment of workers' states.

Washington's wars in Korea and Vietnam were fought during a period of an ascending world capitalist economy. The U.S. rulers' dominance in the world imperialist system was still unchallenged, both economically and militarily. The dollar reigned supreme in world financial markets. But U.S. imperialism's German and Japanese rivals were not under sharp competitive economic pressures that pushed them toward direct military involvement in the Korean or Vietnam conflicts. (In fact, Tokyo took advantage of huge construction contracts during the Korean War to take the first steps toward rebuilding its devastated economy, without having to share the burden of the U.S.-organized military operations.)

Given this global picture that emerged in the second half of the twentieth century, imperialist war was expected to be largely limited for the foreseeable future to the use of military power against the colonial revolution, as well as threats against the workers' states. It was in the colonial world that the main organized, massive resistance to imperialism was continuing to take place—from Asia and Africa, to the Middle East and the Americas. Bourgeois-nationalist leaderships and Stalinist organizations frequently dominated these struggles, but the obstacles posed by this misleadership did not prevent substantial victories from being won by the toilers in their fight for colonial independence.

In some cases radical petty-bourgeois leaderships—responding in a determined way to blows aimed at them by an arrogant imperialism, and under the impetus of worker and peasant struggles against capitalist exploiters in city and countryside—went through an anticapitalist evolution. This was the case with respect to the July 26 Movement in Cuba; a major wing of the Algerian resistance movement; and a few organizations influenced by the Cuban revolution such as the Sandinista National Liberation Front in Nicaragua and New Jewel Movement in Grenada. (Most petty-bourgeois nationalist leaderships, on the other hand, did not evolve in this direction and ended up tailing or being integrated into bourgeois nationalist formations, or, in a few cases, Stalinist parties.)

This was the period of the so-called Cold War. At least from some point in the 1960s, the U.S. rulers operated on the assumption of a nuclear stalemate with Moscow, especially once the Soviet Union developed the capacity to hit U.S. targets with nuclear-tipped missiles. Meanwhile, the privileged castes in the Soviet, Eastern European, and Chinese workers' states, acting as transmission belts for imperialist pressure, combined police-state repression with Stalinist political disorientation to push working people at home increasingly out of politics and keep them isolated from the international class struggle—to the great advantage of the imperialist ruling classes as well.

On the basis of this post–World War II pattern, most revolutionists concluded—correctly for the foreseeable future—that the international class struggle was not heading toward increased interimperialist military conflicts, but toward a standoff between the two major powers with strategic nuclear arsenals—U.S. imperialism and the Soviet Union—and their allies. A third world war, it was assumed, would necessarily find the imperialist powers aligned behind Washington in a conflict with the USSR. The rival capitalist ruling classes would avoid military conflicts among themselves, conflicts that would leave them vulnerable both to the Soviet Union and to the loss of additional portions of the world to anticapitalist revolutions.

I'm presenting a simplified version of this view of the world, but not a caricature. Whatever one-sidedness there was to this assessment, it was grounded in the objective fact that due to the factors just cited there was no drive toward interimperialist military conflict during this initial period of postwar capitalist expansion.

This pattern corresponded with what was actually happening in world politics during the initial decades following World War II, including the generally low level of intensity of the class struggle in the United States and other imperialist countries. We were not heading toward intensified class combat on the picket lines and in the streets. We were not heading toward an ascending working-class movement bursting beyond the bourgeois political framework imposed by the petty-bourgeois union officialdom. We were not heading toward clashes in the streets with growing ultrarightist and fascist movements organized by wings of the employing class to try to take on and crush a class-struggle-oriented vanguard of the labor movement. With a time lag that could not be predicted, it was assumed, the class struggle in the United States and other imperialist countries would eventually turn a corner heading in this direction and begin narrowing the gap with the level of combat in the colonial world. This would lead to prerevolutionary situations that could result in major new advances in the international struggle for national liberation and socialism.

POLITICS AND the class struggle in the Soviet Union, Eastern Europe, China, and other Stalinist-dominated workers' states were largely a nonfactor in this political equation. The existence of a substantial portion of the world where the domination of capitalist property relations had been abolished was recognized as a conquest of the toilers worth defending against imperialist assault. But the workers and farmers of these countries seemed more and more to have been frozen out of the world class struggle for an indefinite period by the repressive and politically stultifying domination of the castes and their police-state regimes—especially following the bloody defeat of the Hungarian revolution in 1956.[14] Meanwhile, as a way of maintaining bargaining leverage with Washington, the Stalinist regimes provided arms and financial aid to national liberation movements and to governments that came in conflict with imperialism in the Third World.

**B**UT NONE of these political assumptions hold any longer in the world situation today—one whose advent was most explosively marked by the 1987 crash of the world's stock markets. The crash was further evidence that the 1974-75 worldwide recession and the sharp and sudden slump of 1981-82 were not simply two more periodic downturns in the capitalist business cycle; they also signaled the end of an ascending segment in the broader curve of capitalist development and the ushering in of a descending segment heading toward intensified class battles on a national and international scale, including among the imperialist powers.[15]

The world pattern today is characterized by capitalism's tendency toward economic stagnation, instability, and vulnerability to breakdowns that can precipitate a global depression and social crisis. It is a world of intensifying interimperialist competition and conflicts. It is a world in which resistance and class conflicts will mount in response to the capitalists' intensifying assault on the rights and conditions of workers and exploited farmers. It is a world in which the disintegration of Stalinist parties and regimes across Eastern Europe will continue, and the crisis faced by the privileged caste in the Soviet Union will deepen, opening up space for the first time in decades for hundreds of millions of workers and farmers in those parts of the world to begin engaging in political life, to recognize and connect with fellow toilers abroad.

Capitalism will not be able to open a new period of accelerated economic development and improving social conditions to the peoples of the Third World under bourgeois regimes, including the Gulf region or elsewhere in the Middle East. Instead, international debt slavery weighs ever more heavily on all these peoples. Struggles for national liberation will increasingly be combined with battles against local exploiters for land, democratic and labor rights, and social justice. These national-democratic and anti-imperialist struggles, in order to be carried through to victory, will more than ever require revolutionary working-class leadership and political perspectives. Conflicts between capitalist governments in the Third World will also increase. In the face of these volatile conditions, the imperialists will be driven time and again to use their military might to defend their power and their profits.

Washington's assault against Iraq is the first of a number of such wars that imperialism will continue fighting against peoples and governments in the Third World. They will be more and more intertwined with intensifying conflicts among the rival imperialist powers themselves. The gap will widen between Washington's military power and its relatively declining economic prowess, while its major imperialist rivals will seek to narrow the gap between their own economic strength and their relatively subordinate military power.

The mounting instability throughout Eastern Europe, in the Soviet Union, as well as in China will not be reversed by reactionary, national-socialist efforts to win economic concessions from imperialism in return for foreign policy favors. The petty-bourgeois misleaders can only ape the world bourgeoisie, not become them, even if they share their values and beliefs. Workers and farmers in these countries will keep pressing their way into politics—domestic and international. So long as major means of production, banking, and trade remain expropriated, these states will continue to come into conflict with the imperialist ruling classes, which will be driven by their profit needs toward taking back hunks of the world and the world's toilers for direct capitalist exploitation. The dangers of imperialist wars against the republics of the Soviet Union and other workers' states will grow, not recede.

Threats and probes against the Cuban and North Korean workers' states—where working people refuse to back down in face of imperialist threats—will continue, and relations between these governments and the U.S. rulers will be exacerbated.

In an early April 1991 opinion column in the *New York Times,* for example, Leslie Gelb called North Korea "the next renegade state." Despite the North Korean government's long-standing efforts to rid the Korean Peninsula of all nuclear weapons (Washington has stationed some 1,000 nuclear missiles in the south), Gelb asserted that they are "likely to possess nuclear weapons in a few years." As a means to force the North Koreans to submit to an inspection of their electricity-generating nuclear reactors, he urged the Japanese government to suspend all trade with that country.

And Jeanne Kirkpatrick, Washington's former UN ambassador, in an April 1 column in the *Washington Post,* called attention to assessments by U.S. government officials that the nuclear power plant that Cuba is constructing in Cienfuegos "could be used to produce weapons-grade plutonium."

So Washington's war in the Gulf is not, as the U.S. rulers pretend, the harbinger of a new world order based on peaceful solutions to strife among states. Instead, in a world of mounting economic crisis and breakdowns, social instability, political conflicts, and unfulfilled demands for national liberation, it can much more accurately be described as the opening guns of World War III.

That is the inexorable historic logic of imperialism in its decline—the class logic that will culminate in world war if the capitalists prevail in the decisive struggles that are ahead.

Intertwined with the historic war logic of the imperialist rulers, however, is the class logic, the historic line of march of the working class: to resist and react, to fight and in the process become revolutionary, to organize independently of the exploiters and identify as a part of a worldwide class, and to wrest the war-making powers out of the hands of the exploiters and oppressors. Whether or not there is a World War III will be decided in struggle between these two historic class forces and their allies. The very continuation of humanity itself rests on the outcome.

The opening guns of World War II came early in the 1920s, in the aftermath of the first interimperialist slaughter and the failure of the working class in Europe to extend the victorious workers' and peasants' revolution in the Soviet Union. Over the next decade and a half, the international working class fought heroically and encountered several revolutionary opportunities to take power out of the hands of the capitalist war makers in Europe. On the basis of a radicalizing working-class and farmers' movement, at the center of which was the rise of the CIO industrial unions, workers in the United States had the opportunity to chart a course toward labor political action independent of the imperialist parties and government. Only as the consequences of Stalinist and social democratic misleadership resulted in accumulated and massive defeats to the working class in Europe did the Second World War become inevitable in the closing years of the 1930s.

Today, as the political consequences of Washington's military "victory" in the Gulf continue to unfold, we need to recognize that this is not primarily a *postwar* period, but a *prewar* period. It is in this context that we say that the slaughter in the Gulf is the first in a number of conflicts and wars that will be initiated by the U.S. rulers in the 1990s, and the opening of a new stage of accelerating imperialist preparations—at home and abroad—for those wars.

But Washington's resort to military power will increasingly set unanticipated and uncontrolled forces into motion that make its "victories" destabilizing and more pyrrhic than lasting in their results. The U.S. government has—and will—become more vulnerable, not more invincible. In this sense, each one of U.S. imperialism's interventions around the world will more and more take on the character of a military adventure.

The task of the vanguard of the workers and farmers in the United States and around the world is to fight for the space to organize our class and our oppressed and exploited allies to win new victories, and to take the power to make war out of the hands of the imperialist ruling classes and their allies among the exploiters and oppressors throughout the capitalist world.

## IV. INVASION WAS A SLAUGHTER, NOT A WAR

ON JANUARY 16, 1991, Washington began its round-the-clock bombardment of Iraq. Several days later the leadership of the Socialist Workers Party released a statement that was featured on the front page of that week's *Militant*. "In the few days since Washington launched the most intensive bombing assault in the history of warfare," the statement opened, "the horrible realities to which hundreds of millions of people closed their eyes for months have become increasingly and brutally apparent.

"The war launched with bipartisan support by the U.S. government will not be short; it will be long.

"It will not be an air war; it will be a bloody ground war.

"It will not be a limited war; it will be a total war, like other mass slaughters of the modern era from the U.S. Civil War through World Wars I and II.

"It will not be a war limited in its aims, allegedly to 'liberate Kuwait.'

"The goal of the U.S. capitalist rulers remains what it has been throughout the escalation of their war drive since early fall: a devastating military defeat of Iraq and the imposition of a de facto U.S. protectorate in Baghdad."

The Bush administration and its bipartisan supporters try to reduce the duration of the war to one hundred hours, or at most to the six weeks between January 16 and February 27. But the truth is that Washington waged a *seven-month-long* war against the people of Iraq. The U.S. government's blockade of Iraq imposed immediately following the August 2 invasion of Kuwait was an open act of war by any definition of the term; it was the most massive military embargo in the history of warfare.

When Washington launched its invasion of Iraq on February 24, what ensued over the next four days was not a ground war but a mechanized slaughter, a military-organized police riot from the land, sky, and sea. The political course of the Saddam Hussein regime was designed, organized, and implemented to ensure that a ground war was never fought. In fact, there were only a few brief rearguard firefights, organized by Baghdad's Republican Guard units as they retreated—taking as much armor, weaponry, and equipment as they could—to regroup and serve as an armed police force to crush internal dissent. The mass of workers and peasants in Iraq's regular army were largely abandoned by Baghdad in Kuwait and southern Iraq. By that time, these Iraqi workers and peasants in uniform—threadbare uniforms, in many cases—were in fact no longer soldiers organized into an army. They had been reduced to unorganized individuals—lightly armed at best, provisioned poorly if at all, with no functional command structure and with only the few officers who had not fled. They were left to face the slaughter on their own.

As for the U.S. invading forces, they emerged from the one hundred hours with practically no tank or heavy equipment losses and a bare handful of casualties. In fact, the toll of U.S. deaths and injuries from the entire seven months of military operations was largely the result of accidents, "friendly fire," and the chance destruction of a barracks in Saudi Arabia by an Iraqi-launched Scud missile. There were very few U.S. combat deaths, either of pilots or of the ground troops that carried out the invasion.

From its invasion of Kuwait on August 2, 1990, right down to the halt of the U.S. offensive at the end of February 1991, Baghdad's entire plan was based on a calculation that it would not have to fight a war against Washington; that it could maneuver, bluff, shuttle diplomats around, buy time, and finally either get away with the annexation or negotiate behind a smokescreen of rhetoric to keep some island port facilities and oil fields. Without a moment's regret, Hussein did offer up tens of thousands of regular army troops to the bipartisan warrior chiefs in Washington. But he never did fight a war.

The Iraqi regime's invasion of Kuwait was an extension of the expansionist course that propelled it to war against Iran in 1980, an assault that lasted for eight long, bloody years. Baghdad's aim in its new expansionist conquest in Kuwait was to increase the Iraqi capitalists' control over oil reserves in the region. They sought to put themselves in a better position to pressure the militarily weak Saudi Arabian regime on pricing and quota policies of the Organization of Petroleum Exporting Countries (OPEC), and at a future point grab some Saudi oil fields as well. In this way, the Iraqi government intended to increase its share of the oil profits garnered by the Gulf regimes and thus contain growing internal dissatisfaction over the mounting economic consequences and loss of life due to the war against Iran.

BAGHDAD'S combined political and military course flowed from the limits of its bourgeois perspectives and its decades-long methods of bombast, bluff, and thuggery. It correctly sized up both the lack of a social base or defensive military capacity of the Kuwaiti and Saudi oil kingdoms—and the fact that these royal families were held in contempt and hatred by the vast majority in the Gulf area and throughout the Middle East as a whole.

Saddam Hussein also acted on the assumption that Washington would not risk the political consequences at home of a military action abroad that would result in substantial U.S. casualties. Baghdad recognized that the initial U.S. deployment to the Gulf (relatively lightly armored and largely airborne units) would not be sufficient for Washington to launch a counterattack. So the Iraqi regime kept on pouring more troops and tanks into Kuwait and southern Iraq and digging them into defensive positions. It anticipated it could buy time to extort a settlement from an administration in Washington that would not fight, because it would fear the domestic consequences of taking the number of casualties that Baghdad itself accepted so casually in its war against Iran.

As part of these calculations, Baghdad banked on being able to play on the rivalries and divisions between U.S. imperialism and imperialist powers in Europe and Japan. In particular, Saddam Hussein anticipated exerting diplomatic leverage through Paris, since French capitalists had a substantial trade and investment stake in Iraq and had been working for more than a decade to use their ties with Baghdad to rebuild French influence in the Middle East. The Iraqi regime also assumed that Moscow would place a high enough priority on retaining its established ties with Baghdad to create problems for Washington's efforts to win international diplomatic cover for U.S. military moves.

The Iraqi regime rejected even the most minimal effort at any real political mobilization and preparation of the Iraqi population to resist an imperialist onslaught. To the contrary, the Baathist regime's propaganda over radio and television basically promised there would be no assault on Iraq. Similarly, Baghdad never issued a serious appeal for regional and international solidarity to halt the impending imperialist attack, or to mount international brigades to help resist such aggression if it couldn't be stopped. Instead, the Iraqi rulers engaged in empty bombast threatening an outbreak of terrorist attacks on imperialist targets worldwide, threats that never materialized. Baghdad also demagogically threatened missile attacks against Israel if war broke out, aiming to unnerve Washington with the prospect of a breakup in its alliance with the Egyptian, Syrian, Saudi, and other Mideast regimes. Each of these steps by Hussein simply added grist to the imperialists' propaganda mill, aiding them in covering up their real goals in the war drive.

Hussein also calculated that Baghdad could isolate Washington in the Arab and Islamic world by justifying the invasion of Kuwait on the basis that imperialism had carved up the region, by utilizing pan-Arab rhetoric, and by cynically manipulating broad popular support for the Palestinian struggle.

But each one of these calculations by Baghdad, all aimed at never having to fight a war, proved to be political misjudgments.

The regimes in Egypt and Syria sent large heavily armored divisions on Washington's side; Turkey's rulers enforced the anti-Iraq blockade, opened Turkey's airfields to U.S. bombers, and massed 100,000 troops along its border with Iraq; and the Iranian regime stayed officially neutral.

B Y EARLY SEPTEMBER at the latest, the Bush administration had settled on a course leading to an all-out war against Iraq. The stated aims of the first stage of Washington's war drive—to respond to requests by the Saudi monarchy for defense against Iraqi aggression—were cast aside, as the U.S. rulers aimed instead at achieving an offensive military capacity in the Gulf.

What followed was beyond anything Baghdad had counted on: Washington stripped its forces in Europe of more than half their troops and tanks and mobilized regular and reserve units at home on a massive scale. By early 1991 an order of battle of more than half a million U.S. troops had been transported to the Gulf (up from some 200,000 in early November) and outfitted with enormous quantities of the Pentagon's best heavy armor, mechanized artillery, most technologically advanced weaponry, bombers and fighter planes, warships, and aircraft carriers.

Washington accompanied its military moves by various "peace" initiatives to gain some diplomatic cover for its inexorable march toward war. This included Bush's offer of talks between Secretary of State James Baker and Iraqi foreign minister

Tariq Aziz, which eventually took place in Geneva in early January. But the Baathist regime misread every one of these diplomatic moves, interpreting them as U.S. hesitation and indecision rather than political camouflage to prepare the next steps in the march toward war. The logic of bluff and bombast fares poorly against the logic of an imperialist war drive.

Saddam Hussein also underestimated the political consequences of Washington's continued military predominance in the imperialist system. In late 1990 Paris and Bonn did take some independent initiatives with Baghdad to stake out their own diplomatic turf. But each of Washington's rivals ultimately had to face up to one central choice: either join in the war drive without hesitation, put your military forces under Washington's command (or pay enormous sums of money, as did Bonn and Tokyo), and get in line diplomatically . . . or suffer whatever consequences Washington can impose later on.

Baghdad misjudged the degree of the crisis of the Soviet bureaucracy and its consequences on Moscow's foreign policy as well. The Stalinist regime placed a much greater priority on promises of a deeper integration into the world capitalist system than whatever secondary diplomatic advantages it has gotten over the years from its ties with Baghdad.

Finally, the Iraqi regime's bombast about drawing Israel into a war also failed in its anticipated aim of bluffing Washington into a settlement. When the U.S. rulers called the bluff and launched the murderous bombing assault in mid-January, Baghdad could do little more than respond by launching some Scud missiles at Israel and Saudi Arabia. Saddam Hussein evidently hoped that what had been intended as demagogy might somehow work. Here too, however, he misjudged Washington's capacity to block Tel Aviv from doing anything that might obstruct U.S. plans and operations.

This course left the population of Iraq unprepared for each stage of the war drive and war. They were literally surprised—shocked—when the bombs started falling on Baghdad, Basra, and other cities, towns, and villages.

The Iraqi people's desire to bring an end to the allied bombing and avoid wider devastation from a war to defend Baghdad's brutal subjugation of Kuwait was shown by the popular celebrations that exploded in the streets of the capital city each time the Baathist regime made a statement hinting it might withdraw. The toilers correctly recognized this as the one sure way that Iraq could be spared a repeat of Saddam Hussein's eight-year military adventure against Iran. But each time, the people of Iraq soon discovered that they were simply pawns in the cynical course of greed and bluster followed by Baghdad since August 2.

## Baghdad's international isolation

In response to the imperialist war drive in the Gulf, communist organizations around the world such as the Socialist Workers Party, and their members and supporters, spoke out immediately in solidarity with Iraq and the oppressed and exploited peoples living and working in that country and throughout the region.

The government of Cuba and the leadership of its Communist Party was another voice that spoke out against Washington's war drive against Iraq. As a matter of basic solidarity, Cuba insisted on keeping its close to 200 medical volunteers in Iraq for the duration of the war.

The Socialist Workers Party was *unconditional* in our solidarity with Iraq and the Iraqi people and in our defense of them in the face of Washington's armed assault. We did not make the mistake of identifying the repressive capitalist regime in Baghdad with Iraq itself, an oppressed Third World country, or with the toilers in Iraq, our brothers and sisters. We were uncompromising in our defense of Iraq against imperialist assault, while unreservedly condemning the Saddam Hussein regime's invasion and annexation of Kuwait, its entire political course, and the monarchical brutalities and oppressions of the rentier al-Sabah and Saudi ruling families.

Despite the importance of this solidarity with the toilers who found themselves in Iraq, Kuwait, and Saudi Arabia on August 2, however, the more general picture was quite a different one. The Iraqi people had less international support in the face of a ruthless imperialist assault than any people who have had to face such devastation since World War II. Nowhere in the world did a government or a major force in the international workers' movement or a national liberation organization issue a call for—let alone begin organizing—sustained mass mobilizations in solidarity with the Iraqi people. No organized political effort was mounted to break through the blockade and get needed supplies to the Iraqi people. There was no call to organize volunteer troops from elsewhere in the region and the world to fight alongside the Iraqi soldiers and people against the coming imperialist invasion.

SEVERAL DEMONSTRATIONS and one-day protest strikes were organized in North Africa and the Middle East, some with support from governments or opposition political parties and organizations. But that was all. And even these were largely perfunctory, despite the genuine solidarity of the working people and youth who turned out for them. But no government or mass organization anywhere charted a clear course to show that—regardless of their opinion of Baghdad and its actions—they were unconditionally determined to mobilize opposition to the horror that Washington was inflicting on Iraq and its peoples, and to continue campaigning until it stopped.

This was different from what happened during the Vietnam War. We correctly credit the Vietnamese people for liberating themselves, but we also know that there was an important international movement in solidarity with Vietnam. I'm not referring just, or even primarily, to the antiwar movement in the United States and other countries that developed late in the war. Vietnam received military supplies and other assistance from governments in the Third World and in the workers' states. Volunteers from other countries and other national liberation movements went to Vietnam to help out in the construction and defense effort.

Similar kinds of international solidarity were extended to the Nicaraguan people during the final year of the fight to overturn the U.S.-backed Somoza dictatorship through the years of the fight against the contra war. Support came not just from other national liberation organizations and political groups all across Latin America, but also from the government of Gen. Omar Torrijos in Panama and from Cuba.[16]

There are many other examples. International support was mobilized in 1973 to help governments in the Middle East defend themselves against the military assault by Israel.[17] There has been international solidarity with the freedom fighters in South Africa, El Salvador, and elsewhere.

*But the Iraqi people were alone* in a fundamental way. From the standpoint of governments or any mass organizations, they were alone.

One reason, as previously noted, was that the Iraqi regime consciously refused to make any serious appeal for regional or international solidarity and aid. That wasn't part of Saddam Hussein's plans; he and his cronies were opposed to it. First, the Iraqi regime wasn't planning on a war ever taking place. Second, appeals for revolutionary mobilizations would have threatened to destabilize other capitalist regimes in the region to which Baghdad looked as a possible avenue for diplomatic deals with imperialism.

Third, and most important, any revolutionary appeals for international solidarity could not have been sealed off from workers and peasants inside Iraq itself. The last thing the ruling gang in Baghdad wanted was for revolutionary-minded working people and youth—from the Middle East or anywhere else—to start pouring into Iraq. That would have opened the door for the Iraqi people themselves to begin organizing resistance to the allied assault. They could have fought to provision the troops in the field and organize relief to areas devastated by bombing raids and the embargo. Fighters willing to lead fellow soldiers in battle could have stepped forward. Calls to arm the population would have been raised, together with demands that Baghdad commit the entire range of its best weaponry to turn back the imperialist attack. But Saddam Hussein wanted no part of any of this. In the wake of such a mobilization, the Iraqi people would have simply swept away the regime—as shown by the deep-going rebellions in the weeks following Washington's suspension of the offensive.

Solidarity with Iraq was also undermined by the fact that there was no anti-imperialist or progressive thrust whatsoever to Baghdad's actions in Kuwait. The occupation of Kuwait was a reactionary act by a bourgeois Bonapartist regime. It presented Washington with the pretext to launch the imperialist war drive in the Gulf.

But the lack of active solidarity with Iraq against imperialist aggression also stems from another reality of world politics that revolutionists must understand to chart an effective course: Never since the end of World War II has the gap been greater than it has become over the past couple of decades between the toilers' aspirations for national sovereignty, democracy, and social justice and the political course of bourgeois misleaderships throughout the Middle East. This fact registers the historical exhaustion of the nonproletarian currents that stood at the head of democratic and anti-imperialist struggles by the toilers and sections of the middle classes in Egypt, Iraq, Algeria, Yemen, Libya, and elsewhere from the 1940s through the 1960s. It marks the political dead end of efforts to advance these goals today in the name of "pan-Arab" or "pan-Islamic" unity—a unity these bourgeois leaderships break at will for national gain and political position.

Today, the framework within which the struggle for national liberation and against imperialist domination unfolds is marked by the consolidation of the various *separate states* in the region. This is not some brand new development. It is not a result of the U.S. war in the Gulf. It is a product of the stage of development of capitalism in these countries, and of their integration into the world capitalist system. It is a product of the consolidation of a national bourgeoisie and substantial middle class, of internal modern class development and class polarization. These bourgeois regimes use their state power—including naked violence and aggression—to advance their class interests against rival regimes, as well as against the workers and peasants at home. And all of them do so under the cover of "Arab unity"—whether Baghdad, to rationalize its land grab in Kuwait; Cairo and Damascus, to justify their alliance with Washington in a war against Iraq; or Amman, to shuck and jive and survive another day to live royally off the toilers.

COMMUNISTS have no trouble in recognizing the need for unconditional solidarity with an oppressed nation against imperialist attack, regardless of the class character of its government, as we've proven once again during the Gulf war. At the same time, communists and other vanguard fighters for true national independence and sovereignty—whether in Iraq or anywhere else in the region—must recognize and act on the fact that there are conflicting classes within these oppressed nations.

The Palestinians are among the biggest victims of the fakery of the bourgeois governments in the region, all of which falsely claim to speak and act in their interests. These blows were dealt to the Palestinians not just by the treacherous Egyptian, Syrian, and Saudi regimes—or by the desperate King Hussein of Jordan, who will turn his guns on the Palestinians again, if he finds it expedient, just as he did in September 1970.[18] No less damage was done by the reactionary demagogy of Baghdad, which postured as the champion of the Palestinian, Arab, and Muslim peoples, while in practice it sapped their capacity for anti-imperialist struggle. Baghdad cynically called for "linkage" of Iraq's partial withdrawal from Kuwait with the Palestinians' demands for national self-determination.

The leadership of the Palestine Liberation Organization also did great harm to the Palestinian struggle by endorsing this demagogic, after-the-fact linkage. This tailing after Baghdad left PLO leaders politically disarmed to explain the *real linkage* that does exist with the Palestinian struggle; the pressing need for *action* in solidarity with Iraq in the face of imperialist assault; the reactionary character of Baghdad's brutal invasion of Kuwait; and the fight against imperialism throughout the region and the world.

The failure of the PLO to chart such a revolutionary course is a reflection of its growing bourgeoisification. This evolution was *revealed* more clearly by the U.S. aggression in the Gulf, but it was not *caused* by the war. The political retreat by the central PLO leadership has been under way for some time.

A political toll has been taken over the past ten or fifteen years by the continued dispersion of the Palestinian people. A whole layer of Palestinian youth have grown up outside the historic lands of Palestine. A PLO apparatus has been built up throughout countries in the Middle East and North Africa hosted and financed by the bourgeois regimes in the region. A few factions of the PLO have become willing tools in the hands of these governments. The blows dealt to the PLO forces in Lebanon over the past decade by the Israeli regime, by the Syrian regime, and by the various Lebanese bourgeois political forces—these have had an additional disorienting and demoralizing impact on layers of the leadership, turning their eyes further away from the ranks of the Palestinian masses inside and outside Israel. The gap has grown between the PLO apparatus and the young Palestinian fighters inside the borders of "Greater Israel," where the liberation fight has been centered more and more.

But this is not a finished process. The PLO remains a revolutionary-nationalist movement with a predominantly petty-bourgeois leadership. The outcome of the PLO's political evolution remains intertwined with the living struggle of the Palestinian people, who have not been cowed or defeated. More of the leadership of the Palestinian movement has shifted to the occupied West Bank, to Gaza, to Jerusalem, and to inside Israel's pre-1967 borders—especially since the beginning of the intifada more than three years ago. More of the leadership is being taken by those who are pressing forward the fight for land, for equality, for national self-determination, for a fully sovereign Palestinian state, and who in doing so are helping to change the world.

Some PALESTINIAN leaders draw important political lessons from the harm done to their struggle by the demagogy of the Saddam Hussein regime. One example can be found in an interview with Hanan Ashrawi run in the May 3, 1991, issue of the *Militant.* Ashrawi was part of a delegation of Palestinian leaders who met with Secretary of State James Baker when he was in East Jerusalem in March and again in April. She teaches on the West Bank at Bir Zeit University (when the Israeli army does not have it shut down). She gave a phone interview to two *Militant* reporters, Argiris Malapanis and Derek Bracey, April 9 from Ramallah on the West Bank.

Ashrawi responded to the statement by some PLO supporters that the confrontation between Baghdad and Washington in the Gulf put a world spotlight on the Palestinian struggle and led to gains for their fight for international recognition. "It's not a question of gains," she said. "There were no gains [from the Gulf war]. The Palestinian question was moved to the fore-

front of the international agenda as a result of the intifada,
which is the Palestinian human voice of resistance, as you know.
Popular resistance."

She continued:

> It is the unfortunate fate of the Palestinian issue to be
> manipulated and used by the Arab leaderships
> historically for their own ends. You see, it is an acid test, a
> source of credibility. It is part of the "credentials" of any
> Arab leader. And most Arab leaders have succeeded in
> oppressing their own people, using the pretext of a
> national cause, which is the Palestinian cause. They have
> manipulated us for their own ends, whether economic,
> political, regional, or international.

Pointing to the popular support for Saddam Hussein that did
build up among many Palestinians in late 1990 and early 1991,
Ashrawi continued:

> In a way, it was a regression to a messianic approach.
> Instead of placing your faith in the power of your own
> people and the determination of the popular movement,
> you started to place your faith in an individual, which is
> against the intifada ethos. The intifada, the Palestinians,
> and the PLO had succeeded in removing the Palestinian
> cause from Arab patronage and manipulation, and
> placed it on its own terms within Palestinian hands and
> under Palestinian sovereignty. We speak for ourselves.

Saddam Hussein's pro-PLO, pan-Arab, and pan-Islamic rhetoric and demagogy dealt a blow to each of the struggles by the
Palestinian, Arab, Islamic, and other peoples of the region oppressed by imperialism. Each of those fights was harmed, not
aided, by being linked by Hussein to his expansionist annexation of Kuwait—a move that gave imperialism a golden opportunity to intervene against the peoples of the region in a way it
had not been able to do for decades. Far from popularizing or
mounting support for any of those causes, Hussein's reactionary
posturing disoriented and demobilized the toilers, setting back
a common struggle against the oppressors and exploiters at
home and abroad.

Well before the January 15 Security Council "deadline" for

Iraq's withdrawal from Kuwait, Washington was fully aware from its intelligence-gathering that the Iraqi people and armed forces were not being organized by Baghdad to defend themselves from punishing bombardment or to resist a large-scale armored invasion backed by U.S. and allied air cover.

The rest of us didn't have as much information as quickly as the Pentagon, so it took us a little longer to begin to see what was shaping up. But we took notice, after the U.S. bombing had been going on for a while, when it became known that Baghdad was sending many of its best fighter planes to Iran. That was a signal that Saddam Hussein wasn't planning to provide air cover for the troops, nor to make the U.S. Air Force pay any price for the ruinous bombardment being inflicted on the people of Iraq night and day. Nor, it became clear, would there be serious air cover for Iraqi soldiers trying to resist an allied ground invasion.

There were other facts we had no way of knowing until reports began to appear following the U.S. occupation of southern Iraq. We now know that Baghdad had begun withdrawing its best tanks and other armor from Kuwait and the southern front before the invasion. The attack helicopters were pulled back— another indication that there would be no air counterattack against allied armor in order to open space for Iraqi ground troops to fight. By the last couple of weeks before the invasion, efforts to reprovision the troops with food rations and adequate clothing and gear had ceased; the caloric intake of the soldiers even began to drop. Nothing was done to maintain the kind of communications network needed by a structured army whose commanders plan to make a stand.

Finally, large parts of the officer caste were organized by Baghdad to get out of the battle zone. By the time Washington invaded, the mass of regular Iraqi troops had been left by the Saddam Hussein regime without any attack helicopters with antitank weapons, without air cover, without communications or coordination, without defensive tactics, without organization or discipline, and without a command structure. They were *no longer soldiers organized in an army,* no longer anything that could function as a fighting force. They had become simply individual workers and peasants—sitting in bunkers, some of them lightly armed, in uniforms—facing massive imperialist bombardment and shelling.

If any revolutionists, any communists had been in those trenches with these Iraqi toilers, we would have known what was being done to the structure, supplies, and morale of the army. We would have known what the inevitable outcome had to be—not a fight, but the slaughter of pawns on whom a cowardly leadership had turned its back. Faced with these conditions during the U.S. invasion, we would have helped organize our fellow workers and peasants to find their way back to Iraq, and to surrender if that was the only way to do so. We would have helped them get out of the killing fields. We would have helped them survive to fight another day. We would have explained what happened and why it showed the need to fight to advance our own class interests, to fight all our class enemies—the imperialist exploiters and oppressors who were carrying out the slaughter, as well as the Iraqi exploiters and oppressors whose reactionary adventure had set us up for it. We would have explained and organized.

ANY OTHER TACTICS or political course would have been unthinkable for communists in that situation. Any other course would have been a blow to the fight for Iraq's national sovereignty, a blow to the fight against imperialism, a blow to the struggle to liberate the working people of Iraq from oppression and exploitation.

Those workers and peasants couldn't defend Iraq from imperialism by fighting. They had been stripped of any capacity to fight by a regime that never had any plan to defend Iraq—only to defend itself. Those Iraqi toilers weren't equipped to defend anything. They were simply offered up to imperialism by Baghdad. The military consequences of the political course of this treacherous bourgeois regime cost more than a hundred thousand Iraqis their lives. And Saddam Hussein and the class he represents could not have cared less. This is a bitter example of why the working class needs its own military policy—and its own class independence to get it.

The Baathist command organized the elite Republican Guards to retreat to serve as its Praetorian guard, to act as a massive, murderous police force against internal rebellions.

The Republican Guards receive better pay, better food, live under better conditions, and have better military hardware. Many of their cadres are drawn from the ruling Baathist Party. They maintain tight links with specialized secret units of the police and interior ministry. These kinds of elite forces are used by repressive bourgeois regimes to crush internal rebellions. They were unleashed by Baghdad against the fleeing soldiers of the regular army that joined revolts by workers and peasants in southern Iraq in the aftermath of the U.S. invasion. And they are the forces that drowned the Kurdish rebellion in blood and drove millions—millions!—from their homes.

O NCE AGAIN, we must understand that the entire political course of the Saddam Hussein regime—from its calculations in annexing Kuwait right up to the U.S. invasion itself—was based on never having to fight a war against U.S. imperialism. Revolutionists understood from the start that this plan was destined for disaster, that Washington had set an undeviating course toward war as far back as September. We said time and again that there was one and only one way to block imperialism's march toward a horrendous war: *for the Saddam Hussein regime to withdraw all its troops from Kuwait.* When he finally did so, it was to protect himself against the people of Iraq, not to spare them the full fury of Washington's final murderous orgy.

As it turned out, after one misjudgment of Washington's moves after another, Saddam Hussein's goal of not fighting a war finally "worked"—but only following the U.S. invasion. Baghdad never intended to fight a war, and in the end it didn't. In one sense, from the point of view of the Baghdad regime, you could say that Hussein won. His gangster-style grab for more turf was pushed back for now, but the core of his regime remains intact along with many of its best troops, aircraft, artillery, and other equipment needed to defend it from the Iraqi people and with which to bully the Gulf sheiks and emirs another day.

Hussein ordered his generals to leave Kuwait in flames. Just days prior to the U.S. invasion, they began to torch oil wells in Kuwait—more than five hundred in all. Within days, one of the worst ecological disasters in history was under way. Thick clouds of black, oily smoke clogged the skies. Two months after the invasion only a handful of the oil-well fires have been extinguished. Due to the blotting out of the sun by the smoke, the average temperature in Kuwait has dropped ten degrees, and truckers and other drivers often have to turn on their headlights during the day. Toilers living throughout the region will suffer directly from the effects: acid-bearing clouds have showered black rain from Iran, to Turkey, to the western shore of the Black Sea.

In his February 27 press briefing just after Washington declared the pause in offensive operations, Gen. Norman Schwarzkopf boasted that the U.S. military "victory" could be attributed to the success of what he presented as the allied command's "secret plan"—what he referred to as the "Hail Mary play." He was referring to the U.S. command's decision to have its ground forces push through southern Iraq toward the Euphrates River and Basra, "flanking" to the north the Republican Guard concentrations, which were positioned closer to the Kuwaiti border, and the regular Iraqi units in Kuwait itself.

But there was nothing "secret" about this plan. It had been discussed on television and published in the newspapers for months. Maps had been featured in the media weeks beforehand charting almost exactly the course followed by the invading U.S. forces.

Gen. Colin Powell, chairman of the Joint Chiefs of Staff, summed up the U.S. rulers' military strategy with terse but brutal accuracy one week after the bombing started: "First we're going to cut it off, and then we're going to kill it." That's exactly what Washington did. But not to an army or a mobilized people.

By the fourth day of the invasion, Washington acted on the assumption that it was well on the way to having a U.S. protectorate in Baghdad. Bush could go on television and claim a military victory over an Iraqi army of half a million, and with only a handful of U.S. body bags. All the U.S. rulers had to do then, as we discussed earlier, was wait for some wing of the Baathist establishment and officer corps to depose or assassinate Saddam Hussein and form a government that was more accommodating to Washington. That was the assumption.

The Bush administration put a stop to the bloodbath after one hundred hours because it was convinced it *had* accomplished the U.S. rulers' war goals in the Gulf to the degree possible, without undermining their related objective at home of putting an end to the "Vietnam syndrome." It could begin "bringing our boys home."

In the following days tens of thousands of toilers in Iraq mobilized in cities in the north and south. They saw the weakening of the regime as an opportunity to wrest some political elbowroom and deal blows to the repressive apparatus of Hussein's government. The Kurdish people rapidly took control of a large section of northern Iraq, either winning over sections of the army or forcing them into retreat. Without prior organization, revolutionary experience, or much leadership in most cases, tens of thousands north and south rallied and confronted the first stage of the Republican Guards' assault. But without a moment's hesitation, Hussein organized the Guards to turn against the Iraqi people the armor and air power that he had refused to use to defend Iraq.

Washington was not predisposed against any political figure or organization in Iraq if one had emerged strong enough to replace Hussein. But the fundamental interests of imperialism, of its allies in the region (beginning with Saudi Arabia), and of the Baathist regime in Baghdad all coincided in certain respects: none wanted the mobilizations in Iraq to continue; none wanted a wider fight for any form of Kurdish autonomy; none wanted the opening of more political space in which Iraqi workers and peasants could organize, resist, and set an example for other toilers in the region; none wanted a prolonged period of political instability in Iraq.

The U.S. rulers did not anticipate the scope of the rebellions by Kurds and other oppressed toilers in Iraq, nor the bloody suppression unleashed by Saddam Hussein and its embarrassing media results at home. But the most important point is that such matters were never part of Washington's calculations one way or the other. The U.S. rulers have no interest in the national rights of the Kurds. The depth of the national pride and determination of the Kurdish people—like that of the Palestinians and other fighting peoples—is a mystery to them; it will always catch them by surprise. To the contrary, Washington's interest is in forging stronger ties of imperialist domination with a subjugated Iraqi government and with other historic butchers of the

Kurds: the Turkish government, the Syrian government, and, to the degree possible, the Iranian government.

Nor did Washington ever have any "democratic" Iraqi political force it was grooming to install in Baghdad. The U.S. rulers don't care about democracy in Iraq.

At the February 27 press briefing, Schwarzkopf dismissed the idea that Washington had designs on Iraq's sovereignty. He bragged that as the U.S. forces rolled across the country there was "nobody between us and Baghdad," should the U.S. command have chosen to press its advance. There is no evidence, however, that Washington considered that necessary to accomplish its aims. And despite Schwarzkopf's pretense that U.S. forces could have breezed into the Iraqi capital, that was never tested.

Since U.S. troops never headed for Baghdad, the invasion never reached a point where the Saddam Hussein regime's interest in its own survival converged, even if temporarily, with the interests of Iraqi soldiers and civilians in defending Iraq against imperialist aggression. Under such conditions, the Baghdad regime might well have deployed the necessary weaponry and equipped and organized the remaining regular army, as well as the Republican Guards, to engage the invading allied forces. But that convergence never occurred, and the workers and peasants of Iraq were never given a chance to fight. Their capacity to resist—if organized and equipped to do so—was never put to the test.

This wasn't inevitable. Being saddled with a political leadership, government, or command structure that is counterrevolutionary does not mean that the toilers are condemned not to fight, or even that they cannot win in some exceptional cases.

THROUGHOUT THE 1930s, for example, the Soviet workers' state was gravely weakened by the political counterrevolution of the privileged caste led by Stalin. Millions of revolutionists and other workers and peasants fell victim to mass, organized police terror. Moscow organized the bloody defeats of revolutions across Europe and in Asia. Stalin carved up Poland in a deal with Hitler's imperialist Germany, turning over thousands of

Communists and revolutionary-minded workers and peasants to the Nazis' murder gangs and concentration camps. The top officer corps of the Soviet army was exterminated in purge trials that began in 1937 and continued up to the eve of German imperialism's invasion of the Soviet Union in June 1941. When Germany invaded, Stalin refused to organize a fight at first. He refused to believe it! The German army captured half a million square miles of the Soviet Union and began to threaten the existence of the regime itself.[19]

Thus, the Soviet workers and peasants entered the war to defend their national sovereignty and the economic and social conquests of the workers' state with a treacherous misleadership that had placed them in an extremely weak position from which to resist. Since Hitler's armies were clearly moving to stop at nothing short of total conquest and the destruction of the Soviet government, however, the Stalin-led regime organized the armed forces and made it possible for the toilers to turn back and defeat the invading imperialist forces. The war under Stalin's domination was never fought with the revolutionary methods that could have dealt the heaviest blows to the class enemy with minimum casualties to the toilers. It was not fought like the revolutionary campaign of 1918-20 under the leadership of Lenin and Trotsky.[20] But by February 1943 the tide was turned to the advantage of the workers and peasants with the decisive defeat of the German armed forces at the battle of Stalingrad.

EVEN DURING the U.S. invasion of Panama in December 1989 there was initial organized resistance by the Dignity Battalions in the working-class neighborhoods. The fighting was sporadic and crushed relatively rapidly as the officer corps of Gen. Manuel Noriega's National Guard refused to do battle and—with Noriega himself at the head of the pack—gave themselves up to the imperialist occupation forces. Noriega headed a corrupt and rotten bourgeois regime. But the embers of the earlier anti-imperialist mobilizations and social upheavals in Panama in the 1960s and early 1970s, during the period associated with Gen. Omar Torrijos, had not been entirely extinguished. Those had been years of an intensified fight to take back the Panama Canal from U.S. imperialism; of bringing the oppressed peoples of Panama more deeply into politics, especially those of African and indigenous origins; of raising the consciousness of Panamanians as Panamanians. That momentum, even after the years of degeneration under Noriega, still yielded the Dignity Battalions, still yielded some capacity among the toilers to find organized ways of resisting U.S. aggression. Although defeated in the end, many veterans of that resistance remained alive to fight another day, and they will have their chance. Fighters throughout the Americas and around the world saw what the Dignity Battalions did for several days and were inspired by this example.[21]

But there was nothing like that in Iraq. There were no Dignity Battalions. And the U.S. forces didn't meet the kind of resistance they ran into—later recalled so vividly by Schwarzkopf—from a few hundred Cuban construction workers and Grenadan antiaircraft gunners during the invasion of Grenada.

Revolutionary-minded workers and peasants in the Middle East and around the world are correctly beginning to sense that the Iraqi people were never given a chance to fight, that they were never organized to resist the imperialist onslaught. Fighters are outraged by massacres such as Washington's "turkey shoot" on the road to Basra; it increases our class hatred of the exploiters and our determination to put an end once and for all to their oppression and terror. But such slaughters don't weigh nearly so heavily on the morale of fighters worldwide as a defeat inflicted by the oppressors on a revolution, on organized and combative toilers who have been forced to bend their knee, or by the failure of an army built by these toilers to fight well.

The Iraqi people have taken horrendous blows at the hands of the butchers in Washington, as well as the wretched capitalist regime in Baghdad. But they never had a chance to resist. They were assaulted as individuals; they faced imperialist firepower as individuals. Their fight was not defeated; it has been postponed.

Like the Palestinians and other working people across the region and throughout the world, they will fight; from proletarian and peasant fighters will come revolutionaries; and from revolutionaries communists can be forged. And they can win.

## V.  WORKER-BOLSHEVIKS
## CAMPAIGN AGAINST IMPERIALISM AND WAR

FOR MOST working people in the United States, the war in the Gulf was the first they have experienced in a world of deepening economic crisis and breakdowns in the capitalist system, similar to that of the worldwide Great Depression of the 1930s. Both the U.S. war in Korea and the war in Vietnam took place during the long post–World War II international capitalist economic expansion. The U.S. war against Iraq, to the contrary, took place not only during a recession, but more fundamentally in a segment of the curve of capitalist development with sharply different dynamics from the previous one.

The segment we are living in today is marked above all by world capitalism's evolution, signaled by the 1987 stock market crash and growing strains on the imperialist banking system, toward a depression and social crisis. This evolution precludes the possibility of alleviating the structural debt slavery to imperialism smothering most semicolonial countries that remain capitalist. It condemns most of Eastern Europe and the Soviet Union to a twilight world of permanent crisis as the workers, bereft of any communist continuity as a result of decades of Stalinist repression and disorientation, struggle to acquire political experience and breadth.

The accumulating impact of the current recession in the United States, Britain, Canada, France, Australia, New Zealand, and other imperialist countries is putting an even tighter squeeze on the livelihoods of hundreds of millions of working people. The toilers of the semicolonial countries face particularly onerous conditions. Most of these countries never pulled out of depression conditions precipitated by the economic downturns in 1980 and 1981-82. Simply keeping up with the interest payments on the enormous (more than $1.3 trillion) Third World foreign debt has devastating consequences on nutritional, health, housing, educational, and other economic and social conditions of peasants and workers. The latest blight is the cholera epidemic that first appeared in Peru and is now spreading throughout South America—the first in many decades; cholera has reappeared in Iraq, as well, as a result of the destruction of water purification and sanitation facilities by the savage U.S. bombardment.

In the United States real wages, working conditions, job openings, and government-funded social services continue to decline, hitting the already worst-off sections of the working class especially hard. Once again the rulers are using the excuse of the growing "fiscal crisis" of state governments and several large city administrations to ram through attacks on public workers and cutbacks in services, while bankers and bondholders fatten their coffers on state and local revenues. Conditions of large sections of the working-class majority of the oppressed African-American nationality are being driven down even more. The growing numbers of immigrant workers continue to confront systematic inequality, discrimination, and harassment. A woman's right and convenient access to abortion remain under pressure by the courts, Congress, and state legislatures. Democratic rights are chipped away at, as the employers and their government take an edge here to expand censorship, an edge there to roll back the rights of prisoners and the accused.

Given this reality, what was the state of the U.S. labor movement and of U.S. politics and the class struggle as Washington's war drive against Iraq began last August? How has it developed since?

As we discussed a few months ago, despite the ongoing capitalist offensive against workers and the oppressed, the employers have not pushed the labor movement off the center stage of politics in the United States.[22] They have not been able to break the resistance by working people to their assaults on our living and working conditions and democratic rights. They have not been able to dissipate working-class solidarity toward anyone who mounts a real struggle.

Coal miners in the United Mine Workers of America (UMWA) fought a successful, nearly eleven-month-long strike battle against the Pittston coal company in 1989-90, with broad support from workers throughout the labor movement. Members of the International Association of Machinists (IAM) waged a twenty-two-month-long strike from March 1989 through January 1991. That battle defeated the union-busting efforts by Eastern Airlines' management (first Frank Lorenzo, then the bankruptcy court's appointed trustee Martin Shugrue) to run a profitable, nonunion airline. After a premeditated lockout by the management of the *Daily News* in New York in late 1990, workers there fought to defend their unions, standing up to company gun thugs and strike-breaking tactics. Hundreds of thousands of working people in the city showed their solidarity with the strike by refusing to buy the scab paper, effectively driving it off newsstands throughout the metropolitan area.

IMPORTANT ELEMENTS of these fights—the stepping forward of rank-and-file leaders in the Eastern and Pittston strikes, the determination by workers to fight despite obstacles erected by the officialdom, the solidarity from other workers and unionists—provide initial experiences and lessons that can be drawn on by vanguard workers in battles to come. A good feel for these strikes and a political explanation of their place in the evolution of the U.S. labor movement over the past decade is provided in a book recently published by Pathfinder entitled *The Eastern Airlines Strike: Accomplishments of the Rank-and-File Machinists.* Judy Stranahan, a staff writer for the *Militant,* draws together twenty-two months of on-the-spot coverage, and Ernie Mailhot, a leader of the strike at New York's La Guardia Airport, evaluates the accomplishments of the rank-and-file leadership that developed.

We've just seen another example of how workers in this country are on the lookout for a fight they can join to push back the employers' offensive. Leading up to the April 17, 1991, expiration of the "cooling-off period" on the contract covering 235,000 rail workers (who've already been "cooling off" for three years), unionists organized discussions, rallies, and other events in a number of areas. The rail bosses, with support from the government, have kept pushing to roll back work rules, chip away at wage levels, intensify speedup, and erode union control over safety conditions on the job. They finally pushed so hard that the top rail union officialdom, under pressure from the ranks to hold the line on further concessions on job conditions and wages, called a nationwide strike in April. (Shortly after Washington's bombardment of Iraq began in January, Dick Kilroy, president of one of the rail unions, the Transport Communications Union, had openly made a no-strike pledge for the duration of the war. "As a patriotic gesture, we're not going to strike and disrupt the war effort," Kilroy said. The other top rail union bureaucrats joined in the bipartisan flag-waving as well.)

Any fight the rail workers could have mounted would have clearly won wide backing from other unionists and working people. They were hungry for such a fight. But in a largely bipartisan vote, Congress—as it has repeatedly done since World War II—adopted legislation just hours after the strike began April 17 declaring it illegal. Not wanting to challenge the "friends of labor" in Congress, or take responsibility for organizing a fight, the union tops quickly ordered the rail workers back to work. A "neutral" board set up by the congressional legislation is now empowered to impose a contract on the unions within sixty-five days if they refuse to submit to some variant of the rail bosses' demands.

Members of the United Auto Workers (UAW) are discussing probes by General Motors and the other auto bosses to force the union to reopen contracts signed just last year and take further concessions. GM threatens that if auto workers don't agree, it will soon run out of money to pay jobless benefits to laid-off union members.

As the working class resists the bosses' offensive, layers of young workers and students have been showing a growing interest in radical ideas. This is reflected, for example, in expanding sales of books and pamphlets containing speeches of Malcolm X and the turnout for meetings and conferences to discuss his political example and legacy. It is shown by the thirst among young women for knowledge about the character and roots of women's oppression and about how the struggle for full equality and liberation can be advanced. It is expressed in the size and seriousness of meetings at which communists from Cuba explain the course of their revolution and its importance for those on the front lines of struggle everywhere. This openness to radical ideas led many high school and college students not only to join in actions protesting the war against the Iraqi people, but also to seek out forums, books, pamphlets, and newspapers, so they could learn about, discuss, and debate the origins of imperialist wars and why the working class needs to chart a course that can lead toward taking power out of the hands of the war makers.

At the same time, the labor movement in the United States continues to retreat under its current class-collaborationist misleadership. The percentage of workers who are organized into unions continues its slow decline. The number of strikes last year was the lowest since this figure has been officially recorded. The purpose of a strike is to use union power to shut down production in order to advance a concrete set of goals in bargaining with the employer, and as a result strengthen the union. But to growing layers of workers, strikes are today coming to be seen instead as virtually equivalent to a decision that scabs—what the bosses call "permanent replacement workers"—are going to be hired to keep production going, and that you and your co-workers are going to have to find a way to wage an enormous fight to get your jobs back, let alone win any of your demands.

This is one of the fruits of the class-collaborationist course of the labor officialdom, which ties the unions more and more tightly into "cooperation with management" to boost profits and fend off the employers' competitors, as well as more deeply into the broader framework of bourgeois politics and the foreign policy interests of U.S. imperialism.

For a classic presentation of class collaboration, let me read a few lines from an article in the March 10, 1991, issue of the *Miami Herald* by Charles Bryan, general chairman of IAM District 100, the district to which the striking Eastern workers belonged. Bryan doesn't say a word about the accomplishments of the hard-fought, nearly two-year-long battle by rank-and-file Machinists. Not a word. Instead, he longingly recounts how the IAM officialdom worked hand-in-glove with Eastern management in the early 1980s—a course that landed Bryan a spot on the company's board of directors and that weakened the union to the point that by the end of the decade Lorenzo thought he could break it. Decrying what he calls "the tragedy of Eastern," Bryan blames "the latecomers who orchestrated Eastern's demise"—he's referring to Lorenzo and Shugrue—who "won't admit that from 1984 until February 1986 we had created a cooperative labor-management model that had solved Eastern's financial problems. For that brief shining moment," Bryan concludes, "there was a Camelot at Eastern Airlines."

That "Camelot" sums up the class-collaborationist course that subordinates the needs and interests of the working class and the labor movement to the employers, their Democratic and Republican parties, and their government. It makes us part of the "Eastern family," not part of the working class. It blocks the workers' path toward using union power in the interests of the working class as a whole: to wage effective strikes, to resist scab-herding and union busting, to organize the growing ranks of the unorganized, to mobilize solidarity with striking workers and fighters in other social struggles, to act against Washington's wars, to break down growing pressures to see workers in other countries as "them" not "us," and to take any steps toward independent working-class political action.

That "Camelot" is still the reality faced by workers who want to fight, to advance tactics that mobilize the ranks to resist the employers' assaults, and to strengthen the unions to the degree possible. We've learned in practice what these limitations are today—and how in some cases they can be pushed at the edges to give the ranks some more space to fight—through participation in building solidarity for the Pittston strikers, by taking responsibility as part of the rank-and-file leadership of the Eastern strike, and from other experiences in the labor movement.

As the bosses keep pushing and probing there will be more fights. There are mounting tensions and pressures in the working class. Millions of workers in this country are on the lookout for a strike that can take on the employers, shut down production, whip them, and end up with the workers going back on the job with a stronger union. Workers will join in any fight when they sense the opportunity, and other working people throughout the country and the world will support them.

The first example of a strike that bursts through the pattern of the past decade can electrify the labor movement, raise the spirit of militancy and self-confidence of the ranks, and inspire emulation. We have no idea where the tension will break, or when, or under exactly what circumstances. But the conditions for such fights will improve as we come out of the current recession and as the employers' leverage to pit workers against each other to extract more concessions from our class and our unions is weakened.

What's more, various steps taken by many capitalists over the past decade to try to slow down and reverse their declining profit rates have actually made them more vulnerable to strike action by the unions. The "just-in-time" inventory systems adopted by the bosses in auto and other industries make the employing class more, not less, dependent on uninterrupted production by suppliers and on freight transportation by rail, truck, and air. The job combinations of white-collar workers and supervisory personnel to cut back payrolls makes it more difficult for management to deploy these employees to keep the production line moving or the freight rolling during a strike.

STRUGGLES THAT ERUPT around a wide range of immediate social and political issues in the interests of working people and the oppressed also help put the labor movement in a better position to reverse its political retreat. The fight against cop brutality is of vital interest to any organization that speaks in the name of the working class. The demand "Gates must go!" needs to be taken up by the unions, not just in Los Angeles but across the United States.[23] The same is true of any battle, anywhere in the country, to defend abortion rights or advance other aspects of the struggle for women's rights and equality, or to defend the space available for the exercise of our rights to free speech, association, and organization.

It will be in the course of an upswing of labor battles and other social struggles, with new advances in labor solidarity nationally and internationally, that vanguard fighters in our class can begin to move forward. That is, to move beyond having to find some tactical maneuvering room to expand solidarity *within* the class-collaborationist straitjacket imposed on the unions by the officialdom and begin to find ways to carve out a class-struggle strategy and course toward independent labor political action.

These contradictory pressures and tensions in U.S. politics and the class struggle were already developing *prior to* Washington's war drive against Iraq that got under way in August

1990. It was in the face of them that the Socialist Workers Party responded to the war drive by organizing to campaign against imperialism and its course toward war in the Middle East. We campaigned by simultaneously going deeper into the unions and reaching out even more broadly to any fighter who wanted to act against the war drive, who wanted to bring the troops home and get Washington's boot off the backs of the peoples in the Mideast.

From the outset we began clearly explaining the facts about the imperialist character of the war drive and its roots in the crisis and decline of the world capitalist system. We explained how the fight against the employers' wars is part and parcel of resisting their assault against workers and farmers at home, and how the methods they use abroad are part and parcel of the brutalities they impose on some working people in the United States today and will attempt to use more and more tomorrow.

We explained that every step taken by Washington from at least some point in September—not only every new escalation of the war drive, but every fake "peace" move too—could culminate in only one end: a massive bloody invasion of Iraq by U.S. air, sea, and ground forces that would have devastating consequences for all the toilers living in the region. And we said that whatever the exact military outcome of such a war, the U.S. rulers would break their teeth on its political consequences. The war would create more problems for Washington in the Middle East; more class, national, and state conflicts; more social and political instability for the imperialist system.

We have been campaigning around the central political demands: "Bring the troops home now!" "End the criminal blockade, including the embargo on food and medicine to Iraq and Kuwait!" and "Foreign troops out of the Mideast!" These demands have stood the test throughout every stage of Washington's bloody course in the Gulf. We embraced the slogan "No blood for oil!" advanced by young fighters against the war, capturing in a popular way a concrete aspect of the war's imperialist character. We demanded "Stop the bombing!" while allied forces were devastating Iraq from the air in January and February.

Given the consequences of the U.S. slaughter and Baghdad's

brutal policies, we have now expanded the demand that Washington end its blockade to include opening the U.S. borders to the Kurdish people and all war refugees seeking asylum. We are demanding that the U.S. government provide massive aid to help the peoples of Iraq and Kuwait rebuild their war-shattered homes, lives, and countries.

While this political estimation of the war drive and orientation of the party against it were right on the mark, the challenge of actually beginning to *campaign* against Washington's war drive proved more difficult to conquer initially. It took us some time and further discussion to cast off routinism and turn boldly toward politically campaigning against the war—not frenetically, but in the way a workers' party carries out a centralized and disciplined campaign. We had to reconquer functioning along the lines of what the communist movement has often called "a campaign party."[24] And every single member and party committee had to internalize this in order to be able to confidently carry out the campaign.

The party has gotten some important experience over the past few years campaigning for justice for Mark Curtis, a unionist and member of the SWP imprisoned on frame-up rape charges in Iowa.[25] During the strikes by Pittston coal miners and Machinists at Eastern Airlines, the party campaigned to build solidarity with those fights—through our unions, on picket lines and at demonstrations, by selling the *Militant,* in public forums, and with the party election slates. But these struggles, despite their importance, were not central enough to world politics to organize a campaign around through which we could reach out to all fights and to all other fighters to explain all other developments in politics and the class struggle. The fight against imperialism and war, the central question of modern world politics, *requires* such a campaign.

We've carried out this campaign through the party's dual structure: the branches, our basic units in cities throughout the country; and the local fractions of party cadres who are members of industrial unions. We've drawn members of the Young Socialist Alliance and supporters and friends of the party into actively campaigning as part of a common communist movement. The increasing energy for the campaign has above all come through the experiences of the union fractions, where the most rapid expansion of leadership has taken place.

We have been well armed with the necessary political weapons to carry out the campaign: the newspapers, magazines, books, and pamphlets that have been produced and distributed by the tens of thousands. We have paid special attention to expanding the subscription base, the regular weekly readership, of the *Militant* newspaper. In December we produced a special issue of the *International Socialist Review* on "The Working-Class Campaign against Imperialism and War" and circulated it to workers and youth throughout the next several months. We widely sold the new Pathfinder book *U.S. Hands Off Mideast! Cuba Speaks Out at United Nations,* which effectively rebuts many of the lies and pretexts used by Washington to justify its murderous war drive against Iraq.

ARMED WITH these and other political weapons, we've been organizing to get out the truth about the war and its ongoing aftermath and to engage in discussions with other workers on the job and in the unions; during weekly sales at plant gates and mine portals; with GIs and their families; with young workers and high school and college students. We campaign among strikers, locked-out workers, farm workers, working farmers, opponents of cop brutality, fighters for Black rights, abortion rights supporters, and all those seeking to defend the unions and democratic and social rights.

Throughout the campaign, we have also been selling the monthly *Perspectiva Mundial* and quarterly *L'internationaliste* to reach out to working people whose reading language is Spanish or French. We have been selling *New International*—including, soon, the issue in which an edited version of this talk will appear. We have been selling the French-language *Nouvelle Internationale,* and we will soon be selling the new Spanish-language *Nueva Internacional.*

We have gotten other books and pamphlets into the hands of fighters drawn into opposing the war who are interested—or who have become interested—in a broad range of other questions of political importance to workers and fighters and to the communist movement. We've sold books such as *Malcolm X Talks to Young People, Cosmetics, Fashions, and the Exploitation of Women,* and *The Changing Face of U.S. Politics: The Proletarian Party and the Trade Unions;* works by veteran leaders of the working-class and communist movement in the United States such as James P. Cannon and Farrell Dobbs; books and pamphlets by Karl Marx, Frederick Engels, V.I. Lenin, Leon Trotsky, and Che Guevara; and much more.

Working people and youth have been attracted to discussions about the war at meetings of the Militant Labor Forum. The number of cities around the country where these forums now take place almost every weekend has grown in the process.

Large slates of Socialist Workers candidates for state and local office have been able to explain more broadly how working people can organize to resist the capitalists' attacks on our rights and living standards at home by fighting against the imperialist system responsible for war, exploitation, racism, the subjugation of women, and other forms of oppression.

IN CARRYING out this campaign, we have consciously avoided the political trap of functioning as communist workers in peace-time, and then sliding toward acting as radical pacifists in war-time. We act as the communist component of the vanguard of the working class, at all times and under all conditions. We have been confident that a working-class campaign carried out in this way will be politically attractive to and will draw in fight-ers—whatever their social background, especially among the youth—who oppose imperialist war, who want to understand the roots of such wars, and who seek ways to *act* on their convictions.

From that standpoint, we joined with others in building united action to organize local, regional, and national demonstrations and protest meetings during Washington's seven-month-long war. We understood how important public protests are in defending the space for political organization and action—both in opposition to the war, and around other labor and social issues. We recognized that these events are arenas where communists can meet and have political discussions with large numbers of young people who can be won to a working-class political perspective, to the fighting traditions of the communist workers' movement.

From the outset, as I pointed out earlier, the fractions of party members in ten North American industrial unions have been providing a special impulse and energy to getting the party on a campaign footing. These worker-bolsheviks are members of the Amalgamated Clothing and Textile Workers Union; International Association of Machinists; International Ladies' Garment Workers' Union; International Union of Electronic Workers; Oil, Chemical and Atomic Workers; United Auto Workers; United Food and Commercial Workers; United Mine Workers; United Steelworkers; and the United Transportation Union.

These communist workers went to the heat—looking for every opportunity on the job and in the unions to explain and discuss the character of, and help organize opposition to, imperialism and its drive toward war. We joined with co-workers and unionists at antiwar protests and continue to bring them to political meetings to discuss the war, its ongoing consequences, and other political questions.

Since the onset of the imperialist epoch at the opening of this century, going to war has never been popular in the working class. Antiwar sentiment has never stopped the imperialists from going to war, however. As they have done throughout this century, they used their preparations for the war against Iraq, and particularly the actual start of the bombardment in January, to push back antiwar opposition and gain majority support. During the seven months of the war drive, bourgeois public opinion in the United States, including in the working class, moved to the right—inconsistently and in a differentiated way, but to the right. Support for the war increased, particularly after U.S. and allied forces began the murderous air war—that is, after the commitment of U.S. personnel to battle.

This prowar sentiment was shallow, however. Throughout the war, communist workers were able to continue civil discussions on the job and in the unions and to sell substantial quantities of materials explaining the war drive's roots and concretely describing its evolution and implications for working people. In the face of attempts by the government, employers, and superpatriotic union officials and co-workers to narrow the space open to dissent, socialists found that many workers—including among those who said they supported the war, or aspects of it—backed our right to express and argue for antiwar opinions and circulate literature.

The war drive led to a political polarization among working people. While attitudes among the majority shifted to the right, many workers and farmers had hesitations or doubts about Washington's policies. Right from the outset there were millions of workers and young people who wanted to discuss the stakes in the war and were open to consider sober explanations of its imperialist origins, character, and implications. Antiwar demonstrations—focused on objectively anti-imperialist demands such as "Bring the troops home now!"—began early in the war, including actions with hundreds of thousands of participants.

The rulers managed to narrow the space for "legitimate" discussion and protest; patriotic pressures to "support our troops when the shooting starts" gained ground. But the rulers couldn't mobilize popular support to tighten things up very much. As soon as the U.S. military offensive operations were called off at the end of February, the rightward momentum promoted by the bourgeois politicians and the press during the war could not be sustained and began to shift the other way. For those who had never pulled back from pressing political discussion and debate, space opened up, both on and off the job, for an even broader exchange of views.

There is less and less gloating among the big majority of the U.S. population over the U.S. "victory" in the war. General Schwarzkopf was quoted the other day by a *New York Times* reporter as having boasted in Kuwait city that the U.S. forces defeated forty-two Iraqi divisions. "Anyone who dares even imply that we did not achieve a great victory," Schwarzkopf said, "obviously doesn't know what the hell he's talking about." But they do know what they are talking about, and they are right.

In fact, for the U.S. rulers, one of the biggest unintended consequences of the Gulf war is that its outcome has made many working people in the United States a little more attuned to the relationship between conditions and struggles at home and broader developments in world politics. The political problems faced by U.S. imperialism in the aftermath of the war, and the truth coming out about the devastation inflicted by Washington on the peoples in Iraq and the Gulf region, have created wider opportunities for the vanguard of the working class to practice politics in the labor movement. It has opened up the possibility for the vanguard of the working class to conquer even greater space than it had prior to August 1990, if we boldly organize to take that space and use it.

With these political openings, workers who are communists today are helping other fighters from our class to understand our fight against the employers' offensive at home from the point of view of the international class struggle, not the other way around. We go to other fighters in this country and discuss and debate the world with them, and how our own struggles are part of that world.

This understanding enables us to champion any just struggle here more effectively—by doing so as citizens of the world. We can put ourselves into the shoes of a worker in another country—whether Iraq, Kuwait, the Soviet Union, Germany, Japan, South Africa, or somewhere else—and try to look at politics and the class struggle as she or he is experiencing it. This arms us to use our internationalist imagination to understand how to organize, who our class enemies are, where to reach out for solidarity, and how to use our collective power.

SOME RAIL WORKERS today, for example, can better see why the no-strike pledge made by top officials of the rail unions during the Gulf war further sapped the potential power of their fight. The back-to-work order by the bipartisan Congress in April was one payoff for class collaboration, for patriotic "forbearance." As it turned out, letting the bosses and their government kill workers somewhere else in the world for a couple of months didn't make "friends of labor" in the Democratic Party more generous to workers here at home.

If the rail unions had thrown themselves into the fight against the war, if they had mobilized solidarity for fellow workers and toilers in the Gulf, then the unions would be better equipped right now to take on the rail bosses, the U.S. government, and the imperialist politicians in the Democratic and Republican parties. They would be in a better position to explain their fight to, and win solidarity from, a broad layer of working people, inside and outside the U.S. borders. That's a little easier to see today than it was a few weeks ago.

It's a little easier to see why the entire procapitalist, pro-imperialist course of the union officialdom will lead the labor movement to disaster if it isn't reversed. Why the working class and labor movement need our own foreign policy and our own military policy. Why the unions are hamstrung when our friends are not other working people, here and abroad, but "friends" in the political parties of the exploiting class—that too makes sense to a few more workers today. As does the need for an independent labor party based on the unions with an internationalist, class-struggle orientation.

O̲R̲ ̲T̲A̲K̲E̲ ̲T̲H̲E̲ ̲F̲I̲G̲H̲T̲ against police brutality, to cite another example. The kind of beating given to Rodney King in Los Angeles in March was not an isolated incident. Workers face cop brutality every night, all the time, everywhere in this country. Many workers have seen the videotape of the beating. Many may also have seen some footage from Washington's "turkey shoot" on the road from Kuwait city to Basra. Many have now watched scenes of Turkish troops beating, and firing on, Kurdish refugees along the border between Iraq and Turkey.

These incidents are connected. The U.S. officer corps in the Gulf used the tank commanders and air force officer corps as punishers in Iraq and Kuwait—as judges and executioners. In the same way, the job of the cops at home is not to investigate and apprehend, but to serve the rulers by dispensing punishment (bourgeois "justice") *on the spot* to workers day in and day out. The beatings meted out, or shootings carried out, by cops in this country are one of the ways the employing class disciplines workers, tries to get us to shape up, just do our jobs, and keep our mouths shut. You don't need to have done anything "wrong"—just be in the wrong place at the wrong time.

If the U.S. rulers are capable of doing what they did to the peoples of Iraq, then they are also—*right now*—acting with more conscious brutality toward more working people here in this country than any one of us could possibly know. We underestimate, not overestimate, the numbers of Rodney Kings, Mark Curtises, and other victims of the rulers' cops and courts in jails, prisons, or the grave.

In this respect there's no difference between General Colin "cut 'em off and kill 'em" Powell, General Schwarzkopf, and Los Angeles cop commander Daryl Gates. All serve the employers and mete out arbitrary punishment to the toilers, at random, to send a message to all those who might challenge the established order. They have the same contempt for working people as less than human. Just shortly before the U.S. invasion, Schwarzkopf said on ABC's "Nightline," that people in Iraq are "not a part of the same human race." Just as Gates once explained that Blacks may be biologically more prone to death from a choke-hold than "normal people."

This helps us understand more concretely how the foreign policy of the U.S. imperialist rulers is an extension of their domestic policy, not vice versa. There can be big differences at any given time as to the amount of force the rulers feel they need to apply in a concentrated way abroad and at home, depending on the depth of the economic and social crisis and resistance by the toilers. But all the methods that the rulers use against toilers abroad will be used when necessary against workers and farmers at home, and build on methods they are already using here. The rulers don't have one set of standards toward working people in Basra and another toward working people in Brooklyn, Des Moines, and Los Angeles.

The fate of the former simply shows the future of the latter, if power is not wrested by the exploited from the hands of the exploiters.

### 'We' versus 'they'

The big-business media, capitalist politicians, and the labor officialdom have consciously sought to confuse working people about who "we" are and who "they" are as we think about—and discuss what to do about—the U.S. war and its consequences for the people of that region and the world. Working to clearly explain and counter this confusion, in the many forms it keeps cropping up, has been central to an effective campaign by worker-bolsheviks against imperialism and war.

For example, the enormous disparity between the handful

of U.S. combat deaths in the Gulf and the slaughter and maiming of hundreds of thousands of Iraqis underlines the political disorientation and chauvinism reinforced by those in antiwar organizations and coalitions who centered their opposition to the war drive on the prospect of large numbers of U.S. body bags returning from the Gulf. This is exactly what the bipartisan war makers in Washington had counted on! For unconditional opponents of the U.S. war drive, the starting point had to be what the imperialist assault was going to mean for *all* the working people in the Gulf—in uniform and out, whatever country they came from. We refuse to make any distinction between the life of an Iraqi soldier or civilian and that of a U.S. soldier or civilian—or a Yemeni, Filipino, Palestinian, Egyptian, Pakistani, or Syrian toiler caught in the wrong place at the wrong time.

WE ARE PART of an international class—the workers of the world—along with our allies among the oppressed and exploited of all countries. Imperialism is a world system. Its victims, *and its gravediggers,* are toilers who have been brought together in a single world by the expansion of capitalism over the past century. For most of the history of humanity, the world's toilers were almost entirely isolated from each other, but we and our fortunes have been tied together by the world imperialist system.

When Washington declared the pause in the offensive at the end of February, I'm sure most of us initially heard some of our co-workers, family members, or others say something to the effect: "Well, at least it was quick. At least not many of our boys got killed. It was a horrible thing, and I'm not sure we should've been over there. But at least it was over quick." But any variant of that attitude ends up as a rationalization for the horrors inflicted by the U.S. rulers on millions of Iraqis, for whom the war and its terrible consequences have been anything but "quick" and are far from being over. It ends up looking at the people of Iraq as being less than fully human.

I noticed that the April issues of a number of magazines ran a full-page advertisement by the Northrop Corporation, the manufacturer of the B-2 Stealth bomber. It shows a big picture of the plane with the following quotation from a Northrop engineer: "Our people had to spend enormous amounts of time to make the surface of the B-2 so fine, every angle so precise. But that's all part of the secret of Stealth. *And Stealth saves lives.*" [Emphasis added.]

When I read that ad, I was struck that in a certain sense it echoes what we have heard from many liberals and middle-class radicals in the antiwar movement. What's Northrop's message? It is appealing to the same patriotic sentiments we've been discussing. Stealth gets wars over quickly. Stealth prevents so many U.S. pilots from being shot down. Stealth makes it possible to send fewer of "our boys" into ground combat. Stealth drops "smart" bombs and minimizes "collateral damage."

Of course, all this is a lie. Stealth and other modern weapons like it, far from saving lives, were used by the U.S. armed forces to carry out one of the most horrendous *taking of lives* in history.

Bending to the rulers' patriotic drive has taken a wide variety of forms since last August. We have had to debate and clarify each one as we resisted efforts by bourgeois liberals and petty-bourgeois radicals to politically divert the struggle against the war.

• We explained to our co-workers and others why the U.S. government is not "our" government, but the government of the employers, of the capitalists, of the imperialist exploiters and oppressors of working people the world over—"their" government. Thus, nothing that "their" government and "their" army did would help *our* class brothers and sisters, fellow working people in the Gulf, throw off the tyranny of landlord-capitalist regimes in the region—whether Saddam Hussein in Iraq, other Bonapartist capitalist regimes such as those in Egypt and Syria, or the varied monarchies in Saudi Arabia, Kuwait, and Jordan.

• We opposed those who argued that "our government" has the right to blockade Iraq and Kuwait—or to intervene in the affairs of any peoples, anywhere in the world. We pointed out the devastating consequences of this act of war for the lives of our fellow working people in the Gulf. We explain that the embargo was part of Washington's war preparations that inevitably culminated in the U.S.-organized bombardment and invasion of Iraq. We call for an end to the blockade, and the immediate exemption of food and medicines. We explained how the effects of the embargo come down on the common people of Iraq—not the privileged or their government.

• We explained why any variant of slogans such as, "Support our boys, bring them home!" is a disorienting concession to the rulers' patriotic prowar propaganda. The GIs, in their great majority, are from our class and its allies; they are workers and farmers in uniform. But the U.S. armed forces are "their troops"—the troops of the U.S. imperialist government and the handful of wealthy capitalist families it represents. (We should also note that, in comparison to the Vietnam War, a substantially larger percentage of the "boys" in the Gulf were actually women—6 percent. At the time of the Vietnam War 1.5 percent of the U.S. armed forces were women, where today the figure has jumped to 11 percent.)

• We insisted that yellow ribbons—no matter who was wearing them, or for what individual reasons—play the same role as an American flag in bolstering patriotic support for the war. It doesn't matter whether the person wearing the yellow ribbon (or a flag) is a worker, a lawyer, or a capitalist; white, Black, Puerto Rican, or Chinese. It doesn't matter if he or she was persuaded to wear it by a neighbor, or is understandably concerned about a son or daughter stationed in the Gulf. We opposed liberals and radicals in the trade union officialdom or various coalitions who suggested attaching yellow ribbons to antiwar buttons, or wearing a different-colored ribbon. This is an objective political question. The ribbon's practical meaning and impact in politics is nothing more than a capitulation to patriotic, prowar pressure in a sentimental guise. The worker can change his or her mind, but the ribbon can't change its function.

• Communists explained that there is also no "we" on the international level that papers over the class division between the capitalist exploiters and exploited workers and farmers, or between oppressed and oppressor nations. There can be no solution to wars in the Middle East or elsewhere enforced by a classless "international community" or "international organization." That is true whether the agency involved is the United Nations or some "Arab peacekeeping force"—the true role of which, in both cases, has been further exposed by the U.S. war in the Gulf.

During the buildup to the U.S. war and during the bombing and invasion itself, these patriotic pressures bore down with increasing weight on the radical currents that politically dominated the leaderships of various antiwar action coalitions on a local and national level. Especially following the large January 26 demonstrations in Washington, D.C., and the San Francisco Bay Area, these forces increasingly retreated from a perspective of mobilizing united actions against the war. It was among young people that the greatest opposition to Washington's war was manifested. Youth- and student-led committees were at the fore of efforts to organize ongoing public protests, such as the February 21 meetings and rallies on campuses and in cities and towns across the country.

## Collapse when the U.S. offensive halted

The various petty-bourgeois currents in the workers' movement in the United States were stunned, impressed, and frightened by what imperialism did during its war against Iraq. They buy Bush, Powell, and Schwarzkopf's claims that the Gulf war showed that U.S. imperialism is all-powerful. Perhaps the clearest example, among the many I've seen, is an article by Irwin Silber in the April 1991 issue of a magazine called *Crossroads.*

As a result of the outcome of the war in the Gulf, Silber says, "The U.S. has unmistakably re-established itself as a superpower." The U.S. government's "display of devastating high-tech military power in the Gulf and its willingness to use it ruthlessly," he continues, "will be an enormously intimidating factor in all future situations where the U.S. declares that its 'vital interests' are involved.

"The 'Vietnam syndrome' has become, at most, a secondary factor in U.S. foreign policy calculations," Silber says, and "The U.S. is now—more than ever—the dominant force in the Middle East." He despairs that the Soviet Union—he means the Stalinist Gorbachev regime—"has a qualitatively diminished capacity to affect the direction and outcome of world events." Calling Moscow's abject support in the UN Security Council for imperialism's economic blockade of the people of Iraq "a not unreasonable decision," Silber adds that the Soviet government nonetheless "doesn't have much to show for its support of the war either. . . . Not only has the U.S. regained superpower status. It is now the only superpower."

Finally, Silber concludes that "George Bush has clearly established himself as the dominating figure in national politics"—perhaps the saddest prospect of all for Silber, to whom Camelot is a Democratic sweep of the White House as well as Congress.

It's not just that Silber is wrong on every count—he is. The most craven thing is swallowing hook, line, and sinker the self-image that the U.S. imperialist rulers seek to project. Not recognizing that Baghdad had no intention of organizing the toilers to fight U.S. imperialism, he mistakes Washington's devastation of Iraq for a grand military victory—and he is terrified and overwhelmed by it. Silber has been so slavish for so long in looking to the Stalinist regime in Moscow for salvation that he is let down by what is simply the privileged caste's continuing class-collaborationist course in face of its deepening crisis. He doesn't say a word about the Kurds and other oppressed peoples in Iraq, whose rebellions were beginning to unfold. And Silber seems to have had not a clue as to the political fiasco that would be developing for Washington in the Gulf as his article went to press.

The monthly newspaper of another U.S. radical group ran the following prominent display quotation in its main article analyzing the political consequences of the war: " . . . having established an army of occupation in the Gulf region, the U.S. military forces are in excellent position to intimidate and overwhelm any revolutionary risings in the areas that threaten to get out of control."

But the last thing that Washington is in a position to do is to "intimidate and overwhelm" a *revolutionary* uprising in the Middle East, or anywhere else. That's exactly the opposite of what happened in the Gulf—unless you think there was some progressive, let alone revolutionary, content to Baghdad's reactionary annexation of Kuwait and its entire previous and subsequent political course. But just consider the political price that the U.S. rulers would have to be willing to pay, abroad and at home, to use military force against the Palestinian intifada, for example, or the freedom fighters in South Africa. As we've already discussed, this is why an imperialist military assault on

Cuba or North Korea today is less likely in the wake of the U.S. war in the Gulf, not more so—despite the exacerbation of Washington's relations with the governments of these two workers' states.

Still other forces among petty-bourgeois radicals in the U.S. workers' movement have reacted to what they perceive as U.S. imperialism's near-omnipotence by turning more deeply toward the Stalinist regime in Moscow and pinning their hopes on it. A few weeks after the end of Washington's offensive operations in the Gulf, for example, the *Guardian* newsweekly ran the front-page headline: "Soviets say 'yes' on union." The article hails the results of the plebiscite staged by Gorbachev in March. The plebiscite was an effort by the regime to justify holding the disintegrating "Soviet Union" together by force and continuing to deny the right to self-determination to oppressed nations and peoples within the USSR. But the Iraqi people—victims of Moscow's vote in favor of every Security Council resolution initiated by Washington as cover for its war drive—might be a better judge than the *Guardian* of the Soviet government's reliability as a promoter of peace and social justice for the world's toilers.

**'Diversion' from domestic issues?**
Another common reaction by Stalinist, social democratic, and centrist currents to imperialism's "victory" in the Gulf war has been to turn their backs on the millions of victims of the U.S. war in the name of concentrating on "domestic issues." Many present the false view that the U.S. rulers launched the war to divert attention from pressing economic and social problems in the United States. They echo the "America first," "charity begins at home" claptrap of the U.S. labor officialdom.

A little more than a week after Bush announced the temporary suspension of offensive operations, for example, the *People's Weekly World,* newspaper of the Communist Party, ran the front-page headline: "Enough War—Time to Rebuild America!" Just consider what working people in the United States already know about the devastation wreaked on Iraq and Kuwait by the U.S. government, and by Baghdad's policies as well, and then think about that headline: "Enough War—Time to Rebuild America!" What about rebuilding Iraq? What about rebuilding

Kuwait? What about aiding the refugee populations throughout the Gulf?

Readers of the *People's Weekly World* weren't left wondering about the answers to such questions. All they had to do was turn to the inside page with a news article headlined: "Hundreds shout: 'Rebuild Brooklyn, not Kuwait!'" That is a headline in the pages of a newspaper claiming to be communist, claiming to be internationalist! But are conditions for the toilers in Kuwait of lesser concern to communists in the United States than those of the toilers in Brooklyn? Can Kuwait simply be equated with the ruling al-Sabah monarchy? If so, then why not equate the residents of Brooklyn with America's wealthy ruling families? Think about it. Think about the chauvinist implications of that headline.

The *People's Weekly World* article itself spells out this reactionary political line even further. It's a news article about a picket line outside the offices of U.S. Rep. Stephen Solarz, a Democrat from Brooklyn. The last paragraph quotes one of the participants in the protest. According to the article: "'Is Solarz representing Kuwait or Brooklyn?' asked Serafina Flores, a life-long Williamsburg resident, who said residents are outraged that Solarz puts his whole focus 'on external problems and neglects the district.'"

But from the standpoint of communists, from the standpoint of proletarian internationalists, from the standpoint of the working class, the crime of Democratic and Republican politicians such as Solarz is not that they pay too much attention to "external [world] problems" at the expense of working people in the United States. Their crime is that they represent the interests of the imperialist rulers in Washington at the expense of the brutal exploitation and oppression of working people— whether in Brooklyn, Baghdad, Kuwait city, or anywhere else. Communists, on the other hand, recognize that the fight against all forms of exploitation and oppression at home can only be advanced as part of an international struggle against imperialism and the horrors it inflicts on toilers throughout the world.

I've been struck over the past few weeks in looking at the front pages of newspapers of groups on the U.S. "left" that virtually none feature the information coming out about the

U.S. destruction of Iraq, the horrors being inflicted on the Kurdish people, or other aspects of the unfolding consequences of Washington's war. Instead, almost all of them contain some variant of the line, "Enough of the war diversions—let's get back to the economic and social problems here at home."

I've seen articles and charts in the liberal and radical press that point out that the price of one "smart" bomb could build three schools in the United States. But that's exactly the wrong point to be making now. No, the down payment on one smart bomb is dead, maimed, and homeless workers and peasants in Iraq. The price paid for a battleship in the Gulf is not the public housing that could otherwise have been constructed. The down payment for that battleship is the carnage of our fellow toilers that are shelled by it.

Of course, there is another liberal fallacy to such arguments. The capitalists already have billions of dollars that could be used to raise the social wage and living standards of working people in this country and around the world—profits they squeeze from the fruits of our labor. Any money shaved from war spending by bourgeois politicians goes to fatten these profits still more, to satisfy the wealthy bondholders of the national debt, not to upgrade "domestic spending." That's the answer to the question all the liberals and middle-class radicals have been plaintively asking of late: "Whatever happened to the 'peace dividend'?" The social services that benefit working people in this country have been won as a by-product of mass political struggles such as those that built the industrial unions in the 1930s and battered down Jim Crow segregation in the late 1950s and 1960s.

COUNTERPOSING the conditions, interests, and struggles of toilers in the Gulf to those of workers and farmers here in the United States is the opposite of a revolutionary approach, of a communist approach. It's as if there is a calibrated scale to measure the worth of human beings from different parts of the world and the horrors we face—one for U.S. citizens, another for Iraqis, Kurds, Kuwaitis, South Africans, and so on.

The Communist Party's *People's Weekly World* recently contained another example of this anti-internationalist political approach, one that dovetails with its "Rebuild Brooklyn, not Kuwait" line. A late April issue of the paper carried a feature article denouncing moves by the Bush administration to lift a range of U.S. trade barriers with Mexico, as part of what is known as the "North American free trade pact." Parroting the chauvinist arguments of the AFL-CIO officialdom, the paper asserts that ending some of these protectionist measures would send "jobs of American workers" to Mexico. (Aren't Mexican workers "Americans," too?) But starting from the standpoint of protecting "American" jobs from "underpaid Mexican workers" makes it impossible for working people—whether in the United States, Mexico, Japan, Haiti, or anywhere else in the world—to chart a common course of struggle against the oppressors and exploiters at home and abroad.

Everything like this is designed, everything is written in such a way as to divide up the human race, and the toilers within the human race, into categories of greater and lesser humanness. And it's all done in the guise of turning our eyes to the pressing issues at home—or even turning to the class struggle. But it's all the most retrograde form of opportunism, of class collaborationism, of economism, of narrow business unionism, of national socialism. It has nothing to do with communism and the interests of the working class—in the United States or anywhere else.

The war in the Gulf was *not* waged by the capitalist rulers to divert attention from pressing social questions at home. Wars fought by the U.S. imperialists have never been a "diversion"; they have always been an *extension* of the rulers' domestic course and a preview of coming attractions at home, if we don't organize to stop them. The U.S. capitalists' efforts to dominate and exploit the world's toilers flow from the same rapacious profit drive that fuels the gutting of our social wage at home, the scab-herding and union busting, the daily cop beatings of workers. The "diversion" comes from the class-collaborationist misleaders of the labor movement, and from the liberal, radical, and pacifist misleaders—who seek to *divert* working people and youth from understanding that we are part of a common struggle, and that we need to unite with our fellow toilers here and around the world to resist imperialism and its wars.

This is one of the fundamentals of communism. Our movement had to defend this principle at the end of the 1920s against the efforts by the Stalinists to gut the proletarian internationalist heart of the program of the Communist International forged under Lenin's leadership. In 1928, commenting on a new draft program for the Communist International proposed by those who were deserting Lenin's course, communist leader Leon Trotsky wrote:

> An international communist program is in no case the sum total of national programs or an amalgam of their common features. The international program must proceed directly from an analysis of the conditions and tendencies of world economy and of the world political system taken as a whole in all its connections and contradictions. . . . In the present [imperialist] epoch, to a much larger extent than in the past, the national orientation of the proletariat must and can flow only from a world orientation and not vice versa. Herein lies the basic and primary difference between communist internationalism and all varieties of national socialism.[26]

That's the truth. That's what communist workers in the United States must explain to others in the vanguard of our class. That's what we're all relearning.

**Deeper into the unions**
If there ever was a day when we should have picked up the intensity of our campaign, it was the morning of February 28, just after Bush announced the unilateral halt in extending the invasion. We were the only political current in this country that had explained to our co-workers, antiwar youth, and other fighters over the previous seven months that Washington was marching inexorably toward a bloody war. And we were the only ones who could explain at the end of February why U.S. imperialism was going to start breaking its teeth on the results of its acclaimed "military victory."

Co-workers needed to know why nothing they were reading or hearing from Bush, Schwarzkopf, and the major media was true. They needed to understand that the war hadn't been a hundred hours for the people of Iraq; it had been seven months of deprivation, brutalities, and death—with more effects of the war still to come. "Just keep watching," they needed to hear, "and you'll see the political fiasco from the U.S. rulers' slaughter and destruction unfold in the Gulf." Moreover, the consequences of Washington's devastation and Baghdad's savage repression of Kurdish and other peoples—which began to unfold within days after Bush's announcement—placed urgent international obligations on us and other thinking workers to continue explaining, discussing, and campaigning.

WHILE THESE WERE the political points that were being emphasized and explained in each issue of the *Militant*, in practice the branches and the union fractions paused, hesitated, and pulled back from campaigning immediately following the end of the U.S. offensive. This pause, in turn, reinforced pressures to fall back into patterns from prior to the campaign, to retreat toward routinism, to let go of the gains we had made in putting ourselves on a politically centralized and disciplined footing, the footing of a campaign party with a weekly rhythm of political discussion and activity sustainable by worker-revolutionists, a footing that increases our striking power and makes us more effective and trustworthy in the workers' movement.

There is a political explanation for this initial pause in our campaigning. It took a while to generalize throughout our movement a concrete and accurate understanding of the chain of events that led to the U.S. government's rout of the Iraqi armed forces without a fight. Like other revolutionary opponents of imperialism, the cadres of our movement wanted there to be organized resistance to Washington's brutal aggression. It took us some time to put together the picture of how the Iraqi toilers had never been given a chance to resist by the course of the Baathist regime in Baghdad, how they had been stripped of everything that would have made it possible for them to fight. We had to get rid of any vestiges of the illusion that there was an iota of will to fight imperialism behind the Saddam Hussein regime's expansionist course and its demagogic abuse of the nationalist, pan-Arab, and pan-Islamic sentiments of the region's peoples to cook up after-the-fact rationalizations for its pragmatic and reactionary maneuvers.

This pause in our campaign threatened to push us back from the ground we had conquered. In those cities where we organized special meetings of party branches on February 28 to collectively discuss Bush's move and organize to respond to it (like the meetings we held January 15 on the eve of the bombing), we were able to respond more quickly and confidently. Had we not caught this pullback, discussed it, and reversed it, we would have missed the opportunity to grab and use the greater space that has now been opened for vanguard workers in the labor movement and broader politics in the United States. Because it can only be used only if it is taken.

In this regard, our entire movement benefited from the political discussions and perspectives that came out of the recent round of national meetings of each of the ten industrial union fractions held in April (the second round of such national meetings during the course of the campaign). Campaigning against imperialism and its march toward war is politicizing and proletarianizing the party's union fractions.

Based on the experience of the fractions over the past half year, the central political conclusion of each of the ten recent meetings is the need for worker-bolsheviks to now go more deeply into the unions—to approach every fight on the job, every issue in the unions, every social and political question from the vantage point of this ongoing campaign. That's how the fractions can more and more become fractions of our class in the unions. That's how, as the pressures and tensions deepen in the class struggle, we are tying together the political points we've been discussing about the outcome of Washington's war with the lessons from the Pittston and Eastern strikes. That's how we'll be in position to respond as a disciplined party of industrial workers to new strike battles that emerge anywhere in this country, as unionists continue to resist the bosses' concession demands and union busting. We'll be in the best position to respond and participate in struggles against police brutality and for women's rights, to join with students demonstrating against tuition hikes or school cutbacks, to champion demands by the unemployed.

The results of Washington's Mideast war—what we have been writing about in the *Militant,* the *International Socialist Review,* and saying to our co-workers, young people, and others—are continuing to develop at an accelerated pace. This is opening doors to deepen political discussions and debates. We've earned the political respect of a substantial layer of our co-workers, unionists, and others by how we stood our ground and didn't back off from advancing our views during the war—despite pressures from the employers, union officials, and small groups of right-wing workers. They know that we not only stand by principles of working-class solidarity, but that we do so in the face of big pressures and can be counted on to act the same way in other fights.

MANY OF OUR co-workers have been listening to what we said, and thousands have bought copies of the *Militant*, the *International Socialist Review, U.S. Hands Off the Mideast!* and other literature and read them. Many have bought the April issue of the *International Socialist Review* containing the report of a United Nations commission detailing the devastation of Iraq. Right now, as Washington's "victory" unravels, many of them are more open to our views than they have been at any time since August 2, 1990. The big majority still don't agree with us. What's more, the most important things we are discussing with them are exactly the questions where there often won't be immediate agreement. These political questions are not the kind we "settle" in one discussion. We encourage them to read the *Militant*, then come back to the discussion; read the *New International* and come back at it from another angle; go through some more experience and come back at it again.

More and more workers think we may have had a point or two about Washington's aims in the war and its inevitable results. Many are less confident about the truthfulness of the U.S. government, of the officer caste, and of the press. Some suspect they might have known more and thought about things a little differently if freedom of the press hadn't been restricted so sharply by Washington during the war—and if the big-business media hadn't submitted so abjectly to this censorship and so actively promoted the patriotic hype. What about *other* freedoms, like the right to strike, during the next war? Do the employers have their eye on those rights as well?

Many workers are less willing right now than they were a few months ago to share in the responsibility for "our country's war"—and its horrendous aftermath for the peoples of Iraq, Kuwait, and throughout the region.

This continued political attention and interest in the war and its consequences gives us the opportunity to help other working people see the aspects of the class struggle that affect us directly in one factory, in one city, or in one country through the lens of the opening guns of World War III. Workers in the United States don't have the choice of remaining isolated from the world; we are inexorably drawn into it by what the U.S. capitalists must do to advance their class interests. We can all understand more concretely the need to approach politics more broadly in world and class terms, to think socially and act politically.

Selling a co-worker the forthcoming issue of the *New International* on "The Opening Guns of World War III," or a copy of *The Eastern Airlines Strike: Accomplishments of the Rank-and-File Machinists,* or *Malcolm X Talks to Young People*—this is all part of what worker-bolsheviks are doing in campaigning against imperialism and war. Co-workers and other fighters who subscribe to the *Militant* are able each week to follow news and analysis about what's happening in the Gulf, protests against the beating of Rodney King, Congress's back-to-work order against striking rail workers, new attacks on women's right to abortion and resistance to them, student protests against tuition hikes in New York City, Washington's efforts to drive the Kurds back into Iraq, Gorbachev's efforts to crush resistance by workers and oppressed nationalities, the growing stakes in the fight led by the African National Congress for democracy and social justice in South Africa.

It is along this road that the communist movement will attract militant workers and unionists, fighters against racism and for women's rights, and youth who come into action against the wars and other horrors of capitalism and who are attracted to radical ideas. Through our campaign against imperialism and war, young workers and students have been drawn toward our movement and into the Young Socialist Alliance, and more can and will be in the weeks and months to come.

In order to be won to communism, to be recruited and

integrated into a proletarian communist party such as the SWP, these young fighters must be systematically trained and educated in the political experiences and continuity of the revolutionary workers' movement. If they are drawn *through* the YSA *toward* the party, toward its proletarian orientation, toward its communist politics and history, toward its traditions of disciplined class combat, then they can be won as working-class revolutionists.

To the degree it is strong enough to do so, a youth organization like the YSA needs to develop its own organizational identity—its own meetings, its own leaders, some of its own literature, its own political buttons and T-shirts. But the YSA has *no separate political identity* from the communist party, from the SWP. It is only through the party that these young people can be drawn into understanding and identifying with the historic experiences and lessons of the working class. Party members must help YSA members open the door to that revolutionary political continuity.

YSAers need to read and study books by James P. Cannon such as *The History of American Trotskyism, The Struggle for a Proletarian Party,* and *Socialism on Trial,* which explain how a communist organization prepared to continue advancing the class struggle in the face of the oncoming Second World War and forged a stronger proletarian party in the process. They need to study *Teamster Rebellion,* the opening book in a series by Farrell Dobbs that tells the story of how communists operated in the trade union movement in the 1930s to try to build the nucleus of a class-struggle leadership that could use the power of the labor movement to fight the capitalist employers and their imperialist system and its wars. They need to learn how communists have been uncompromising in championing the struggles of all the exploited and oppressed during imperialist wars, in the face of union and other misleaders who urge working people to "sacrifice" and "defer" our demands during wartime—lessons recounted in books such as *Fighting Racism in World War II.*

If proletarian revolutionists consciously work with young fighters won to the YSA, participate alongside them in struggles, get revolutionary literature of this kind into their hands, and patiently but forthrightly discuss and argue with them as political people—then new cadres can be won to the working class and its methods of work and struggle. New cadres can be forged for the communist party in this country and the communist movement worldwide.

❖

**W**ASHINGTON'S WAR against the Iraqi people signaled the opening guns of broadening class, national, and interimperialist conflicts. These are inevitable. What is far from inevitable is that these battles will culminate in a third world war that would set back the progress of humanity beyond our capacities to imagine. That will depend on the outcome of the class battles in the years ahead, in the course of which workers and farmers will have our chance—the opportunity to win revolutionary victories and take the power to make war out of the hands of the imperialist ruling classes.

Such victories, however, can be won only if proletarian communist parties can be built as part of a world revolutionary leadership of the toilers. Such a party can and must be constructed here in the United States, where the power of the most violent imperialist ruling class in history must be taken on and replaced by a revolutionary government of the workers and farmers.

That's why communists in the United States go to where the fights by workers and our allies are taking place. We are always looking for fighters from our class or fighters who can be won to our class. Because we know from history that communist parties aren't built by looking for communists, by looking for people with "good ideas." They're built by communists who are fighters and revolutionists looking for other fighters. As these fighters go through experiences in class battles, they too can become revolutionists. And from revolutionists of action, who are ready to think and consider the lessons of past struggles, the working-class cadres of a communist party and an educated and confident communist world movement can be forged.

It is along that road that the fighters who set out at the beginning of the 1950s to throw off the U.S.-backed Batista dictatorship in Cuba led a victorious revolution in 1959 and forged a Communist Party with revolutionary leaders of the caliber of Fidel Castro and Ernesto Che Guevara. It is through uncompromising struggle against imperialist oppression and capitalist exploitation that Maurice Bishop of Grenada and Thomas Sankara of Burkina Faso were won to a communist perspective. During the last year of his life, Malcolm X arrived at anticapitalist and increasingly prosocialist political conclusions through his intransigent battle against the oppression of Blacks in the United States and his internationalist solidarity with all those struggling against imperialist and racist domination the world over. It is through the vanguard fighters of the African National Congress and their battle for a democratic, nonracial republic that a communist leadership will be forged in South Africa.

And, whatever the concrete forms, it will be from the fighting workers, exploited farmers, and youth in the United States that the revolutionary cadres of a communist movement will be forged in battle in this country as well.

By campaigning against imperialism and war, the members of the Socialist Workers Party are ourselves being changed. We are communists who responded as revolutionists of action to U.S. imperialism's assault on our fellow toilers throughout the Gulf. We are responding as fighters seeking out other fighters in the working class and among other opponents of Washington's wars and attacks on the rights and conditions of workers and farmers here and abroad. In the process, we are becoming better fighters, more self-confident, more disciplined, more political—cadres of a politically stronger and more confident workers' party.

Join us!

# NOTES

1. During the Spanish civil war the German air force aided Spanish fascist forces. They bombed and strafed the fishing village of **Guernica** in April 1937, killing more than 1,600 men, women, and children and wounding nearly 1,000. The people of the Japanese city of **Hiroshima** were the first target of an atomic bomb,

dropped by U.S. forces August 6, 1945; Washington was responsible for the death and maiming of more than 100,000 people and the destruction of 90 percent of the city. Five firebombing raids against the German city of **Dresden**—a city with little military significance—during the spring of 1945, killed some 100,000 or more civilians and consumed most of the city in flames just weeks before the German government's unconditional surrender. Some five hundred unarmed men, women, and children in the South Vietnamese village of **My Lai** were lined up and shot by U.S. forces on March 16, 1968, after their houses had been dynamited and burned—all on orders of the U.S. officer corps.

2. In September 1864, U.S. government troops under Union Gen. William T. Sherman captured Atlanta, a major supply depot of the eleven seceding Confederate States of America, and burned a large part of the city to the ground. Sixty thousand troops under Sherman's command then marched more than two hundred miles to the Atlantic Ocean, cutting what remained of the Confederacy in half and destroying as many economic resources as possible along the way. This blow helped prepare the ground for the military defeat of the slaveholders' regime in the spring of 1865.

3. This article from the December 1990 *International Socialist Review* is reprinted elsewhere in this issue under the title "The Working-Class Campaign against Imperialism and War."

4. The *intifada* is the sustained uprising—including protests, strikes, rallies, and resistance to land confiscations—begun in December 1987 by Palestinians and their supporters in Israel and in other Arab territories occupied by Israel following the June 1967 war.

5. In June 1967 the Israeli government invaded Egypt, Jordan, and Syria. By the time a cease-fire took effect after six days of fighting, Israeli forces occupied East Jerusalem, the West Bank, the Golan Heights, the Gaza Strip, and the Sinai Peninsula. Nearly 1,000 Israeli soldiers were killed and 4,500 wounded. Some 4,000 Arab combatants were killed and 6,000 wounded.

The 1973 war lasted from October 6, 1973, when Egyptian and Syrian forces attacked Israeli units occupying the Sinai and Golan Heights, until a cease-fire took effect on October 24. Contingents from Jordan, Morocco, Saudi Arabia, and Iraq also took part in the fighting. In the course of the war 2,800 Israelis were killed and 7,500 wounded. More than 8,000 Arab combatants were killed, 19,000 wounded, and 8,000 taken prisoner.

Accords between Egyptian president Anwar al-Sadat and Israeli prime minister Menachem Begin were signed under the auspices of

U.S. president James Carter at the presidential resort at Camp David, Maryland, on September 17, 1978. Under terms of a subsequent peace treaty, signed in Washington March 26, 1979, Cairo extended formal diplomatic recognition to the Israeli state; Tel Aviv withdrew from the occupied Sinai Peninsula in 1982.

6. The Kurdish regime held power for nearly a year. When the Iranian monarchy moved to crush the two governments and reoccupy the areas in December 1946, the Soviet government opposed the resistance efforts by the Azerbaijani and Kurdish peoples. This led to a split in the Azerbaijani leadership, with the majority following Stalin's dictate and calling off armed resistance. The Stalinist leadership in Azerbaijan capitulated without a struggle. The fall of the Azerbaijani government quickly led to the fall of the Kurdish republic. Kurdish forces, however, organized a fighting retreat.

The retreat was organized by Mustapha Barzani, the military commander of the Kurdish Republic of Mahabad, who had earlier led Kurds from Iraq to join the republic in northern Iran led by Ghazi Muhammad. Fighting the shah's army, they crossed the border into Iraq, where they came under attack by the armed forces of the Iraqi monarchy backed by British imperialism. Barzani then led his forces in a fighting retreat through Turkey and Iran into the Soviet Union. They remained there until the overthrow of the Iraqi monarchy in the July 1958 revolution when they returned to Iraqi Kurdistan and continued the struggle for self-determination.

7. Geronimo, an Apache warrior, was an outstanding leader of the struggle by the American Indian peoples against the U.S. government's genocidal policies and dispossession of Indian lands and rights. In May 1885 he and his followers broke out of the San Carlos reservation in Arizona, where they had been driven by U.S. government forces. They then went to Mexico, where they were ultimately pursued by five thousand U.S. soldiers, a force equivalent to nearly one-third of the U.S. army's combat strength, as well as thousands of Mexican army troops. Geronimo and a few dozen followers finally surrendered in September 1886. The entire band was then deported to Fort Marion, Florida.

8. For more information on the rise and defeat of the workers' and farmers' government in Nicaragua, see "Defend Revolutionary Nicaragua: The Eroding Foundations of the Workers' and Farmers' Government." This resolution, adopted in August 1990 by a convention of the Socialist Workers Party, was published in the *International Socialist Review* supplement to the September 7, 1990, *Militant*. Selected speeches and writings of Sandinista leaders are found

in *Sandinistas Speak* (New York: Pathfinder, 1982), which includes the 1969 Historic Program of the Sandinista National Liberation Front, as well as in *Nicaragua: The Sandinista People's Revolution* (New York: Pathfinder, 1985).

9. For an account of the Grenada revolution in the words of its central leader, see *Maurice Bishop Speaks: The Grenada Revolution and Its Overthrow, 1979-83* (New York: Pathfinder, 1983). For a detailed evaluation of the political legacy of the revolution and the lessons of its overthrow, see the introduction by Steve Clark to *Maurice Bishop Speaks* and the November 1983 speech by Fidel Castro reprinted as an appendix to that volume, as well as Clark, "The Second Assassination of Maurice Bishop," in *New International*, no. 6, pp. 11-96.

10. *Granma International*, March 24, 1991.

11. At the start of the 1950-53 Korean War, the United Nations Security Council adopted a series of resolutions providing diplomatic cover for U.S. imperialist military intervention on the side of the landlord-capitalist regime in the south. The Soviet Union, which as a permanent member of the Security Council could have vetoed the measures, was boycotting Security Council meetings at the time to protest the UN's refusal to seat the People's Republic of China.

12. The eighteen amendments by Cuba were made to Security Council Resolution 686, outlining Washington's conditions for Baghdad's surrender, which was adopted March 2, 1991. All of Cuba's amendments were defeated. One of these requested "all member states, the United Nations, the specialized agencies, as well as other international organizations to provide, on an urgent basis, humanitarian assistance, including foodstuffs and medical supplies to Iraq and Kuwait." This amendment was defeated by a vote of 5 in favor (Cuba, Ecuador, India, Yemen, Zimbabwe), none against, and 10 abstentions (according to the UN Charter, nine affirmative votes are required for the Security Council to adopt a proposal). Another amendment, calling for immediate release of all prisoners of war, was defeated by a vote of 2 in favor (Cuba, Yemen), none against, and 13 abstentions. Another, calling for speedy withdrawal of foreign military forces from Iraq, was defeated by the same vote. The Soviet government followed Washington's lead in abstaining on every amendment; China abstained on all but one. When Resolution 686 came to a vote, Cuba cast the sole opposing vote, with China, India, and Yemen abstaining.

13. The **Kurile Islands** are a chain of islands north of Japan colonized by Tokyo in the late nineteenth and early twentieth

century and seized by the Soviet Union following the Second World War. During Gorbachev's trip to Japan in April 1991, he stated that sovereignty over these islands would be subject to negotiation between the two countries.

In September 1990, the Soviet Union established full diplomatic relations with the government of **South Korea,** followed by an April 1991 visit by Soviet president Gorbachev to South Korea. Gorbachev hailed the "new relationship" between the two governments, which includes Seoul's pledge to Moscow of $3 billion in economic aid. During the visit, Soviet officials stated that if the North Korean government refused to accept international inspection of its Yongbyon nuclear reactor, Moscow would stop providing nuclear fuel and technology. In addition, Gorbachev indicated that if Pyongyang continued to oppose separate entry into the United Nations by the two Koreas, Moscow would back Seoul's entry.

Also in September 1990, the Soviet government and **Israel,** which had broken diplomatic relations after the 1967 war, agreed to establish consulates in each other's countries. In February 1991, the Soviet Union and **South Africa** announced an agreement to open interest sections in each other's countries.

In January 1991, for the first time in three decades, the Soviet Union began to require **Cuba** to conduct much of the trade between the two countries in hard currency at world market prices. While terms to help buffer this change have been negotiated for 1991, these cushions are being phased out. There have also been increasing shortfalls and delays in deliveries of oil, wheat, and other items imported from the Soviet Union. This sudden deterioration in the scope and terms of trade with Havana's largest trading partner has caused severe shortages and dislocations in the Cuban economy.

14. The 1956 Hungarian revolution began in late October following attacks by Hungarian secret police and Soviet troops on demonstrations demanding democratic rights. Workers formed revolutionary councils, took control of a large section of the country, and battled several divisions of Soviet troops. The uprising was crushed by Moscow within several weeks, though strikes continued into mid-December. Also in 1956, a workers' rebellion in Poland was put down by a combination of armed repression and the establishment of a "reform" regime under Wladyslaw Gomulka. Three years earlier, in June 1953, Soviet troops and armored vehicles crushed an uprising in East Germany that included a general strike by more than 200,000 workers.

By the time of these rebellions in the 1950s, the Stalinist regimes and parties, through a combination of murderous repression and political disorientation, had decimated any vestige of communist leadership of the working class in these countries. These revolts, however, were the last in Eastern Europe to involve layers of socialist-minded workers who in their youth had been won to communist perspectives prior to the consolidation of the Stalinist counterrevolution in the Soviet Union and Communist International in the early 1930s.

The Prague Spring in Czechoslovakia was a period of mass radicalization during the early part of 1968 that initially succeeded in winning some democratic concessions and political space from the Stalinist regime. It was crushed by the August intervention of more than 650,000 Soviet and Eastern European troops. No communist leadership existed during this rebellion to organize resistance by working people and students, or to forge a nucleus of a revolutionary internationalist vanguard of the working class in the aftermath of the defeat.

15. For more information on the meaning of the 1987 stock market crash and of the 1974-75 and 1981-82 world recessions, see the Socialist Workers Party resolutions cited in note 1 of "In This Issue." See also *An Action Program to Confront the Coming Economic Crisis* (New York: Pathfinder, 1988); and Jack Barnes, *The Changing Face of U.S. Politics: The Proletarian Party and the Trade Unions* (New York: Pathfinder, 1981).

16. Panama was the first government to recognize the provisional government established by the Sandinista National Liberation Front, June 16, 1979, in territory liberated from the U.S.-backed Somoza regime. Among the internationalist brigades that fought alongside the Sandinistas was the Panamanian Victorino Lorenzo Brigade, led by Hugo Spadafora, the country's deputy health minister. Thousands of teachers, doctors, technicians, and military advisers from Cuba, as well as substantial assistance in food and agriculture, construction materials, and medical supplies, were provided to the new revolutionary government.

17. One of the most noteworthy acts of solidarity toward the Arab peoples came from Cuba, which sent a contingent of volunteer troops to help defend Syria from Israeli attack.

18. In September 1970, King Hussein's army, with the support of Tel Aviv and Washington, launched an all-out attack on Palestinian refugee camps and communities in Jordan, aiming to blunt the growing militancy of the Palestinian freedom fighters and maintain stable relations with Israel. More than eight thousand Palestinians were killed in the assault, a massacre that has become known as

"Black September."

19.  For an account and political analysis of the weakening of the Soviet workers' state under Stalin during the 1930s, see Leon Trotsky, *The Revolution Betrayed: What Is the Soviet Union and Where Is It Going?* (New York: Pathfinder, 1972) and Trotsky, *In Defense of Marxism: The Social and Political Contradictions of the Soviet Union*, 3d ed. (New York: Pathfinder, 1990).

20.  Within months after the October 1917 revolution, a civil war broke out as the Russian capitalists and landlords sought to regain their power. Backed by the intervention of troops from a dozen countries, including the imperialist governments of the United States, Britain, and France, the counterrevolutionary forces opened a war on numerous fronts. In response, the young Soviet republic mobilized the workers and peasants through the newly built Red Army and successfully defended the revolutionary government. V.I. Lenin was the central leader of the Soviet government and Communist Party; Communist Party leader Leon Trotsky was the chief commander of the Red Army.

21.  See Cindy Jaquith et al., *Panama: The Truth about the U.S. Invasion* (New York: Pathfinder, 1990).

22.  See the section "March Toward War and Depression" of the article "The Working-Class Campaign against Imperialism and War" printed elsewhere in this issue.

23.  In Los Angeles March 3, 1991, a gang of more than two dozen cops savagely beat Rodney King, an unemployed construction worker who is Black. The brutal assault, videotaped by a nearby resident and broadcast around the United States and world, led to protests demanding the ouster of Los Angeles police chief Daryl Gates.

24.  The course toward building a campaign party of the working class on the model of Lenin's Bolshevik Party was codified in a series of resolutions adopted by the Socialist Workers Party between 1938 and 1940, and has remained at the center of its political and organizational principles to this day. The political resolution adopted by the July 1939 SWP convention, states: "The serious advance of the party in the mass movement depends upon its adoption of the campaign principle in its activity. As in the case of a military campaign, a political campaign means the concentration and coordination of all available forces in advancing toward and achieving a concrete and definite objective or set of objectives. For the party, it means gearing in the entire national organization and every aspect of its activities . . . as a single unit revolving around the specific axis of the campaign." James P. Cannon et al., *The Founding*

*of the Socialist Workers Party* (New York: Anchor Foundation, a Pathfinder book, 1982), p. 346.

Other works by communist leaders and documents of revolutionary organizations that explain how such a fighting party of the working class can be built are Cannon, *The Struggle for a Proletarian Party* (New York: Pathfinder, 1972), *Letters from Prison: The Communist Campaign against Wartime Repression* (New York: Pathfinder, 1973), Farrell Dobbs, *The Structure and Organizational Principles of the Party* (New York: Pathfinder, 1971), the 1965 SWP resolution *The Organizational Character of the Socialist Workers Party* (New York: Pathfinder, 1970), and Barnes, *The Changing Face of U.S. Politics: The Proletarian Party and the Trade Unions.*

25. Mark Curtis, a packinghouse worker, antiwar fighter, and member of the Socialist Workers Party, is serving a twenty-five-year sentence in Iowa. His fight for justice has won widespread support around the world. Facts in the case are detailed in Margaret Jayko, *The Frame-Up of Mark Curtis* (New York: Pathfinder, 1989).

26. Leon Trotsky, *The Third International after Lenin* (New York: Pathfinder, 1970), p. 4.

# The Changing Face of U.S. Politics

## The Proletarian Party and the Trade Unions
### by Jack Barnes

"When we say that the working class is moving to center stage in American politics, we mean two closely intertwined things:

"First, the industrial workers are the central target of the rulers' offensive. To drive up their profits the employers have to take on the big industrial unions which are the most powerful institutions of the oppressed and exploited.

"Second, we mean that the working class is moving to the center in the resistance to the offensive."

"The ultimate contradiction facing American imperialism is that it must be able to intervene militarily around the world or else capitalism will be overthrown piecemeal. But to do so, the rulers have to take on the American working class, which more and more sees that it has no stake in Washington's military adventures abroad. And this contradiction is the most decisive in world politics."

*Reports and resolutions adopted by the Socialist Workers Party examine the process of building a revolutionary workers' party in today's world of imperialist wars, economic crises, and assaults on the working class—a world where labor's fighting rank and file will play an increasingly central role. 346 pp., $18.95*

SEE PAGE 2
FOR DISTRIBUTORS

# THE EASTERN AIRLINES STRIKE

## ACCOMPLISHMENTS OF THE RANK-AND-FILE MACHINISTS

*by Ernie Mailhot
Judy Stranahan
and Jack Barnes*

The story of the 22-month strike—spearheaded by rank-and-file members of the International Association of Machinists—that defeated the attempt to turn Eastern, one of the world's largest carriers, into a profitable nonunion airline.
 91 pp., plus 16 pp. photos. $8.95

*NEW COLLECTION*

---

## TRADE UNIONS IN THE EPOCH OF IMPERIALIST DECAY
*by Leon Trotsky*

## TRADE UNIONS: THEIR PAST, PRESENT, AND FUTURE
*by Karl Marx*

Two historic leaders of the revolutionary workers' movement discuss the tasks of trade unions under capitalism and their place in workers' fight for economic justice and political power.
 156 pp., $13.95

SEE PAGE 2
FOR DISTRIBUTORS

# THE WORKING-CLASS CAMPAIGN
# AGAINST IMPERIALISM AND WAR

*by Jack Barnes*

O N NOVEMBER 1, 1990, the National Committee of the Socialist Workers Party issued a statement calling on working
people around the world to "put at the center of their
political activity campaigning against the horrendous war Washington, London, Paris, and their allies are preparing in the
Middle East." The statement emphasized, "We can have no
illusions. The war preparations are now accelerating."

Today we can confirm the accuracy and urgency of that statement. What's more, events since then have brought a murderous war in the Middle East even closer.

On November 29 the United Nations Security Council
adopted a resolution giving Washington the green light to unleash its massive military force following a January 15, 1991,
deadline for the Iraqi regime to withdraw from Kuwait.

Previous Security Council resolutions had condemned the
August 2 invasion of Kuwait and called for the immediate withdrawal of Iraqi troops; demanded that Iraq rescind its August 8
annexation of Kuwait; called on the Baghdad government to
immediately release all citizens of other countries without
harm; demanded revocation of the order closing embassies and
consulates in Kuwait and a halt to violations of the diplomatic
immunity of their personnel; and condemned the mistreatment
of citizens of Kuwait and of other countries by Iraqi occupation
forces.

---

*This article is based on talks presented in Washington, D.C., November
17, 1990, and in New York City December 1, 1990. It was first
published in the* International Socialist Review *supplement to the
December 21, 1990, issue of the* Militant. *Jack Barnes is national
secretary of the Socialist Workers Party.*

The U.S.-initiated measure adopted November 29 reaffirmed these demands from previous Security Council resolutions. It did something more, however. The new measure not only authorized "all member states . . . to use all necessary means" in order to "fully implement . . . the foregoing resolutions," but also "to restore international peace and security in the area." The Security Council called on "all states to provide appropriate support for actions undertaken" by Washington and its allies.

This wording, drafted by Washington, provides the U.S. government with an even more open-ended basis than before to rationalize war against Iraq under the cover of enforcing UN decisions. For the U.S. rulers, "peace and security" in the Middle East has only one meaning: peace and security for imperialist interests. It would require the imposition of a regime in Iraq that, in political terms, is largely a U.S. protectorate in the region. It would require inflicting a massive defeat on the Iraqi armed forces and toppling the current government. Washington's minimum aim is to end up with an Iraq qualitatively more vulnerable to Washington's dictates and continuing military threats.

Secretary of State James Baker told the Senate Foreign Relations Committee December 5 that if the UN conditions are not met and war is launched against Iraq, Washington will strike "suddenly, massively, and decisively."

Abdalla Saleh al-Ashtal, Yemen's chief UN representative, could not have been more correct in telling members of the Security Council November 29 that "in the annals of the United Nations this will long be remembered as the war resolution." That's what it was.

It was also a foregone conclusion. Virtually every aspect of the Security Council proceedings had been carefully staged by Washington through prior meetings with other supporters of the war drive against Iraq. These backers included Soviet foreign minister Eduard Shevardnadze, who feigned indignation when he warned the Iraqi government: "If even one Soviet citizen is harmed, I cannot say what the consequences might be, but they would be very, very serious." (Shortly after that, the Baghdad regime announced that all Soviet citizens in Iraq were free to leave the country. A few days later all foreigners held until then as hostages in Iraq were permitted to depart.)

The government of Cuba strongly opposed the Security Council measure as a dangerous new step in Washington's massive military buildup and preparations for aggression. Paraphrasing the title of a novel by Gabriel García Márquez, Cuba's foreign minister Isidoro Malmierca termed the resolution "the chronicle of a war foretold."

## WASHINGTON'S BIPARTISAN COURSE TOWARD WAR

O N NOVEMBER 29, the day of the Security Council vote on the war resolution, U.S., British, and Saudi troops went on the highest alert short of combat. The agreements are now all in place for the British and Saudi units to fight under U.S. command when the shooting starts.

The day after the UN vote, Bush sought to plug a loophole in his political rationale for war by going through the motions of "exhausting all the channels" before resorting to arms. Bush announced he was inviting Iraqi foreign minister Tariq Aziz to Washington and sending Secretary of State Baker to Baghdad. Baker's job is to look Saddam Hussein straight in the eye and state: "There'll be no 'face-saving' way out. Comply to the letter of each of the UN resolutions or else."

The next day, December 1, Pentagon officials announced that 300 more fighter bombers were being sent to the Arab-Persian Gulf, bringing the number of U.S. warplanes in the region to some 1,900—not to mention several hundred more provided by Saudi Arabia, Britain, France, Canada, the Netherlands, Italy, and others. (This is the first time since the Korean War that the Canadian government has sent combat forces to participate in an imperialist war. Unlike Australia and several other governments, Ottawa sent no troops to fight alongside Washington in Vietnam.) The Iraqi air force, by comparison, is estimated to have some 600 less-advanced planes.

All told, more air power has already been mobilized by Washington in the Gulf region than at the high points of the U.S. saturation bombing during the Korean and Vietnam wars. The air force and other Pentagon brass who have appeared before the Senate Armed Services Committee have all testified that the U.S.-led forces are capable—during the first week and a half of intensive bombing alone—of hurling more destructive power against Iraq than during the entire Korean War. In recent weeks, the air assault units that have been training since their arrival in Saudi Arabia have been moved closer to the border.

Britain announced just before the adoption of the UN Security Council vote that it was expanding its troop commitment from 15,000 to 30,000—with the backing of the top leaders of both the Tory and Labour parties. This amounts to some 10 percent of its total active-duty forces. By comparison, the highest estimate for the number of British ground troops involved in the assault against Argentina's Malvinas Islands in 1982 is some 8,500 (although with a substantially larger offshore armada of some thirty to forty British ships). In addition, London plans to send virtually every tank it has in continental Europe, as well as additional ones from Britain itself.

Following the Security Council vote, the National Party government of New Zealand announced it was sending its first contingent of three hundred military personnel to the Gulf.

President Turgut Özal has proposed that the Turkish government, already cooperating by mobilizing nearly 100,000 troops along its border with Iraq, may dispatch a contingent to join the U.S.-led forces in Saudi Arabia itself soon. He also offered to make the Incirlik air base in southern Turkey available to Washington if war breaks out. The government of Pakistan recently announced that it is sending another 10,000 troops to Saudi Arabia, bringing their combat strength up to 15,000 before January 15.

The Syrian minister of defense was quoted on ABC, NBC, and CNN television news December 1 as having said at a news conference that his government is prepared to commit half a million troops to combat if war actually breaks out. That's in addition to the 19,000 troops in heavy armored divisions already in place or on the way to Saudi Arabia.

Before the end of January, the U.S. government will have close to 450,000 troops there; the combined force of U.S. and allied troops will be 650,000 strong. Some 40 percent of the U.S. Army and about half of its combat troops are in the region or on their way. This includes more than half the U.S. Army units formerly stationed in Europe. Some two-thirds of the U.S. Marine Corps combat units will be in the Gulf. Half the U.S. armored forces in Europe are being sent to Saudi Arabia, bringing the number of modern U.S. tanks to 1,200. There are to be six U.S. aircraft carriers and naval battle groups in the seas around the Arabian Peninsula.

As the troops and armor relentlessly mount up, Washington is also escalating military maneuvers carried out in close proximity to Iraq's forces, such as Operation Imminent Thunder, which took place at the end of November. These massive operations by hundreds of fighter bombers and air assault units, the mock landings by invading forces—these are not primarily training exercises. They are aimed to be indistinguishable from the opening moves of the military assault itself. The longer they continue, the more provocative they become. As each day and each week passes, the fateful decisions confronting Iraq's armed forces in the face of the provocations become more and more difficult.

If the fighting does not break out soon, or if Washington is unable to score a relatively rapid military victory, then there is no way to sustain a mobilization of this size without reimposing the draft. So many U.S. combat forces are already committed to the operation in the Arab-Persian Gulf that there is no other way to replace and rotate forces over the long haul. Already, some politicians—especially liberal Democrats—have begun to call for reinstituting capitalist conscription, allegedly to redress the current class and racial imbalance of the armed forces. But as anyone knows who thinks for a minute about the troops who fought in Vietnam, a conscripted capitalist army would be no less working class and no less Black and Latino than the current volunteer force. Communist workers maintain our historic position: Not one cent, not one man—or woman—for the imperialist army!

## The U.S.-imposed blockade

Alongside this ongoing imperialist military buildup, and the diplomatic maneuvers to give it cover, the economic blockade against Iraq has been reinforced. U.S. and allied war vessels continue to use armed might to prevent tankers and merchant ships from bringing imports into and transporting exports out of Iraqi ports. It is easy to forget that this is the most effective

embargo—in fact, the only real blockade—of a country in decades. Its scope, and the disparate economic and military power
of the two sides involved, is unique in modern history. By any
definition, it is an act of war.

It's sometimes said that Iraq is the third country since the
founding of the UN in 1945 to be targeted by such a Security
Council–sanctioned measure, the other two being Southern
Rhodesia during the years of the white-minority regime and
apartheid South Africa today.[1] But the UN actions against these
two racist regimes have involved only sanctions, not a blockade.
They were openly cheated on by Washington itself. There were
no mechanisms of enforcement whatsoever—let alone by massive naval, air, and ground forces of the mightiest imperialist
power on earth!

We often speak of the "blockade" against Cuba. But there's
not a naval or air blockade of Cuba either, although the brutal
U.S-orchestrated ban on trade and aid has had much more
devastating economic and social consequences than the UN
sanctions against the racist regimes in southern Africa. (There
*was* a U.S. naval blockade of Cuba for a few days in October
1962, when Washington declared its intention to intercept and
turn back Soviet ships transporting nuclear-armed missiles.)[2]

Even during the Vietnam War, the U.S. government never
sought to interdict Soviet, Chinese, or European ships bringing
armaments and other matériel into North Vietnam. In fact, the
U.S. Air Force attempted to avoid sinking or damaging such
vessels during repeated bombing assaults on Haiphong harbor.

With regard to Iraq, on the other hand, there *is* an actual
embargo. Any ship that seeks to run the blockade risks being
blown out of the water—with the blessing of Security Council
Resolution 665, which euphemistically calls upon governments
"deploying maritime forces to the area to use such measures
commensurate to the specific circumstances as may be necessary . . . to halt all inward and outward maritime shipping."
With that reality in mind, no Iraqi or other tanker or merchant
vessel has so far run the blockade once hailed, although several
have been the target of warning shots across the bow before

*ENDNOTES FOR THIS ARTICLE BEGIN ON PAGE 214.*

agreeing to turn back or be boarded by imperialist forces.

The U.S. government estimates that the blockade has cut off 90 percent of Iraq's imports and 97 percent of its exports and slashed nonmilitary economic production by some 40 percent since September. Even if these figures are exaggerated, the effects of this brutal blockade are already taking a heavy toll on the peoples of Iraq and Kuwait. As Cuban foreign minister Malmierca explained before the Security Council November 29, the adoption of "a resolution implementing a total blockade that did not exempt foodstuffs and medicines" has "turned millions of elderly people, women, and children . . . into hostages of hunger and death.

"There are already children and those suffering illnesses among the civilian Iraqi population who have died as a result of the lack of medicine in the hospitals," Malmierca said. "The presence of more than two hundred Cuban doctors and nurses, who have been rendering their services free of charge in that country for more than twelve years, enables us to testify to this fact."

There is already a lack of milk vital to infant health in Iraq, and its price has shot up by 400 percent. The prices of other basic staples are also rising sharply.

FROM THE OUTSET of the imperialist-orchestrated efforts to impose the blockade in August, socialist Cuba has taken the moral high ground on this issue. Cuba's UN ambassador Ricardo Alarcón explained to the Security Council in September: "Cuba regards as completely inadmissible the very idea of claiming that hunger can be used to deprive peoples of what is an absolutely fundamental human right of every single human being in every part of the world and in any circumstance—that is, the right to receive adequate food and appropriate medical care. We do not believe that anyone has the political, juridical, or moral authority to apply inhuman measures such as those whose sole and exclusive victims would be innocent civilians."[3]

Consistent with that position, the Cuban government has refused to cancel its food export agreements with Iraq or to withdraw its volunteer medical brigade from Iraqi hospitals.

The August 2 Iraqi invasion of Kuwait and the subsequent U.S.-organized war drive have also resulted in the forcible uprooting and displacement of entire populations.

At the November 29 session of the Security Council, the ambassador from Yemen reported that some 900,000 Yemeni workers—many of whom have lived and worked in Saudi Arabia their entire lives—have suddenly had their work permits jerked by the Saudi government and been sent packing back to Yemen over the past two months. Why? Because the Saudi monarchy didn't like the way the government of Yemen had voted on resolutions in the Security Council.

"Comparatively speaking," Yemen's ambassador explained, "it is like having 30 million jobless Americans come back home within a short period of two months. You can imagine the economic strain that will be caused by this demographic dislocation."

The comparison is even more striking when you consider the low level of economic development and already meager living standards in Yemen. What's more, the governments of Saudi Arabia, the Gulf emirates, and other Arab countries lined up behind Washington's coalition have cut off virtually all economic assistance to Yemen since August. And to top it off, as reported in the *New York Times* December 2, just minutes after the Yemeni ambassador cast his vote against the U.S.-initiated war resolution, "a senior American diplomat was instructed to tell him: 'That was the most expensive no vote you ever cast'— meaning it would result in an end to America's more than $70 million in foreign aid to Yemen."

In addition to the Yemeni workers expelled from Saudi Arabia, many Jordanian and Palestinian immigrant workers have shared the same fate at the hands of the monarchical Saudi and Gulf regimes. The Palestinian people have been shoved around by the Baghdad government, as well. More than 180,000 Jordanian citizens previously working in Kuwait, many of them Palestinians, have been expelled by Iraqi occupation forces.

In addition, an estimated two million noncitizens from other countries remain in Kuwait and Iraq, a substantial majority of them against their will, with no government or international agency willing to foot the bill of transporting them back to their homelands. Of these, some 98 percent are from Third World countries. These include 90,000 from Pakistan, 65,000 from Sri Lanka, 55,000 from Lebanon, more than 20,000 from India, 15,000 from Bangladesh, 14,000 from Vietnam, nearly 6,000 from the Philippines, and nearly 5,000 from China.

### Washington's goal: a U.S. protectorate

When the Iraqi regime ruthlessly swallowed up Kuwait in August 1990, the U.S. rulers saw that Saddam Hussein had served them on a silver platter the best chance in a decade to achieve one of their key strategic goals in the region. These goals have to do with safeguarding and advancing Washington's economic and strategic interests in the Middle East, not defending national sovereignty in Kuwait or anywhere else. The U.S. rulers' aim is to shift the relationship of class forces in the Middle East to its advantage, to take back some of what has been lost over the past three decades. The most recent big blow to Washington's power in the region came in 1979 with the victory of the Iranian revolution.

Prior to the overthrow of the shah, Iran had been one of Washington's most reliable client states. In the configuration of imperialist props in the region, the shah's "peacock throne" had formed the third leg of a tripod. The other two were Israel—by far the strongest leg, in its capacity as a massively armed junior imperialist power—and the Saudi and Gulf state monarchies, the weakest.

For more than ten years the U.S. rulers have been trying to recoup some of what they lost with the overthrow of the monarchy in Iran. For much of the past decade they did so by providing encouragement to Saddam Hussein's war against Iran and supporting the course of their imperialist allies, especially the French government, in supplying arms to Iraq for the war effort. That conflict, launched in 1980 with a massive Iraqi invasion of southern Iran, has been among the most slaughterous conflicts in this century, with hundreds of thousands of deaths and injuries. Despite Washington's thinly disguised aid and comfort to Baghdad, however, that murderous eight-year war brought the U.S. rulers no closer to their goal of establishing another subservient regime in the region directly beholden to imperialist interests and reliant on imperialist military support.

Since August, however, the U.S. rulers—with bipartisan Democratic and Republican support—have grabbed the opportunity presented to them. The Republican and Democratic party leaderships agree that military action is justified to achieve their goals, including all-out war against Iraq if necessary. They support the Bush administration's stated policy of rejecting negotiations with the Iraqi government (although behind-the-scenes talks have undoubtedly been under way from the outset, as they are prior to—and during—most armed conflicts).

Congress supported the Bush administration's decision in August to begin pouring massive U.S. ground, air, and naval forces into Saudi Arabia and the Arab-Persian Gulf region. There was bipartisan agreement with Washington's move to organize its imperialist allies, various bourgeois regimes in the region, and other governments—thirty-two in all by now—to throw troops, armor, air and naval power, war matériel, and financial backing into this mammoth military mobilization.

There has been bipartisan backing above all for the brutal and unilateral U.S.-organized war already being carried out by Washington in the Gulf—the war of attrition aimed at starving the workers and peasants of Iraq and Kuwait into submission through a criminal and inhuman blockade of imports and exports, including food and medicine.

Acclaim has been showered on the White House by Democrats and Republicans alike for winning international political cover for this unilateral aggression through after-the-fact endorsement of each new step by the UN Security Council—with unanimous help from the council's other four permanent members: Britain, China, France, and the Soviet Union. Imperialist politicians on both sides of the aisle in Congress have hailed Washington's achievement in bringing the bourgeois regimes in Saudi Arabia, the Gulf states, Egypt, Syria, Turkey, and others in tow behind the U.S.-led military operation to crush Iraq. They have been heartened by imperialism's success in scrambling all past alignments and sharply exacerbating conflicts among the rival bourgeois ruling classes in the Middle East.

### A war they'll break their teeth on

The U.S. rulers' main problem is not a military one. It's true that not many decades ago Washington and other imperialist powers were in the practice of taking on countries the size of Iraq with a relative handful of marines, some gunboats, several planes, and a few paid-off traitors. Someone even coined a term for it: "gunboat diplomacy." That's over!

But, as shown by the mammoth size, modern character, and rapidity of Washington's mobilization in the Middle East, a relative decline of military power is not the source of its weakening. To the contrary, military power remains the U.S. rulers' single most dominant advantage over its imperialist allies and other governments. Instead, their problem is twofold.

First, sections of the ruling class are concerned about Washington's capacity to win a war against Iraq that yields greater gains for U.S. imperialism than losses from the uncontrolled social and political forces it sets in motion. What will be the outcome of such a war beyond the borders of Iraq and Kuwait? Will a military victory simply end up exacerbating the very failures of imperialism in the region that made it necessary for the U.S. rulers to launch the war in the first place? Will it be a pyrrhic victory?

The answers to these questions are not ultimately subject to control by Washington. This dilemma registers the consequences for U.S. imperialism of the ongoing shift in the international relationship of class forces to its disadvantage. The rulers of the declining U.S. capitalist empire confront the prospect of never again winning an unambiguous victory in a protracted war, as they did in the First World War and Second World War in the opening half of the twentieth century.

The second major problem confronting the U.S. rulers as they gear up for a war in the Middle East is how, or whether, they can win a military victory quickly enough to forestall destabilizing social and political consequences at home. How long can such a war go on, how many body bags can be flown back, many ruling-class politicians want to know, before organized antiwar opposition replaces grudging support or fatalism in the working class and begins to make the political price of the operation greater than the benefits? How long before they are compelled to reinstitute conscription?

The capitalist rulers will not be stopped from going to war by antiwar sentiment in the population; they never have been in this century, in the United States or anywhere else. But the bourgeois politicians and military officer corps are united in their determination that any war against Iraq, if it is launched, must be a war that can be completed quickly and successfully. The slogan of opponents of U.S. wars is today given a different content by the imperialist ruling class of the United States: "No more Vietnams!"

The U.S. rulers proclaim they will not let a war against Iraq become another Vietnam. But whether or not such a war would turn out the way the U.S. rulers hope, and as rapidly as they intend, is their biggest problem. That is the source of their tactical divisions and hesitations, and of their periodically shrill arguments with one another as they preen and prance across the television screen.

It's important for opponents of imperialism's war drive to take a closer look at these considerations, in order to guard ourselves from becoming subject to disorientation and resulting demobilization by the weekly or daily ebbs and flows of debates over tactics in the ruling class and diplomatic maneuvers by the contending forces in the Middle East; from becoming pushed and pulled by bourgeois public opinion. Only with a clear understanding of the U.S. rulers' objectives and problems can communists maintain an independent and steady working-class campaign against the growing danger of a war being organized by Washington—a war whose consequences in death and destruction will be horrible for working people, in and out of uniform, throughout the Middle East, in the United States, and around the world.

### The 'peace party' in Washington

While the "loyal opposition" in Washington never questioned the U.S. buildup of 230,000 U.S. troops in the Gulf between mid-August and the beginning of November, some have expressed hesitations over the Bush administration's subsequent decisions that will roughly double the size and firepower of that order of battle by the end of January.

Bush's actions are no mystery. The military might concentrated in the Gulf in early November was nowhere near sufficient to win a rapid victory in a war against the Iraqi regime. There were not enough troops, tanks, bombers and fighter planes, attack helicopters, warships, logistical units, and so on.

The U.S.-organized force was not yet a credible threat to the Saddam Hussein regime.

The tactical differences in the rulers' twin parties and top brass are *not* over whether military action is justifiable, or whether at some point war is likely to be the correct and necessary next step. On those questions there is overwhelming accord.

The real tactical debate among the rulers—reflecting their different weightings of the pros and cons of the two fundamental problems they face—boils down to: *How long will it take for the U.S.-enforced blockade of Iraq to weaken the regime sufficiently to make possible a relatively more rapid military victory or perhaps to achieve Washington's goals some other way?*

Washington should first try "squeezing [Saddam Hussein] to his knees" through the embargo, Sam Nunn, the chairman and ranking Democrat on the Senate Armed Services Committee, said on a television news program December 9, and then move on to a "viable military option if that fails." At the Armed Services Committee hearings two weeks earlier, Nunn spelled out what he means by a "viable military option." He called for opening up the attack by waging war "over the horizon with air power"—that is, sustained massive bombing of Iraqi cities and troop concentrations to minimize subsequent U.S. losses in a ground assault.

Adm. William Crowe, a former chairman of the Joint Chiefs of Staff, appearing before the Armed Services Committee, also advocated tightening the militarily enforced economic chokehold on the Iraqi people before launching a war. His testimony was accompanied by that of Gen. David Jones, another former chairman of the Joint Chiefs of Staff. After giving the blockade some more time to strangle Iraq, Jones said, "If we take military action, we're not going to stop in Kuwait."

Caspar Weinberger, Ronald Reagan's secretary of defense, wrote in the *New York Times* in early December that the blockade "will bring Iraq to its knees if we and our allies have the patience to keep it tightly in place, and the willingness to wait until its full effect is felt."

Weinberger added, "Of course, we must keep our own military strength . . . in place and ready to be used if necessary. The objections to President Bush's recent strengthening of our force make little sense: If we are in the Gulf because we have to be, every military consideration dictates that we should be there with overwhelming power."

And then there's the ultimate antiwar senator, Edward Kennedy. He proposes an anniversary present for the Iraqi people. After a full year of starving them out, Kennedy suggests that a war be launched only after August 2, 1991, if the Iraqi regime has not yet withdrawn from Kuwait.

These are the most prominent voices of the "peace party" among the Democratic and Republican politicians and in the Pentagon! They are the most vocal advocates of laying a grim, months-long economic siege of Iraq—enforced by the largest naval armada assembled since the end of World War II. And, we can add, these are the most vocal advocates of reinstituting imperialist military conscription as well.

As Bush caustically points out, his critics in Congress won't even call themselves back into session!

The most important thing for opponents of imperialist war to recognize, however, and to help their co-workers and others prepare for, is the fact that when the shooting starts, the two capitalist parties in Congress will close ranks behind the flag.

**Pattern for the 1990s**
These are not problems the U.S. rulers confront just for the moment, or just in one part of the world. They are permanent dilemmas facing the foreign and military policy of U.S. imperialism at this point in its decline. This will be the pattern for the 1990s.

In fact, one element not accounted for by those in Congress and the Pentagon who recommend prolonging the squeeze on Iraq before launching a war is the fact that the rest of the world will not stand still for them in the meanwhile—nor will the Iraqi or Israeli regimes. The deepening crisis of the world's capitalist economies and of the imperialist system will keep driving the U.S. rulers and their allies to war, if not in the Middle East then in Asia, if not there, somewhere else. And the handwringing in Washington will continue.

Military power is the main advantage left to the U.S. rulers in their decline relative to their imperialist competitors and to the world's toilers. While U.S. capitalism still has enormous economic power, as well, its position has slipped substantially in recent decades vis-à-vis its German, Japanese, and other rivals. Moreover, the entire world capitalist system itself has become more vulnerable and crisis-ridden than at any time since the Great Depression.

Washington has not undergone anything approaching a comparable weakening of its relative world strategic military power, however. One fact is sufficient to illustrate the point: it is impossible to conceive of any other single imperialist power—or even any coalition of other imperialist powers—capable of mounting a military operation in the Gulf to take on the Iraqi regime and have a reasonable chance of a military victory.

British imperialism certainly couldn't. And Britain was the former colonial power in Iraq and Kuwait, as well as in Egypt and in Palestine (what is now Jordan and Israel). The Thatcher government would not have been able to defeat the Argentine regime in the Malvinas war without decisive transport, intelligence, and logistical support from Washington. Nor could French imperialism, the former colonial power in Syria and Lebanon.

Moreover, there's not some clever trick being carried out by the German and Japanese ruling classes, who haven't committed any military forces to the Gulf. They aren't waiting in the wings to somehow grab part of the spoils of war when it's over. It's not for lack of desire that the German and Japanese ruling classes are not more involved. They are simply too weak politically to confront the consequences at home of trying to commit major military forces abroad for the first time in half a century. And they will pay a price in international imperialist political relations for this weakness, just as the British and French rulers will gain a bit of edge from the relatively big—though far from decisive—roles that their troops, tanks, planes, and warships are playing in the operation.

Washington's preparations for previous wars in this century have not been characterized by any similar lack of confidence. In fact, prior to World War I the main protagonists on all sides thought they knew what was going to happen. They thought they were going to win and profit greatly from the outcome.

The same was true prior to the outbreak of World War II. In the United States, Wall Street and its bipartisan representatives in Congress had concrete goals that they were confident could be met by crushing their Japanese and German imperialist rivals. Of course, as it turned out they didn't exactly get everything they had hoped for, even with their victory over Tokyo and Berlin. They hadn't planned on being unable to crush the Chinese revolution, to cite just one example. Or on the scope of anticolonial struggles throughout Asia, the Middle East, Africa, and the Americas that received an impulse from the inter-imperialist conflict. Nonetheless, the U.S. rulers had been overwhelmingly united and confident in going into that war.

The same was true prior to the Korean War and the Vietnam War. In each case the U.S. rulers were confident they could win, advance their strategic interests, and reorganize those countries and regions to the greater good of imperialism. In Korea they thought they could roll back the expropriation of imperialist and other capitalist property in the North (and perhaps even push on into China), and in Vietnam they thought they could at least hold the line at the seventeenth parallel. As we know, of course, the outcome in both Korea and Vietnam did not match up to Washington's initial expectations. But the rulers embarked on both these wars with confidence.

That is not true today. They are not confident they know how the war they are preparing will actually turn out. So both sides in the tactical disputes in the U.S. ruling class argue on.

The U.S. rulers got away with an easy victory in Grenada in October 1983 because the popularly supported workers' and farmers' government led by Maurice Bishop had already been overthrown in a bloody counterrevolution by the Stalinist faction led by Bernard Coard. The Grenadian toilers, who only a few weeks earlier would have fought hard to defend their revolution, had been disarmed—physically and politically—and demobilized and demoralized by the murderous actions of the Coard gang.[4]

The U.S. rulers were able to roll back the workers' and farmers' government in Nicaragua without the use of U.S. troops because the leadership of the Sandinista National Liberation Front, after having organized the toilers to militarily defeat the U.S.-organized contras, turned their backs on a revolutionary course and sought to come to terms with the capitalists and landlords.[5]

Washington made short work of the National Guard in Panama in December 1989 and early January 1990 because the corrupt and cowardly leadership around Gen. Manuel Noriega refused to organize a fight. It left the anti-imperialist-minded workers and peasants mobilized in the Dignity Battalions without any organized support or direction, while Washington used massive firepower to overwhelm the courageous resistance that was put up in many working-class neighborhoods in the first days.[6]

In each of these cases, the U.S. rulers were able to achieve their bipartisan goals by military means and without a conflict of the scale and duration that either threatened their broader class interests in the region or undermined social and political stability in the United States in any big way.

But nobody in the U.S. ruling class expects an assault on Iraq to be another Grenada or another Panama, nor can a 500,000-strong, heavily armored contra army be found to do the job.

### Stability in Middle East?

The actions already taken by Baghdad and Washington have irreversibly shaken up long-standing political alignments throughout the Middle East.

The historic and oft-betrayed hopes of many workers, peasants, and even middle-class layers in the region for pan-Arab unity in the fight against imperialist domination and Israeli dispossession of the Palestinians have been pushed back even further.

The Iraqi regime brutally seized a neighboring Arab-ruled country and now faces along its borders an imperialist military force that is larger—and many times more deadly in modern firepower—than that mobilized for the invasion of Normandy in 1944.

The government of Saudi Arabia—which despite its long political collusion with Washington had never previously permitted U.S. or other foreign armed forces to station troops on its soil—now has half a million soldiers there poised for an assault against Iraq. Moreover, the Saudi rulers have placed their own troops under U.S. command in the event of war. They have found the first of many problems they cannot buy their way out of.

The U.S. rulers have also brought the governments of Egypt and Syria—only recently at sharp loggerheads in the Arab League—under a common umbrella, both dragging their people toward a war in alliance with imperialism. As part of the deal, Washington has given its tacit blessing to the bloody partition of Lebanon by the Syrian and Israeli regimes. Syria has mobilized massive forces along Iraq's northwestern border, putting itself in a position to open up a second front and perhaps annex some territory. The more and more divided government of Turkey has followed suit along its border with Iraq.

The governments of Pakistan, Bangladesh, and other countries with largely Muslim populations have fallen in step behind U.S. imperialism. On the other hand, Jordan's King Hussein, previously one of Washington's most pliant collaborators, fears the price he might pay at this point for open participation in the U.S.-organized operation, given what could be loosed among the country's majority Palestinian population. The government of Yemen—strangled by the Saudi ruling families because of its failure to fall in step—doubts the honorable intentions of that regime toward Yemeni sovereignty. And the list goes on.

No matter what happens, the changes already brought about in the region mean that the Arab League will henceforth be seen as an even more transparent fake than before as an instrument for defense of common interests and shared aspirations of the toilers of the Middle East.

The Organization of Petroleum Exporting Countries (OPEC) and relations among the ruling classes and governments of its member states will never be the same. Washington and the capitalist families who own the U.S. oil monopolies have bolstered their position against the ruling classes of all the oil-exporting countries—not to mention vis-à-vis U.S. imperialism's Japanese and German competitors, both of whom are heavily dependent on Mideast oil.

The U.S. rulers' deals with the various bourgeois Arab regimes involve Israel, too. None of them dare admit to this, of course, for fear of the consequences at home. But many of these governments are ready to recognize the State of Israel. They hope an agreement can be reached whereby some of the borders of the so-called occupied territories are shifted. They want to finally get the Palestinian question off their backs. After all, there's not a single one of these bourgeois regimes on either side of the impending war that doesn't itself have the blood of Palestinians on its hands: the Syrians, the Jordanians, the Egyptians, the Iraqis, the Saudis. None of them.

But U.S. imperialism has a problem with delivering on that kind of a deal too: the Israelis may not accept it. So that's not a straight road to greater stability in the region either.

Washington also fears what the Israeli rulers themselves may do if the U.S.-led forces go to war against Iraq. The U.S. government wants Israel to stay out, since its involvement would threaten the internal stability of Washington's allied Arab regimes. The Israeli rulers themselves have mixed feelings about getting involved, since they too recognize the uncontrolled forces that can be set in motion, redounding to the disadvantage of the interests of Israel's capitalist ruling class.

At the same time, the Israeli rulers have their own direct, strategic military stake in preventing a possible attack by the Saddam Hussein regime if war breaks out. On that the Israeli rulers will take orders from nobody. They will use whatever military force they can muster—short of their strategic nuclear arsenal—to prevent such an attack. If they're convinced that missiles capable of reaching Israeli soil have not been taken out of commission by preemptive U.S. air strikes, then they will move to do so themselves—the consequences be damned.

THE U.S. RULERS are extremely pleased with themselves over what they have been able to accomplish in so short a time. Who would have imagined even a few months ago that any of this was possible without social upheaval in the Middle East? Without the fall of one or more governments?

But the chips have not yet been called in. The U.S. rulers pose the questions: How can we stabilize Syria and U.S. relations with the Syrian regime? The government in Turkey? The Egyptian regime?

None of the Democratic or Republican politicians have any answers to the underlying social and economic problems that produce and reproduce crises throughout the region. None have any proposals as to how these countries can be turned into prosperous, stable societies with some degree of space for the big majority of the population to organize and engage in politics. Not that they care about the conditions of the toilers. But none even claim to have any proposals on this level.

The structure of imperialist exploitation and domination and the deepening crisis of world capitalism preclude any such solutions in a bourgeois framework. So all that the politicians in Congress have to propose are various tactical military solutions. They may emerge from a war in worse shape to stabilize capitalism in the region. But the political spokespeople for a declining empire have little else to offer.

For opponents of the coming war, this problem confronting the U.S. rulers should underline the fact that the argument "Who wants to die fighting to defend feudalism and put a royal family back on its throne?" is not a very powerful or convincing one.

Not that we shouldn't remind people that Washington's closest regional ally in this effort—the Saudi Arabian government—did not declare slavery illegal until 1962. Or that its ruling family has made it a state offense for a woman to drive a car. Or that the Kuwaiti ruling family gave voting rights to less than 10 percent of the population, excluding the overwhelming majority of those who worked and produced the wealth of the country from even the most basic civil rights and freedoms.

But the slaughter being prepared by Washington will not be a war for these reactionary and exploitative ruling families. It will not be a war for feudalism. *It will be a war for capitalism*—a war to advance U.S. imperialist economic, political, and military interests in the Middle East against the toilers there.

### The danger of denial
Right now, at this stage in the rulers' war drive, perhaps the biggest hazard that faces the working-class vanguard, including communists among them, is the danger of denial.

These hazards are compounded for those who are buffeted by the day-to-day swings and tactical divisions reflected in bourgeois public opinion. One day the news covers a tough-talking press conference by Bush—war! The next day, a sharp exchange at congressional hearings between Baker and several senators—war has been pushed back. The UN Security Council adopts a new resolution—war! The Iraqi regime releases the hostages—

war has been pushed back. Several returning hostages call for bombing Baghdad—war! And so on.

The political vanguard of the working class must steel itself against such impressionistic reflexes. The workers' movement has always faced a double problem leading up to every imperialist war.

On the one hand, the capitalists and bourgeois politicians who are themselves preparing the war always claim to be acting in the interests of peace—and of freedom, democracy, and national sovereignty as well. They are the most *fervent* opponents of war! They publicly agonize, as cameras roll and reporters fill up their notebooks. The bosses and politicians do this in order to maintain support for actions they must take to preserve their social system.

But it's not just the bourgeois propaganda that is disorienting. Individuals and currents from the petty bourgeoisie—sometimes because of the depth of their shock at the horrors of war, and their fears of its consequences—lose their moorings and get drawn into the undertow of one or another section of the war makers and their political parties. These middle-class currents have a bigger direct impact on layers of fighting workers and farmers since—unlike the employers and most bourgeois politicians—they frequently function in or around organizations of the labor movement and in broader radical politics. They often make common cause with petty-bourgeois bureaucrats in the unions and other workers' organizations—whether social democrats, Stalinists, or the homegrown U.S. business-unionism variety. These middle-class layers, whether well intentioned or incurably corrupted, serve as a culture for the growth of all varieties of bourgeois ideas and pressures inside the working-class and labor movement.

Based on the facts, communists can provide an independent working-class answer to the question of whether the capitalist rulers are pushing us closer to war. The answer is yes. The danger of a bloody slaughter in the Middle East is greater today, and the need for a working-class campaign against the imperialist war drive is more pressing.

It is closer, first of all, because Washington is nearer to having in place in the Gulf the forces it needs to fight a war and win it militarily.

There is a second reason as well. Marxists understand that economic relations—or more precisely, the social relations of production that constitute the economic structure of society—are ultimately the determining factor in the evolution of history. But the specific actions that make history at any given time are the product of political decisions by human beings.

While politics has correctly been called "concentrated economics," there is no precise time in the ripening of economic and social contradictions that determines when or how a particular political decision will be made. Big events are determined in their timing and in the character of their outbreak not by the broadest economic and social factors underpinning them but by the political decisions of organizations and individuals reflecting the conflicting interests of various classes operating in the larger historical framework. And this includes "accidents."

We can all think of specific examples: social revolutions that break out when the revolutionary classes are still young and weak in historical terms; strikes that erupt before conditions are really ready, or conversely long after conditions have become overripe; workers initially being stunned by the impact of an onslaught against their living conditions and only later beginning to fight back as pressures mount and openings accumulate. There are innumerable examples of this unevenness in politics and the class struggle.

In this regard, there's something else we need to keep in mind as we follow Washington's buildup in the Middle East day in and day out, and its stiffening enforcement of the embargo. Just as politics is concentrated economics, military force is the carrying out of politics by specific means—by violent and explosive means that have their own momentum in the short run. In fact, over the past month the very weight, speed, and massive character of the order of battle that the U.S. government is putting in place in the Gulf pushes politics and conflicts in the region toward resolution by military means. Never in this century has an imperialist ruling class assembled such a gigantic military force without these preparations eventuating in a full-blown war.

The events pushing humanity toward carnage and devastation in the Middle East have already been set in motion by Washington. They have already produced permanent, and potentially explosive, shifts in the balance of class forces in the region. There is nothing pessimistic or fatalistic about recognizing this reality. To the contrary, only by looking at it and refusing to blink in the face of it will vanguard fighters in the working class in the United States and other countries be prepared to act in an effective way against the war drive.

The positions advanced on all sides by the bourgeois politicians and military brass in Washington have nothing in common with the interests of workers and farmers in the United States, the Middle East, or anywhere in the world. As Mary-Alice Waters explains in the introduction to the Pathfinder book *U.S. Hands Off the Mideast! Cuba Speaks Out at the United Nations:*

"This war drive and its results are being orchestrated by the bipartisan government of the United States. But the people in whose name this is being done—those whose economic livelihoods will be devastated and whose sons and daughters will die in combat—have no say. No political party of working people sits in Congress, and no mechanism gives citizens of the United States—in or out of uniform—the right to debate the issues and vote on a declaration of war. That prerogative is reserved to the representatives of the twin imperialist parties that control the Congress and White House. After much argument and debate over tactical alternatives—and unanimous protestations of a desire for peace—those same parties have already dragged the people of the United States into four horrendous world wars this century: in 1917, 1941, 1950, and 1964. They are on the verge of doing it again, with all the unspeakable consequences it will entail in the Mideast and in the United States itself."[7]

## SHORING UP A DECLINING EMPIRE

WHAT ARE THE configuration and dynamics of the world in which this war buildup is taking place? Vanguard workers must understand this if we are to organize effectively against the imperialist war drive.

When I spoke in New York City in November, a very good question was asked during the discussion period—one that provides a useful framework for looking at the state of world politics and the class struggle. I briefly addressed the question at the time, and I'd like to return to it tonight. It was a three-part question that I'll paraphrase.

The first part was: "Doesn't Washington's capacity to mount this kind of military mobilization, and pull such a broad coalition of governments behind it, indicate that we may be living through the coming together of a new world order? Or isn't this at least what the U.S. and other imperialist rulers are attempting to accomplish and think they can bring about?" The phrase "new world order" has been used in recent years by Gorbachev, and by Reagan, Bush, and various commentators associated with both the Democratic and Republican parties.

The second part of the question was: "If the above is true, then some prominent figures in the U.S. ruling class and government must believe they have won the Cold War. Isn't that how they read the disintegration of Stalinist parties and regimes throughout Eastern Europe and the deepening social crisis and devolution of the Soviet Union? Aren't the imperialists now trying to take advantage of that shift, as they see it, by upping the ante in the Middle East more than they might otherwise seek to do?"

Finally, the third part of the question was: "Aren't the U.S. rulers and some of their imperialist allies, then, operating with a 'triumphalist' view of their world position? Doesn't this register the culmination of proclaimed successes during the 1980s of what came to be seen as Reagan- and Thatcher-style 'free market'—and internationally aggressive—capitalism? Aren't the imperialists operating from a position of greater strength? Don't communists have to face that reality?" (The limits of the "success" of Thatcherism are probably denied a bit less than they were before her personal defeat and retreat to the Tory back benches in November 1990.)

Answering these questions will help us think more clearly about the place of the military blockade and the war drive in the world class struggle, about some broader implications of the deeply shared bipartisan war course, and about the tactical divisions in the U.S. ruling class. What should workers organizing opposition to the war anticipate about the impact of the conflict on U.S. and world politics? How can that help us explain to other workers fighting at our side against the employers' offensive at home why our struggles are interconnected with uncompromising opposition to imperialist war as well as to debt slavery and the exploitation of the wages system?

## Seeking to salvage the old order

First, what the U.S. rulers are doing in the Middle East is in fact the opposite of any attempt to establish a new world order. The point is not the words they may or may not use, but the economic, social, and political reality behind those words.

World orders *have* been put together by exploiting classes at different times in history. They've been built following major defeats of the working class and revolutionary upsurges by the toilers. They've been consolidated and extended on the basis of sustained periods of economic expansion. Sometimes under these conditions the ruling groups have been able to maintain themselves in power for decades, influence the course of world politics, and deal further blows to working people fighting for democratic liberties, for liberation, for socialism, or simply for the most elementary justice.

But what the U.S. rulers are doing by using military power to move toward a virtual protectorate in Iraq has nothing to do with establishing a new world order. To the contrary, it's aimed at trying to stave off a further crumbling of the old capitalist world order.

Following World War II the imperialists succeeded in the Middle East, as in other parts of the world, in adjusting their system of world domination to the new situation they faced with the victory of decolonization and spread of national liberation movements. The former colonies were largely transformed into politically independent countries with bourgeois social relations and ruling classes, and integrated into the world capitalist system. These new capitalist regimes often absorbed—and put to the service of both local and foreign exploiters—substantial elements of feudal, semifeudal, and other preexisting forms of social organization.

But the organization and exploitation of labor in these countries remains subordinated to the world system of imperialist plunder. The ruling capitalist and landlord classes—even in countries such as Iran, South Korea, or Brazil, where there has been a relatively substantial degree of industrialization—maintain their own power and privileges by brutally enforcing a neocolonial social system that traps the toilers in economic and social conditions far below those of even the weakest imperialist countries. The debt crisis is just one prominent manifestation of this reality.

The gap in economic development and living standards between the handful of imperialist countries and those of the great majority of the so-called Third World has widened over the past two decades, as has class differentiation and polarization within them. The neocolonial capitalist structure of these countries is a permanent barrier to long-term, stable bourgeois democracy or any political and social equilibrium. Various sections of the national ruling classes alternately conflict with the imperialists and conspire with them to drive these countries more deeply into indebtedness—at the expense of the peasants and workers, whose labor is savagely superexploited to cover the staggering interest payments. These countries and their toilers are hit the hardest by explosions of inflation, sudden rocketing of oil prices, intensified protectionism by the strongest imperialist powers, and slumps in the world capitalist economy.

This bitter fact of the world imperialist system confronts the vast majority of humanity. Capitalism creates the very conditions that lead to increasing breakdowns and social instability; that result in the incapacity of the bulk of these countries to develop, and the consequent social disintegration; that deepen the class polarization and give rise to struggles by workers and farmers even in the handful of Third World countries that do experience industrial development. The expansionist drives of the neocolonial ruling classes themselves erupt in border disputes, land grabs, and wars.

Today these countries also face a mounting threat of a world depression, one that will have a devastating impact in Asia, Africa, and the Americas—areas of the world that have already been through the wringer of a decade-long decline in the 1980s. All these conditions created, reproduced, and perpetuated by imperialism increasingly destabilize its poorest capitalist countries and block their development.

The massive Third World debt combines with the balloon of corporate debt and the results of a decade of real estate speculation in the imperialist countries to threaten collapse of the international banking system. Imperialist-backed austerity drives imposed by neocolonial capitalist regimes to squeeze interest payments from the blood and sweat of the toilers result in unanticipated explosions. These conditions are the product of the decline and disintegration of the old world order, not the emergence of a new one. They are the real underpinnings of the political crisis that makes inevitable the U.S. drive toward war in the Middle East.

### The capitalist regime in Iraq

In Iraq the imperialists do not confront a workers' and peasants' government that they seek to crush in order to reverse the tendency toward expropriation of capitalist property. In that sense, too, Iraq is not another Korea, Vietnam, Nicaragua, or Grenada. The government of Saddam Hussein is a corrupt, brutal, expansionist capitalist regime—a regime of imperialist democracy's own making, in large part.

Despite the Iraqi capitalists' sometimes sharp conflicts with imperialism over the division of the spoils from pillaging the Iraqi toilers, the regime there—as with many other neocolonial regimes—has served as an agency to organize the exploitation and suppression of the workers and peasants to the benefit of Wall Street and Washington and other imperialist powers. It has helped imperialism police the toilers elsewhere in the region as well, not only by waging a bloody war to weaken the Iranian revolution but also by organizing repeated repression of Palestinian militants and of any class-conscious workers' leaders who try to organize.

But Saddam Hussein also heads the government of an Iraqi capitalist class that has its own national interests, which it seeks to advance at the expense of its rivals in the region and—to the degree possible—by wresting concessions from the imperialist bourgeoisies. That's what led to the invasion of Kuwait. It's not complex. The Iraqi capitalist rulers, like all capitalist ruling classes, think and act pragmatically, not on the basis of science or theory. They do what they judge they can get away with at a given time to boost their profits, expand their base, and defend and advance their national class interests.

By invading Kuwait, the Iraqi capitalists hoped to gain what every capitalist class hopes to gain when it goes to war. They want Kuwait's oil, they want its territory, they want its deep-water port. So, when they figured the time was ripe, they took them. (As it turned out, they figured wrong. They may even have been entrapped by the U.S. State Department.)[8]

They'll hold on to Kuwait as long as they think they can do so. They've held on to Kuwait since August; now they've got another six weeks or so until January 15, they figure. They'll wheel and deal, see what happens, and then try to cook up something else. Hope for a deal, perhaps offer some territorial concessions. They'll act pragmatically, just like Bush and company. And the history of humanity over the past several hundred years teaches us that wars—often started through "miscalculations"—are the result of this pragmatic capitalist expansionism and maneuvering for advantage. The workers and farmers, in and out of uniform on both sides, always pay the highest price.

The Saddam Hussein regime started the war against Iran back in 1980 for the same reasons. Yes, Iraq's bourgeois rulers felt threatened by the revolution and wanted to deal a blow to it if they could. But they also wanted Iran's oil fields, its refineries, and its tanker ports. They hoped that the recent disintegration of the shah's army would work to their benefit. They had one big advantage, too: they were backed and to some degree armed by the imperialist powers, who feared above all the deepening or extension of the Iranian revolution. So the Iraqi rulers launched an eight-year war at an appalling cost in deaths, injuries, and destruction. What did they end up gaining? One relatively small strip of land. And then they gave that back to Iran one month after their invasion of Kuwait to gain some diplomatic advantage and relieve military pressure on their eastern border in face of the imperialist buildup.

It's important not to fall into thinking that the only wars that take place in the capitalist epoch are imperialist wars. They are a minority of the armed conflicts, although usually the largest ones. Capitalism itself is an expansionist social system. There were capitalist wars of conquest and plunder before the consolidation of the modern system of imperialism, and there have been many since then—including wars between capitalist ruling classes of countries oppressed by imperialism.

Despite Saddam Hussein's services to imperialism, his regime has proven too unreliable, too unpredictable, and too destabilizing in a part of the world where imperialism has enormous economic stakes—*oil, above all*—and where all varieties of national, social, and political conflicts are very explosive and can be very costly in their consequences for the imperialists.

The U.S. rulers need a government in Iraq that they can dominate much more directly. This is because of what Washington has failed to accomplish, because of imperialism's weakness, not its strength. But even if Washington succeeds in imposing such a subservient regime, this new regime would be no more capable than its predecessor of bringing development and stability to Iraq or to the region.

The rulers in Washington, in pursuit of their class interests, may well subject the Iraqi people to a massive bloodbath—and the result will be to reestablish a new version of the neocolonial capitalist regime that has failed and brought them to this point in the first place. Another Syngman Rhee—installed as president of South Korea by U.S. armed forces in 1948, preserved in power by a massive U.S.-organized war, only to fall a decade later in the face of a popular uprising. Another Guillermo Endara—sworn in as president of Panama on a U.S. military base.[9]

That's what Washington's bloody victory would put in place in Baghdad—another regime to oversee the brutalization of workers and peasants on a scale beyond our imaginations, another series of cynical and betrayed promises of economic development, another failure for the world capitalist system.

So WASHINGTON'S accelerating drive toward war against Iraq is not the product of some strengthening of the imperialist system, some new period of its expansion and stabilization. To the contrary.

Nor is it built on the capacity of the rulers in Washington, London, or other imperialist centers to smash the working class and labor movement at home, as the capitalists succeeded in doing in Italy, in Germany, elsewhere in Europe, and in Japan in the 1920s and '30s.[10]

Nor is it based on the imperialists' ability to offer substantial enough economic and social concessions to layers of the working class to ensure relative social peace for a decade or so. That's what the U.S. ruling class was able to do following World War II on the basis of a sustained period of capitalist economic expansion in the 1940s, '50s and '60s—itself the product of the prior smashing of the working-class movement in Europe; U.S. imperialism's victory in the war; and the political derailing, bureaucratization, and narrowing of the unfolding social movement that the CIO industrial union movement exemplified.

Nothing comparable to either one of these previous situations exists for the imperialist ruling classes today. During the 1980s the employers in the United States and other imperialist countries did deal some big blows to the labor movement and were able to push down the living and job conditions of the working class. But nowhere did the imperialists' antilabor offensive accomplish enough to break the resistance of the working class, smash its elementary institutions of defense—the unions—and thus lay the foundations for a prolonged period of capitalist economic expansion and political stability. It hasn't gotten rid of the workers' tendency to find ways to fight back against the antilabor offensive.

What the bourgeois commentators hailed as the "Reagan-Thatcher revolution" of the 1980s has come a cropper. It failed. We've just witnessed one small chapter in that unfolding story with Thatcher's stepping down in Britain amid rising unemployment and double-digit inflation and interest rates.

The U.S. rulers have entered a recession with corporate indebtedness, the banking system, the mammoth insurance business, commercial real estate, and the stock market all in the worst shape they've been in on the eve of an economic downturn since the Great Depression of the 1930s. This will be a worldwide recession for sure, and one rife with potential for breakdowns and sudden failures that could send the international banking system tumbling.

In short, what Washington is racing toward in the Middle East is the first major war in the twentieth century prepared by the U.S. rulers from a position of relative weakness, not strength—economic, social, and political weakness combined.

## U.S. imperialism lost Cold War

That brings us to the second part of the question: Didn't U.S. imperialism win the so-called Cold War?

The answer is no. Week after week, month after month, the

evidence keeps getting stronger.

At the end of November 1990 a conference was held in France of the heads of state of the United States, Canada, and thirty-two European countries—including imperialist powers, all the Eastern European governments (except Albania, but they'll be there soon), and the Soviet Union. With great bally-hoo they signed a "Charter of Paris for a New Europe." These thirty-four strokes of the pen, we are told, put a formal end to the Cold War—and, I guess, opened the prospects for a "new world order" (although that term is less popular in Europe, where it has some bad echoes from the 1930s and early '40s).

But the truth is, what's shaping up in Europe for the capitalist ruling classes is a debacle, not a new order. As recently as several months ago it was common to hear on television and to read in the financial pages of major newspapers, or in magazines like *Business Week,* the *Economist* of London, and *Newsweek,* how the West German capitalists were on their way to becoming the world's dominant economic power as a result of the unification with East Germany. This was supposed to give a united Germany a big investment and trading edge with Eastern Europe and the Soviet Union. This was going to be a way forward for world capitalism, a powerful locomotive of sustained growth.

Today, however, the hosannas are fading. The German and other Western European ruling classes are looking at Eastern Europe as if it's a massive brood of poor relations who've dropped in to visit and overstayed their welcome. And this is not just a manner of speaking; it's literally true. Today, the preoccupation of the capitalist rulers throughout Western Europe—who supposedly won the Cold War a year ago—is how to forestall massive migrations of working people from the Soviet Union and Eastern Europe seeking to flee the rapidly deteriorating economic and social conditions there.

In place of the Berlin Wall that was knocked down a little over a year ago—an act supposedly symbolizing the "new world order"—capitalist governments are today talking about erecting a new political wall dividing Western Europe from everything to its east. The aim of this new wall—consisting of immigration restrictions enforced by border cops, roundups, and deportations—is to prevent freedom of travel, freedom to look for jobs, freedom to live and work where you choose. To prevent the very freedoms promised to working people just a few months ago. (The appearance in what was previously West Berlin of T-shirts with the cynical and reactionary message, "Bring back my wall," is an omen of these coming restrictions.)

It is now clear, as communists have recognized from the outset, that no stable regime has been or will be established soon anywhere in Eastern Europe or in the Soviet Union itself. The remnants of the ruling bureaucratic castes, and those privileged layers who to a greater or lesser extent have supplanted (or incorporated) them at top governmental levels in some countries, will seek to maintain whatever degree of centralized power they need to keep themselves in command. They will maintain strong police, military, and semimilitary forces to preserve their power in the face of growing economic, social, and political instability.

These regimes and the privileged personnel who administer them continue to bank everything on their hopes of being integrated more and more into the world capitalist system. They have no other plan for a way out of the economic and social crisis in these countries.

At the same time, none of these countries is any closer today than they were a year ago to reestablishing stable capitalist property relations in the basic means of industrial production and wholesale trade, or to winning acceptance of the social relations of production that must accompany them. The very efforts of the ruling groups to maintain themselves in power, and to ensure their continuing access to the comforts made possible by the labor of workers and farmers, creates constant obstacles to achieving the conditions necessary for the restoration of capitalism.

Most decisively, the working class itself in these countries will have to be fought and defeated before the capitalist system can be reimposed. One of the first major strikes of workers in what was formerly East Germany broke out recently. It was a strike of railway workers protesting massive layoffs planned by the government and demanding wage parity with railway workers in the western part of the country. The determination of the regime of Chancellor Helmut Kohl to make German workers pay for the fiasco in that country will not meet with ready acceptance either. There have been strikes, farmers' demonstrations, and other protests in Poland, Hungary, the Soviet Union, and elsewhere, as the privileged ruling layers seek to make working people bear the brunt of the crisis and of the increasing reliance by these regimes on capitalist market methods.

## Accelerating disintegration of Soviet Union

The crisis in the Union of Soviet Socialist Republics continues to accelerate, including the pace of the disintegration of the so-called Soviet Union itself. The USSR hasn't been soviet nor heading toward socialism for decades. It hasn't been a workers' republic since the late 1920s either. Now it threatens to cease being a union as well. In fact, it may be the most misnamed country in the world.

The communist course of the Bolshevik leadership in the opening years of the Soviet republic—a course that guaranteed the right of national self-determination to the oppressed peasants and workers in the tsarist prison house of nations—was reversed by the Stalinist counterrevolution in the late 1920s and '30s. A new prison house of nations was erected by the Stalinists, not only in the Soviet Union but to a greater or lesser degree within each of the Eastern European workers' states as well. Today that involuntary "union" is coming apart.

The economic and social crisis in the Soviet Union is worsening as well. Shortages of food and other basic necessities are growing more acute. Demonstrations and defensive strikes continue to occur to protest the devastating consequences on working people of this downward spiral.

In the face of this mounting instability, we should be prepared for the Gorbachev regime to deepen its Bonapartist course and to lash out with increasing violence and repression against resistance by workers and farmers.[11]

Gorbachev has already unleashed murderous assaults on oppressed nationalities, so far almost entirely against those in non-European parts of the Soviet Union such as Azerbaijan. The central government has also used economic sabotage and blackmail against the national aspirations of the peoples of Estonia, Latvia, and Lithuania.[12]

Most recently, under the cover of populist demagogy against price-gougers and profiteers, Gorbachev has set the stage to legitimize the organization and unleashing of paramilitary thugs against food protests, strikers, or others who can be labeled as "economic saboteurs." He has prepared the way for more aggressive use of the militarized police units.

How long Gorbachev himself will be able to survive this deepening social and political crisis, however, is still to be determined. It's hard not to believe that late at night Saddam Hussein doesn't get satisfaction out of thinking that even with his own prospects, he may well outlast the treacherous Gorbachev.

It's not only Gorbachev and the Stalinists who decry this outbreak of demands for national self-determination in the Soviet Union and in Eastern Europe. The editorial writers for the *New York Times* and many other ruling-class mouthpieces have also warned of the destabilizing consequences for the world capitalist system of a breakup of the Soviet Union and the nationalist forces that this development could accelerate elsewhere in the world. A few days ago, *New York Times* senior columnist Flora Lewis wrote an article under the headline, "The Bane of Nations." Speaking of the "new partition threatening Europe," Lewis cited approvingly the warning of an unnamed high-ranking "Western leader" against "the risk of a new 'fragmented Europe of tribal states.'"

But growing demands for national rights are inevitable today. They are the consequence of what capitalism and imperialism have wrought over the past century. They are the consequence of what the Stalinists carried out by reversing in blood the Bolsheviks' efforts to forge greater internationalist unity among toilers of all nations and nationalities through an uncompromising fight against national chauvinism and oppression.

Capitalism and the imperialist system reproduce and deepen economic and social inequalities among peoples of different regions, nationalities, skin colors, languages, and so on—more sharply than ever during periods of economic crisis and decline such as today. The disintegration of the Soviet Union and of the regimes in Eastern Europe inevitably lead to an explosion of national demands by peoples long oppressed by more powerful nations.

There will be an upsurge of the demand for national rights as the old world order continues to come apart. It's important for the communist movement to stick strongly to what we've said many times before: that the national question will not diminish in today's world but will increase; and that the uncompromising championing of the right to national self-determination of oppressed nations and nationalities is a precondition for any successful revolutionary advance toward socialism and proletarian internationalism.

This right must be assured not only to those who are a nation in the economic and social sense. It must also be guaranteed to all those driven down by capitalism and imperialism who, through struggle against that oppression, come to recognize themselves as a people or a nationality. Certainly that is one of the lessons learned from Lenin and the Bolsheviks that was reinforced by the Nicaraguan revolution and the central place in it of the autonomy process among the Black and Indian peoples of the Atlantic Coast.

## Regimes of permanent crisis

What exists throughout Eastern Europe, and in the Soviet Union itself to an accelerating degree, are regimes of permanent crisis, with a disintegrative aspect to all of them. Far from being a boon to the imperialist economies, this threatens to place new economic pressure and strains on the world capitalist system.

So the answer is no: the imperialist ruling classes of the United States and Europe did not emerge as the victors from the Cold War. In fact, they have suffered a historic defeat with the ongoing disintegration of the Stalinist parties and weakening of these bureaucratic regimes. This is the case because this process was not accompanied by a decisive defeat of the workers; by the "appearance" of capitalist property relations; or by an increase in the number of revolutionary-minded workers who look to the Soviet regime and thus can be politically misled by it. Just the opposite has occurred.

The Cold War was imposed on the imperialists in the years following World War II by their inability—due to the international relationship of forces—to carry out by means of a hot war, a shooting war, their goal of restoring capitalism in the Soviet Union and other countries where it had been overturned. They were not strong enough to do so right on the heels of World War II, in part because of organized resistance by U.S. GIs to being used as cannon fodder in China or Eastern Europe rather than being demobilized and sent home.[13]

The U.S. rulers' failure to achieve their aims in the 1950-53 Korean War was another relatively early test of the limits on what Washington could accomplish through direct military might. Rather than rolling back the overturn of capitalist property relations, the war actually accelerated the deepening of the anticapitalist revolution both in Korea and in China.

So during what came to be called the Cold War, the U.S. rulers had a standoff with the privileged castes in the Soviet, Eastern European, and Chinese workers' states. The capitalist ruling classes watched the Stalinist regimes break the revolutionary continuity of the workers' movement in those countries, demobilize and demoralize working people, turn them away from internationalism, and isolate them from struggles by workers and peasants around the world. This was deeply in the interests of the imperialists.

The counterrevolutionary castes sought stable relations with imperialism. They aided revolutionary struggles against imperialism and capitalist rule only to the degree necessary for their own defense and diplomatic leverage. In fact, Stalinist political corruption and miseducation—the Soviet Union's universal export, the "invisible goods" that came along with the aid—became the biggest obstacle throughout the world to forging revolutionary leaderships capable of organizing workers and farmers to defeat their class enemies and carry through to the end the uprooting of imperialist oppression and capitalist exploitation.

Throughout this period, Washington and its allies continued to wage hot wars, launch armed aggression, and organize mercenary armies throughout the Third World—in Korea, Vietnam, Algeria, the Congo, the Dominican Republic, and Nicaragua, to name just a few well-known examples. Meanwhile, they hoped that what became known as the Cold War—that is, the pressure exerted on the workers' states through the transmission belt of the bureaucratic castes—would weaken these states sufficiently that they could at some point in the indefinite future be toppled militarily and capitalism restored by force of arms.

As we've seen over the past year, however, that's not how things turned out. The brutally repressive regimes that had blocked the workers and farmers of these countries from entering into politics and acting in their own class interests are crumbling. The regimes that have replaced them are in irresolvable crisis. And the imperialists have no prospect of restoring a stable capitalism, or even reasonable social equilibrium, without a fight against the toilers—a fight whose consequences they cannot foresee.

The crisis will deepen in all these countries. It will get worse. The assaults on the living standards, on what workers and farmers in these countries have come to recognize as social rights, will intensify.

But working people will resist these attacks. And through these defensive battles workers in these countries will find ways to link up with fights by other workers, not only elsewhere in Europe but around the world—an opportunity they were denied for half a century by these regimes.

Permanent crisis and instability, mounting struggles by workers and farmers—that is what will mark the months and years ahead in Eastern Europe and the Soviet Union. The outcome, like everywhere else in the world, will be determined in struggle.

Moreover, the Stalinist misleaders—not only in these countries but in the imperialist countries and throughout the Third World—are less able than ever before to disorient and betray revolutionary workers who look to them under the illusion that their policies point the road out of oppression and exploitation and toward socialism.

**Imperialist war**
With this understanding of the world in mind, we can see more clearly why the word *triumphalist* is not an accurate description of the imperialists' world position.

In one way, the war that is being prepared by Washington in the Middle East today is a "post–Cold War" war. That's because, unlike any other war they've prepared since 1945, the U.S. rulers can't present this one as part of the battle against communism or the Soviet threat. This too will be a pattern from here on out. The wars that Washington fights will be more nakedly imperialist wars—and imperialist in every sense of the word.

Imperialist, first of all, in the most popular sense—like imperial Rome and its legions. The legions of a dominant power that exaggerates its contributions to human culture and ideas in order to rationalize marching off to dominate other parts of the world. A war fought by an imperial army, claiming imperial rights and prerogatives for an imperial race. A war against illogical heathens with strange gods. A war aimed at economically draining, politically oppressing, and militarily subjugating another people. An imperial power—often with high-flown rhetoric and practiced apologists—that claims the right to police the world.

It's good to use the term this way. There's nothing wrong or "unscientific" about it. It *is* an imperialist war in that most classical, most popular sense. It goes back thousands of years, and rings a bell with people throughout the world.

Moreover, it's completely accurate in another sense, too. Because Washington—the last of the world's massive, brutal, imperial powers—is now embarking on a series of final wars to try to hold together a crumbling order, the capitalist order. And in the course of these conflicts—regardless of how long it takes— that empire will go down to defeat under the combined blows of workers and farmers at home and abroad.

### War for Big Oil

It's also an imperialist war in the popular economic sense—a war over oil. It will be a war to guarantee that the profits derived from the organization and control of petroleum remain in the hands of Big Oil, of the monopolies and the imperialist governments that defend their interests. That's the sense in which you hear people say, "I'm not sure oil is worth a single life over there."

We shouldn't be hesitant to use the word *imperialist* in that sense, either. There's a great deal of truth to the statement that the war is being fought over oil. It's a battle over resources—a battle by the U.S. rulers to stop another capitalist class, in this case the Iraqi capitalists, from gaining too much control over those resources, directly or indirectly.

We should remember that the U.S. capitalists alone use 26 percent of the world's oil production. Moreover, every aspect of the world oil market—right down to the gas pump—is highly monopolized by a handful of superrich capitalist families in the

United States, Britain, and other imperialist countries.

Today, while the price of a barrel of oil remains well above what it cost four months ago, substantially more is being produced, sent through pipelines, and put on tankers than prior to the Iraqi invasion of Kuwait. In fact, in November world oil production reached a six-month high. Washington has played up information about the Saudi Arabian government bearing a big load in financing the U.S. military buildup there. But the windfall profits to the Saudi ruling families from the rise in oil prices since August 2 has produced five times as much income for them as they've laid out for Operation Desert Shield.

But it's not the Saudi throne or the ruling classes of the OPEC countries that are the biggest victors of this price-gouging—although they do benefit, and at the expense of both the workers and peasants in their own countries and those in non-oil-producing countries throughout the Third World.

The big winners are the wealthy families who own the imperialist oil monopolies. They more than anyone else—more than OPEC—influence the world price of oil. This is true even though most of the Mideast oil fields have been nationalized in the decades since World War II, as well as those in many other semicolonial countries. The imperialist-owned monopolies not only own and operate their own massive oil fields, but also dominate world petroleum refining capacity, transportation, and distribution networks. The government of the Soviet Union, the world's largest oil producer, has also benefited from recent price increases, helping to offset falling revenues from the declining output of its crisis-wracked petroleum industry.

The great losers economically—not to mention from the slaughter that is being planned—are working people in the United States and around the world. The majority of humanity—those in the semicolonial world—are being hit the hardest by the monopoly-rigged leap in oil prices. The Third World is being devastated. The working people of Eastern Europe are special victims too. They have been hit by the price hikes, the cutoff of Iraqi oil, the failure by the Soviet government to come through with contracted supplies, and—beginning January 1, 1991—with the necessity for the first time in decades of paying for Soviet oil in hard currency at the world market price.

So the war that is being prepared is an imperialist war in that sense too—a war for Big Oil.

There's a third way in which it's an imperialist war—the way Marxists have used the term for most of this century. It's a war waged by finance capital. It's a war over economic domination and control—redivision—of a big piece of the semicolonial world. It's a war against other propertied classes in other countries for the domination of raw materials, markets, and access to the superexploitation of low-paid labor.

It even has the aspect of a war to redivide world power and influence among rival imperialist ruling classes. Despite the broad backing of the world's capitalist ruling families for the war drive, the massive military operation in the Gulf is not a "coalition" effort. It's not a partnership of equals. U.S. imperialism is calling the shots.

The bottom line, however, is that this will be a war in which all the imperialist powers—U.S. imperialism above all—stand to lose. It will be a war of a declining, not an advancing, imperialist power.

## REVOLUTIONISTS AND COMMUNISTS

WITH THIS UNDERSTANDING of the crisis of world imperialism today, and how the war that Washington is preparing fits into its grinding decline, we should take a look at the political leadership working people need in order to advance toward national liberation and socialism. Because world capitalism, no matter how deeply crisis-ridden it should become, will not collapse into socialism under its own weight. The imperialist ruling classes and the various bourgeois agencies of exploitation and oppression throughout the world will have to be replaced in the course of revolutionary struggles.

Thus, when we point to the accuracy of Cuban president Fidel Castro's statement that "in the world of today and tomorrow being revolutionary means, and will increasingly mean, being communists, and being communists in the full revolutionary sense," we're not just repeating a well-turned phrase. We're not simply restating what communists have always held about the need for proletarian leadership.

Today, to become and remain a revolutionist increasingly necessitates becoming a communist. That is a political judgment. It flows from our assessment of the evolution of the world system of capitalist exploitation and imperialist oppression, the weight of this evolution in international politics and the class struggle, the stage of the crisis of Stalinist parties, and the tasks confronting revolutionists at this point in the twentieth century.

This assessment underlies the necessity of forging a revolutionary leadership of the workers and farmers in every part of the world. The particular problems and challenges in accomplishing this task, however—the weight and priority of various demands—differ substantially depending on the class structure of a given country, the degree of exhaustion of previous leaderships and misleaderships, and the living continuity of communist experience in the workers' movement.

In the Soviet Union and Eastern Europe, for example, there is no continuity of revolutionary leadership anywhere today. There are no communist currents and no unbroken historic link with the experiences of a communist leadership in the working class. For all practical purposes, the human material that represented that communist continuity was decimated, demoralized, or broken over the course of the 1930s, '40s, '50s, and '60s. It will have to be rebuilt. In the course of the big class struggles that lie ahead, workers and farmers in these countries will forge links with fighters and revolutionists elsewhere in the world, and that will contribute to the process of forging communist leadership on an international level.

In the semicolonial world, the task of forging revolutionary leaderships is no less challenging. There the battle for national liberation has gone through a particular evolution and important changes as the twentieth century has unfolded. These cumulative developments have altered the class character and caliber of the leadership necessary to take the next steps in the struggle against imperialist domination, semifeudal oppression, and capitalist exploitation.

Only fifty years ago, with the outbreak of World War II, a great movement for decolonization began to sweep the world. At the opening of that war, the vast majority of what are today independent countries were colonies. When the United Nations was launched at the close of the war in late 1945, it initially had only

51 members; today there are 159.

This political independence was not granted by the imperialist colonizers out of the goodness of their hearts. Independence was conquered through struggle—by the peoples of India and Iraq to throw off British rule; by the Indochinese, Algerian, and Syrian peoples against French rule; by the Filipino people against U.S. colonial rule; by the Indonesian people against Dutch imperialism; by the Congolese people against Belgian colonialism; by the peoples of Angola and Mozambique against Portuguese rule; and many others.

If you don't count Hong Kong as a colony—and I don't anymore; its rapid integration into China is not only a foregone conclusion, but actually running ahead of the scheduled 1997 formalities—then the largest colony left in the world today is Puerto Rico. If anything, this fact increases the importance of the anticolonial struggles that remain to be settled, particularly of numerous islands in the Caribbean, the Pacific, the Indian Ocean, and so on. But the scope of the post–World War II decolonization conquests is impressive.

While in each case there were landlords, merchant capitalists, and other indigenous exploiters who collaborated with the colonial powers to the bitter end, the decolonization movements nonetheless mobilized broad united fronts behind the fight for national independence. Representatives of different classes, with directly counterposed social interests, carried substantial weight in these battles.

Independence struggles were fought and led to victory under leaderships that were often bourgeois or petty bourgeois both in program and social composition. The workers and peasants were the most self-sacrificing fighters, the courageous battalions without whom the battle could not have been won. But the dominant political leaderships were not proletarian or communist in the vast majority of cases. Most of the regimes that came to power were bourgeois, not workers' and peasants' governments.

The victories of the decolonization movement gave an impulse to a second set of conquests in the struggle for national liberation—ones that were often intertwined with the anticolonial fight itself. This was the struggle to wrest back from direct ownership by imperialist interests the most basic resources and infrastructure—the national patrimony—of countries in the Third World. These struggles marked much of the 1950s and '60s, and continued even into the late 1970s with the Iranian revolution.

In 1956 the Egyptian government headed by Gamal Abdel Nasser took back the Suez Canal from British and French finance capital, for example. Regimes throughout the Middle East, Latin America, and elsewhere nationalized oil fields and mineral rights. Class lines in these battles were drawn more sharply than in the decolonization battles themselves, since layers of native exploiters had economic interests that were directly tied to major imperialist-owned banks and monopolies. Workers and peasants often took advantage of these confrontations with imperialism to press demands on the neocolonial regimes for land reform and labor rights, and in the process won some greater space to organize and practice politics.

But in the big majority of cases these resources taken from the direct domination and exploitation of the imperialists were transferred to the domination of local, rising capitalist classes, either directly to private owners or indirectly through the neocolonial regimes they controlled. Once again, the conflicts that culminated in the nationalization of these former imperialist properties were carried through largely by bourgeois and petty-bourgeois leaderships and without the establishment of workers' and peasants' regimes.

THE MOST PRESSING tasks that confront workers and peasants in most of the Third World today, however, require a different class character and caliber of leadership if they are to succeed. The tasks of national liberation, of carrying through to the end the liberation of the toilers from imperialist domination and super-exploitation, cannot be advanced short of a struggle against the local capitalist and landlord classes, whose interests are completely intertwined with those of the imperialists. Thus, the political challenges before national liberation movements in tackling this next set of historic tasks require greater political clarity and working-class leadership.

That's the road forward to lasting economic and social development. That's how to rid these countries of social structures and institutions that ensure their permanent subjugation to imperialism. That's the only way to prevent the gains from even limited economic and social development from ending up in the hands of a thin layer of capitalists, the government bureaucracy, and the military officer corps, while the vast majority of workers and peasants are driven into deeper impoverishment and brutally repressed when they resist. That's the only way to carry through land reforms that are thoroughgoing and that don't—through the mechanism of the capitalist rents and mortgages system, and domination over credit, marketing arrangements, and sources of agricultural equipment and supplies— simply end up reproducing massive landlessness and class differentiation in the countryside.

These pressing tasks confronting anti-imperialist fighters in most semicolonial countries today are the product of the crisis of the imperialist system itself, of the failure of capitalism. It is capitalism that has robbed workers and peasants the world over who fought courageously—and at great sacrifice—for their national independence, only to find themselves today the debt slaves of imperialist banks. Only to find themselves still subject to the dictates of the great oil cartels, the giant merchants of grain, and other imperialist interests.

The imperialist enemy can no longer be fought successfully in the same ways as in past decades. Colonial independence has been achieved in most countries. The national patrimony of land and other mineral resources has been nationalized in many cases.

In the most direct and immediate sense, the problem for the toilers is not that the bourgeois and petty-bourgeois parties and organizations are ineffective as instruments in the struggle for socialism; that's always true. But the social reality that above all poses the demand for working-class leadership is that the bourgeois ruling classes have become the main prop of imperialist domination of these countries at this point in history, even if in great conflict with this or that imperialist power for periods of time. So it is impossible to carry through to completion the struggle for national liberation under their leadership; they have to be fought against and replaced.

Just look at the utter incapacity of any of these bourgeois

leaderships even to take a united stand against the imperialist banks and say: "No! We're not going to pay one more cent on the interest payments that are devastating our countries. Cancel the debt!" In 1985 Cuban president Fidel Castro launched an international effort to convince not only popular movements and labor unions but the heads of state of various Latin American and other Third World governments to join together in a campaign to press for this demand. There were no preconditions, no pressure to bring in other questions—just a collective stand to refuse to pay the foreign debt that was strangling these countries.

But Castro did not find even a single taker. And, as he sharply underlined several years later, a historic opportunity to confront imperialism when it was vulnerable was lost. The neocolonial ruling classes cannot and will not help lead a fight to cancel the debt, because such a campaign endangers the very mechanisms of capitalist banking and credit that these local exploiters themselves benefit from and depend on.

The kind of struggle necessary to take on the next tasks of national liberation requires the organization of the workers and peasants politically independent of the capitalists and landlords, who block the progress and development of the nation. It requires a strong worker-peasant alliance. It requires the fight for political space to organize and engage in struggles. It requires an internationalist orientation toward the battles of other toilers, not only elsewhere in the Third World but in the imperialist countries and throughout Eastern Europe and the Soviet Union. It requires an anticapitalist program and proletarian leadership. And it requires the fight to replace the current neocolonial bourgeois regimes with workers' and peasants' governments.

### Revolutionists and communists

This is why we are convinced (1) that struggles to carry through national liberation to the end will be a stronger, not a weaker, force in world politics in coming years; and (2) that in the great majority of these countries, to be an effective revolutionist today and tomorrow is to be a communist. Over the past three decades we have seen how such leadership can and will develop in the course of revolutionary struggles against national oppression.

On the one hand, we have seen how the development of capitalism itself in semicolonial countries—even its limited and distorted forms—continues to create a stronger working class and new layers of toilers in the city and countryside from which new generations of fighters will come forward and form revolutionary organizations.

At the same time, we have seen communist leadership of world-class caliber emerge from hard-fought battles for national liberation around the world. We have seen the leadership of the July 26 Movement around Fidel Castro and Ernesto Che Guevara forge a communist party as they led the workers and peasants of Cuba to carry through to the end the liberation of that country from Yankee exploitation and oppression.

We have seen the development of outstanding communist leaders such as Maurice Bishop in Grenada and Thomas Sankara in Burkina Faso. Right here in the United States we have experienced the evolution of Malcolm X—through his uncompromising struggle against the national oppression of Blacks, and his revolutionary opposition to U.S. imperialism's oppression of the peoples of Africa and elsewhere in the Third World—to openly anticapitalist, and increasingly prosocialist, political views.

These examples alone, and there will be many others, are sufficient confirmation that new advances in the struggle for national liberation will contribute mightily to forging leadership of the caliber needed to rebuild a world communist movement.

Building a revolutionary leadership of the fight for national liberation is set back by any equivocation in recognizing the reactionary character of the Iraqi regime's expansionist grab for land and oil in Kuwait. Anti-imperialist fighters, communists, and other revolutionary-minded workers and farmers throughout the world demand the immediate withdrawal of all U.S. and other foreign troops from the Middle East. They advocate a victory for Iraq over the blockading imperialist-organized armies, navies, and air forces and will unequivocally hold to that position if a war breaks out. But they will be fighting the imperialist invaders *despite* Saddam Hussein, not with him. They know—or if not, they will rapidly learn—that this bourgeois regime and its officer corps will disorganize and weaken an effective defense of Iraq in the face of such an onslaught.

THIS IS NOT something new for communists and other uncompromising opponents of imperialism in this century. We actively supported the defeat of German imperialism when it invaded the Soviet Union during World War II. But we did so in spite of Stalin, whose counterrevolutionary course would have ensured defeat had it not been for the sacrifice and determination of millions of Soviet workers and peasants who fought and died to defend the conquests of the October 1917 Russian revolution. We fought the imperialist invasion from within the armies commanded by Stalin only because the vanguard of the working class was too weak to replace him with a proletarian leadership. We never gave up our perspective of replacing the leadership that beheaded the toilers with a leadership of the toilers.

Communists and other revolutionists fought for the defeat of Japanese imperialism when it invaded China in the 1930s, but we did so despite the leadership of the Chinese army by the reactionary butcher Chiang Kai-shek.

That's our stand with regard to the Baghdad regime and the defense of Iraq against imperialism today. We say: "Get the imperialist troops out now! End the blockade! Let food and medicine through!" A defeat for imperialism would open up the greatest possibilities for workers and peasants to burst free of bourgeois misleadership and build their own power and their own organizations. The Saddam Husseins of the world feed off imperialist pressure as a justification to tighten the space for political life and to crack down with savage brutality on trade unions, peasant organizations, and political parties of working people.

The biggest blow of all dealt by the Iraqi regime's occupation of Kuwait and treatment of the workers there (a tiny minority of workers are Kuwaiti by national origin) has been to the struggle of the Palestinian people for their national self-determination. At a time when the *intifada* had opened millions of new doors to support and sympathy for this struggle in recent years, the actions of the Iraqi regime have pushed the Palestinian movement out of the center of political attention in the Middle East.

The invasion of Kuwait has diverted attention from the increase in brutal Israeli repression—an opening the Israeli rulers immediately took advantage of. It has weakened the campaign in the Middle East to place negotiations with the Palestinians at the center of all demands against Israel and its backers.

Saddam Hussein's demagogy about "linkage" between Iraq's invasion of Kuwait and Israel's occupation of Palestinian territories could not be more cynical. It's an obstacle, not an aid, to the efforts of the Palestinian people to win a hearing for their demands from workers, farmers, and democratic-minded people around the world.

What possible "linkage" is there between the Palestinians' just demand for national sovereignty in face of Israel's dispossession of their homeland and Baghdad's reactionary assault on the national sovereignty of Kuwait? Absolutely none. They're the opposite.

Hussein's claim that he launched his invasion of Kuwait in order to advance prospects for a "settlement" of the Palestinian question is a bald-faced lie. He was after oil. He was after territory. He was after booty. That's all he's ever been after the entire time he's been in power. Iraqi troops subjected Palestinian workers in Kuwait to the same callous and brutal treatment meted out to hundreds of thousands of other immigrant workers there. To connect these actions in any way with the Palestinians' fight for national self-determination is a criminal diversion from that struggle.

The Iraqi regime's blow to the Palestinians has been compounded by the refusal of the leadership of the Palestine Liberation Organization to unequivocally condemn the invasion of Kuwait, demand that the Iraqi troops get out immediately, and, on that principled basis, declare to the world that the PLO will fight to the death alongside its Iraqi brothers and sisters to resist any imperialist assault. This harm has been made still worse by PLO chairman Yassir Arafat's public statements backing Baghdad's proposal tying talks on the withdrawal from Kuwait to "an overall settlement" of conflicts in the Middle East. Because of the esteem accorded the Palestinian people for their decades of courageous resistance, these positions of the PLO leadership help pretty up the Iraqi bourgeois regime and sow confusion among layers of other fighters worldwide.

## Cuba's leadership in fighting war drive

The role played by the revolutionary Cuban government and Communist Party in world politics today is an example of the profound difference that the class character and orientation of a leadership makes in the fight for national liberation, including in the fight against imperialist war.

That's why one of the most effective political weapons in a working-class campaign against Washington's war drive is Pathfinder's *U.S. Hands Off the Mideast! Cuba Speaks Out at the United Nations.* As Mary-Alice Waters explains in the introduction:

"Mobilizing world public opinion—and U.S. public opinion in particular—as a counterweight to Washington's drive toward war is the goal of all those concerned about the future of humanity. That is why the role that the representatives of the Cuban government are playing in the United Nations Security Council today is important. As they have done before, leaders of the Cuban revolution are using the United Nations as a tribune from which to speak out and chart a course of action in defense of the interests of working people around the world."

The book contains ten U.S.-initiated resolutions adopted by the UN Security Council between early August and the end of October 1990, followed by speeches by Cuba's UN representative Ricardo Alarcón. In these speeches Alarcón explains his government's opposition to Iraq's invasion of Kuwait, while uncompromisingly exposing Washington's drive toward war and its use of a blockade to deny even food and medicine to the Iraqi people. The book also has several related letters by Fidel Castro and a portion of a recent speech by him.

Cuban foreign minister Isidoro Malmierca's November 29 speech before the Security Council reaffirms these positions and condemns in the strongest terms the new UN war resolution.[14]

Prior to that session of the Security Council, Malmierca had met in New York with U.S. secretary of state James Baker—the longest meeting at a high governmental level between the United States and the Republic of Cuba since 1960. Since the chair of the Security Council in November was held by the U.S. government, Washington was formally obligated to meet at least once with each member of the council to try to come to agreement on a common resolution. That was a diplomatic convention that the U.S. delegation had to abide by. And Baker himself was to occupy the chair for that special session.

This was perhaps the only thing surrounding that entire meeting of the Security Council that Washington hadn't planned on—having to hold the first formal meeting in thirty years with Cuba's foreign minister. Most of Baker's other meetings were useful to the U.S. government—carving out agreement on the exact date of the deadline to Baghdad, working out wording to provide some cover at home for various delegations, and so on. They were like business luncheons to settle the price and nail down the deal.

But the meeting with Malmierca was different. The Cuban foreign minister spoke with Baker, and then upon leaving the meeting simply reported to the press that Cuba intended to vote against the resolution and continue pressing for a peaceful solution. Moreover, unlike the governments of some other members of the Security Council, Cuba did not receive a follow-up invitation from Baker for meetings in Washington. Nor was Cuba compelled to hold a news conference a few days later denying any connection between a sudden new aid package or International Monetary Fund loan and how it had voted on the UN resolution.

In his remarks to the November 29 meeting of the Security Council itself, Malmierca reiterated Cuba's uncompromising opposition to the Iraqi government's invasion and annexation of Kuwait, as well as its holding of foreign nationals as hostages. These actions, Malmierca said, weaken "the unity and solidarity that [Third World countries] sorely need in order to face the challenge of overcoming underdevelopment."

Malmierca went on to condemn the UN Security Council–sanctioned war moves by Washington against Iraq, including the inhuman embargo. He expressed Cuba's concern "about the enormous and increasing concentration of military forces from the United States and its allies in the Gulf and over the danger of the outbreak of a war that . . . would bring enormous destruction to the countries of the region, beginning with Kuwait and Iraq and their neighbors, in addition to the losses by the attacking forces."

Malmierca reaffirmed Cuba's long-standing solidarity with

the struggle for national rights by the Palestinian people and condemned the hypocrisy of the U.S. government in acting to block Security Council consideration of a resolution—drafted by Cuba together with Colombia, Malaysia, and Yemen—calling for a UN commission to monitor the Israeli government's treatment of Palestinians in the territories it occupies. At the same time, Malmierca said, Cuba continues to reject "any linkage between Iraq's withdrawal from Kuwait and the Arab territories occupied by Israel."

The Cuban foreign minister then pointed to the example of Korea to underline the horrible consequences for humanity of the last time that the UN Security Council gave its blessing to a U.S.-organized war. The case of Korea, Malmierca said, "is an example of how—after three years of war, hundreds of thousands of victims, and enormous material destruction—the use of force under the banner of the United Nations ended in an armistice that even today keeps that country divided as it was before the conflict broke out. There are still tens of thousands of soldiers and foreign military bases in the southern part of that territory."

Malmierca concluded with the remarks I cited earlier, terming the UN resolution "the chronicle of a war foretold."

THE COURSE CHARTED by Cuban revolutionists from the outset of the Gulf situation has been a courageous, consistent, principled, and internationalist one. It is correct not because it is a communist position that advances the fight for socialism—although it is certainly the only conceivable position for communists to take. But you don't need to be a communist to stand up and be counted alongside the Cuban revolutionists in championing this course.

Cuba's stand is correct above all because it helps advance the fight against imperialism in the Middle East, because it is the only principled position on behalf of the fight for national liberation. It is the only correct and revolutionary position for any anti-imperialist fighter and national liberation movement anywhere in the world.

Cuban revolutionists know they will suffer consequences for

this principled stand against the war drive led by U.S. imperialism. They know Washington will do what it can to make things rougher for them—and that if a war is unleashed against Iraq, the going will get rougher still. More than any other people on the face of the earth, Cuban revolutionists know what a massive and bloody war in the Middle East will mean for every single fighter anywhere in the world who is standing up to imperialist oppression and plunder. They know the pressures that will be brought to bear on revolutionists, including in the United States. They know the greater squeeze that will come down on democratic rights and the space to organize and resist. They know the increased dangers of imperialist military moves in other parts of the world.

An imperialist war in the Middle East would open the way for the bipartisan gang in Washington to throw even more weight behind the murderous regime that protects the property and privileges of the landlords and capitalists in El Salvador. It would bring greater pressure—political and military—on the Farabundo Martí National Liberation Front, which is continuing to press its revolutionary struggle against the U.S.-backed regime there.

A Mideast war would inevitably be accompanied by further retreats by the imperialist governments from their supposed good wishes toward the African National Congress and the fight it is leading to destroy the apartheid system in South Africa once and for all.

Such a war would be a blow against the fight for the reunification of Korea—where the presence of some 45,000 U.S. troops, along with military bases and nuclear-armed ships, makes it second only to the Gulf region today as a zone of U.S. imperialist military power. *Rodong Sinmun,* the North Korean daily, pointed to this reality in a December 3, 1990, news analysis pointing to the war dangers posed by the recent Security Council resolution. "The adoption of the resolution approving the use of armed forces against Iraq under conditions of sharp confrontation of ultramodern means of war and huge armed forces massed in the Gulf region," the North Korean article explained, "cannot but be a danger signal that a war might break out in the region. . . . Should a war break out in the Gulf region, an irrevocable situation will be created in the region and it will pose a serious danger to the peace and security of the world."

## An exemplary model

To the best of our knowledge, the Iraqi toilers are confronting the prospects of a brutal imperialist onslaught today without the existence of any organized revolutionary current among vanguard workers, peasants, and youth. Revolutionary-minded militants in Iraq face extremely repressive conditions—imprisonment, torture, assassinations.

There is one example from the recent history of the region, however, of how communists conducted themselves in the face of an imperialist-backed war.

During the opening years of the Iraqi government's war against the Iranian revolution, launched in 1980 with Washington's blessing, there was a communist organization in the working class in Iran called the Workers Unity Party—in the Farsi language, Hezb-e Vahdat-e Kargaran, the HVK. The HVK was the victim of repression by the capitalist government in Iran; its members faced harassment by government-organized thugs and even imprisonment.

HVK members were among the draftees and the volunteers from the factories who fought and died at the front defending the Iranian revolution against the Iraqi regime's reactionary assault. They acted on the conviction that communists had to be the best fighters to defend the gains wrested by the toilers in Iran through the revolutionary overthrow of the U.S.-backed regime of the shah.

At the same time, these same HVK cadres deepened their participation in and support to struggles in the factories against efforts by the capitalist government to intensify the exploitation of workers—under the cynical cover of the need to sacrifice for the war effort, while the capitalists themselves raked in profits. The HVK championed the fight by peasants for land and for government-supplied means to work it. Nothing could have raised more sharply the peasants' determination to resist the imperialist-sponsored Iraqi invasion. The HVK joined in the fight for democratic rights in the face of the government's increasingly brutal crackdown on all forms of independent political expression and organization by the toilers.

The HVK gave unconditional support to the national rights of the Kurdish and other peoples oppressed by the Iranian capitalist regime. It explained that deepening the fight by workers and peasants for their class interests was the only way to consolidate the conquests of the Iranian revolution and prevent the defensive war against Iraq from becoming a slaughterous stalemate that drained the blood and energies of the most courageous and self-sacrificing revolutionaries. They pointed to the need to establish a workers' and peasants' government in order to carry through the job of freeing Iran from oppression and exploitation by imperialism and all of its agencies, inside and outside the country.

This communist course was explained in a resolution adopted by the HVK in 1981. It was translated into English and published that year in the magazine *Intercontinental Press.*[15] It's a magnificent example for revolutionists, anti-imperialist fighters, and communists everywhere in the world.

## MARCH TOWARD WAR AND DEPRESSION

THE SAME WEEK in November 1990 that the UN Security Council adopted Washington's war resolution, top U.S. government officials were finally forced to admit that the recession already unfolding in Canada had also begun in the United States. (Some voiced their apprehension that this could turn out to be a deep one—for North America and much of the world.)

It was also the same week that the federal government announced that for the fourth year in a row the average life expectancy of Black people in the United States had *declined*—declined in absolute terms. That decline was large enough to result in a drop of the overall average life expectancy in the United States. Moreover, this decline has been very class-divided, resulting from rapidly deteriorating health conditions among the worst-off layers of the working class, not limited to those who are Black.

The very fact that average life expectancy can drop in the last decade of the twentieth century in the world's wealthiest imperialist power—and that it can decline for four years in a row for working people from an oppressed nationality—is a sign of the depth of the underlying capitalist economic crisis. Intensifying exploitation and deepening class polarization are both reinforced by capitalism's continuous regeneration of institutions of racist oppression as it reproduces the social relations of production necessary for its own existence.

Behind this statistic lie many others, and all of them point to the truth about what is coming, about the character of the international social crisis we are heading into, and about the stakes for working people in the battles that lie ahead. We can't predict the exact timing or how events will unfold, but we can say with certainty that the imperialist ruling classes are marching workers and farmers toward war and depression.

As the working class in the United States goes into the current recession, we have already been the victims of a more than decade-long offensive by the employing class against our living and working conditions. Workers' real wages have fallen some 10 percent over the past decade alone. In fact our buying power has dropped so sharply that it is now at the same level as in 1961. Since 1980 our pensions, health benefits, and insurance protection have dropped about 15 percent on average in real money terms. As a result of the pressures from this assault on workers' incomes, the debt burden on working-class families has skyrocketed as they desperately seek to somehow buffer the blows to their living standards.

With unemployment already rising sharply, only one-third of those out of work in this country are currently receiving jobless benefits, due in large part to major government slashes in the form of stiffer eligibility requirements. This contrasts to more than three-quarters of jobless workers during the 1974-75 recession and about half during the deep capitalist downturn in 1981-82.

Working farmers are in for another round of accelerating indebtedness, bankruptcies, and foreclosures. The capitalist farm crisis that drove tens of thousands of exploited producers off the land in the early and mid-1980s—the worst times since the 1920s and '30s—is far from resolved.

The capitalists are weighed down under an enormous debt structure that reached historic heights during the 1980s. Investment in new, capacity-expanding plant and equipment stagnated throughout the decade. Meanwhile, there was an explosion of real estate speculation, debt-financed buy-outs and mergers, and junk bonds, plus growing instability on the stock and commodities markets. The Third World debt continued to climb to staggering levels, devastating the workers and peasants in those countries and putting new strains on the imperialist banking structure. The banks, savings and loan institutions, and giant insurance companies in the United States—as well as the funds available to government agencies that supposedly protect depositors and beneficiaries—are in their weakest condition in decades.

Sudden breakdowns or partial crises on any one or more of these fronts—all of which are more vulnerable given today's capitalist downturn—threaten to turn a recession into a collapse of the international banking system that can plunge the world into a major depression and social crisis.

The employers, their government, and the Democratic and Republican party politicians continue to press their anti-working-class, union busting offensive. The ultimate solution to all the country's economic problems, they insist, is to guarantee workers the "right" to work in a "union-free environment." More and more they act as if the only good worker is a "permanent replacement" worker.

The bosses continue to demand take-back contracts—such as the recent pacts accepted by the United Auto Workers officialdom—that deepen divisions in the working class by agreeing to trade off wages, conditions, and job opportunities for younger workers and new hires in return for the will-o'-the-wisp of "job security" for a declining number of higher-seniority union members. The employers continually push to gut health and pension benefits, speed up production with less union control over safety on the job, and ravage the environment.

City and state governments around the country—as in the mid-1970s—are complaining of "declining tax revenues" and "tightening budgets." They "reluctantly" point to the need to sharply cut the rolls of public employees and impose take-back contracts. Governors and mayors are slashing expenditures on basic health services, education, child care, and other social programs that millions of working people depend on. Bridges and roads continue to deteriorate dangerously.

So workers and farmers in this country face a double march today: a march toward a horrible war and a march not only into a recession but toward a seemingly inexorable worldwide depression and social crisis.

This reality is sensed by growing numbers of working people. And it poses big challenges and responsibilities for every thinking worker, every rank-and-file union militant, every communist.

## Labor movement not pushed out of politics

The U.S. working class and labor movement have suffered blows; our unions have been further weakened by the class-collaborationist and proimperialist course of the labor officialdom; and we have been put on the defensive by the accelerated onslaught of the employers in the 1980s. But we have not been defeated. The labor movement has not been shoved out of the center of politics in this country. Our capacity to resist has not been broken.

Since the middle of the 1980s, as resistance by the working class and unions in the United States has evolved, a pattern has emerged. Despite the difficulties, despite the blows, workers and unionists in the United States pushed to the wall by the employers' assaults have found ways to fight. Layer after layer have found ways around simply being handcuffed, chained, and prevented from organizing to defend themselves. They have done so even when the bosses and labor bureaucrats have combined to block them from using standard union tactics that have brought victories throughout the history of the labor movement—that is, even when they are blocked from organizing union power and solidarity to shut down production.

As workers have moved into action in the face of these odds, other working people have expressed solidarity with their battles. Important experiences rich in lessons in how to forge unity, overcome divisions, and wage an effective struggle have begun to be accumulated by a small vanguard of fighters in the labor movement. These defensive efforts are waged from a position of weakness. The ranks are not in a strong enough position to push aside the current labor officialdom and replace it with another leadership that has an alternative, class-struggle strategy. Their efforts have to take place largely within the limits of the strategy imposed by this ossified bureaucracy. But this fact makes these experiences no less important as the arena where rank-and-file fighters find each other and test each other.

All this is being experienced right now as the *Daily News* strike unfolds in the greater New York City area. This is a strike that began in October 1990 as one of the most cold-blooded, brutal, militarily organized lockouts by management in years. The ranks of the drivers, press operators, and other unionized employees were forced into a fight without any preparation by the officialdom, who hoped against hope that it would not happen. The ranks have no democratic union structures through which to organize, make decisions, argue out tactics, strive for greater unity among themselves, or reach out for broader solidarity from the rest of the labor movement. They have no union structures available to them to bring their real potential power to bear.

Management, on the other hand, was well prepared. Production never stopped. The *Daily News* didn't miss a single edition. It had scabs lined up months in advance to do everything from writing copy, to typesetting and printing the papers, to transporting them throughout the metropolitan area. The scabs were at their posts within a matter of minutes—together with armed thugs to go after the unions. The rest of the New York media joined in the company's violence-baiting of the unions.

But then something happened that management had not anticipated. They could write the paper, print the paper, and truck the paper with "permanent replacements." But they couldn't get working people to buy it! The working class in the New York area pulled together to keep the *Daily News* off the newsstands. They put pressure on the owners of the newsstands they patronize not to carry the scab paper; they argue with them, try to convince them. Some of these small shopkeepers have put up solidarity signs announcing, "We don't carry the *Daily News*."

Workers argue with co-workers on the job and with friends and family members not to buy the paper. They've made buying the *Daily News* an immoral, rotten, unconscionable act for any working person with an ounce of decency, human feeling, and solidarity. Unionists have volunteered to go out and ring doorbells to urge people to cancel their subscriptions.

There are thousands of retail outlets that carry daily newspapers in greater New York. Prior to the strike, the *Daily News* was the second-largest-selling metropolitan daily in the country. Yet, today it's difficult to find a newsstand that carries it. This was not accomplished by centralized organization. It took the actions of tens of thousands of workers and unionists. Newsstand owners found that carrying the *Daily News* was considered an insult by regular customers—people they've gotten to know, made friends with, depend on for steady business. These kinds of factors play a role in labor and other social struggles, and they are having a big impact on the *Daily News* strike.

THE POINT HERE is not to try to predict what the outcome of this strike will be, given the character of the officialdom in these unions and the overall state of the labor movement.[16] To keep moving forward against the *News* management, space must continue to be opened by the printing trades officialdom for the ranks to operate, and the ranks must have time to find ways of organizing and structuring themselves, as we saw happen in the Eastern Airlines strike. The ability to gain solidarity from other unionists and workers—the growing hatred of the working class for the antiunion assault—opens some unexpected space even if the strike does not have the ability to shut down production. Other expressions of struggle and solidarity are not a substitute for the strike; they are a supplement to it. They become a way for the ranks to assert themselves and prove that union busting is not a sure winner for the bosses. All this is very important right now, and deserves the active support of all workers, regardless of the duration or expected outcome of the effort.

The *Daily News* strike is just the most recent example of the pattern that has emerged from the labor struggles in this country in recent years. It is an uneven pattern, one with gaps and breaks. But the pattern is nonetheless clearer today than when it began to take shape back in August 1985 with the strike of the packinghouse workers against the Hormel Company and other battles in meat-packing over the following eighteen months.[17]

Since then there have been other fights: by paperworkers, by cannery workers, by coal miners both in the eastern and western fields, by telephone workers, by hospital employees. All have been defensive in character, waged by workers pushed deeper and deeper into a corner by the employers. They've had various outcomes: some substantial setbacks or defeats, some standoffs, a few victories. The most weighty victory in the recent period has been that won by members of the United Mine Workers of America and their supporters against the union busting of the Pittston coal company.[18]

But through all these fights you can watch not just the cumulative impact of the assaults, but also the cumulative effect of workers finding ways to resist for slightly longer, or surprising the employers a bit more with what they are able to accomplish, and thus giving greater confidence to other layers of the working class who will find themselves in struggle.

The strike by members of the International Association of Machinists (IAM) against Eastern Airlines that began in March 1989 has been a little different from the rest. There, through the initial months of the battle, a rank-and-file leadership of the strike came forward and had enough time to structure itself. It kept reaching out to maintain maximum unity while drawing in broader solidarity from elsewhere in the labor movement. These strikers demonstrated the capacity to take the blows and withstand the shocks that came their way and to outlast and outfight the employers. And it was not your run-of-the-mill boss they were up against. Frank Lorenzo was the man the employing class considered the union buster of the decade, a model for them all.

The Eastern strikers blocked Lorenzo from imposing on them the kind of nonunion operation he had rammed down the throats of workers at Continental Airlines in 1983. In fact, the IAM strikers drove Lorenzo out of the airline industry, and their nearly two-year-long fight has brought both parts of Lorenzo's former Texas Air empire—Eastern and Continental—to bankruptcy. They have made the government step in and openly take direct responsibility for Eastern's future—to the horror of its individual stockholders and creditors. This has made other employers, suppliers, and bankers—inside and outside the airline industry—less confident that blatant union busting, "Lorenzoism," is the high road to high profits that it seemed to be in the mid-1980s.[19]

The labor movement is not on the offensive against the employers. There are no developments anywhere in the unions that represent the organized beginnings of an alternative, class-struggle strategy. The labor movement is still being weakened by the class-collaborationist course of the officialdom in the face of the rulers' continuing offensive. All that is true.

But that is not the entire story. The pattern of resistance by workers and unionists over the past half-decade, the search for ways to bring class solidarity to bear, the openness to reaching beyond themselves, beyond the union movement, beyond the country to seek and extend solidarity—these facts, too, have to be brought into the picture. And they are among the *decisive* facts on the basis of which communist workers, who are part of this working-class vanguard, must chart our strategy and tactics—including in campaigning against the imperialist war drive.

### Independent working-class political action

These struggles bring additional experience to a vanguard layer of workers, making them more open to seeing themselves as part of a class with interests different from and opposed to the employers, the employers' political parties, and the employers' government. The unity workers have needed to forge in order to advance their own fights, and the solidarity they have reached for, help clear away some of the divisions and reactionary prejudices promoted by the employers. This increases the capacity to recognize common interests with other working people both in this country and around the world.

These shifts are important for communist workers, because they provide new opportunities—grounded in common experiences of rank-and-file union militants—to win broader understanding of the need for a labor movement that operates on the basis of democracy, class solidarity, and independent working-class political action. For a labor movement that rejects the narrowness of unionism as conceived by a timid officialdom, and instead fights for a movement that thinks socially and acts politically—in the interests of its own class, not that of the bosses. This becomes more necessary than ever in the face of increasing imperialist war moves.

The tactical divisions in the ruling class are real, and we haven't found it difficult to explain the reasons for them. They enable us to see the dangerous character of the con—promoted by the bourgeois press—that the debate in Congress pushes us further away from war. The truth is the opposite. The imperialist assumptions and goals shared by both Democratic and Republican party politicians, and the bipartisan policies they have already set in motion, are the very ingredients propelling forward the probability that the siege war will become a massive ground war (perhaps with a devastating air war as a prelude).

Workers and farmers, as well as any authentic opponent of Washington's course toward war, have no voice, no representatives in Congress of any kind. There have been tactical divisions and squabbles among bourgeois politicians in Congress, and between Congress and the White House, prior to every imperialist war in this century. There has also been a growing concentration of governmental power in the executive branch. But without exception, whenever the president has asked Congress for support in a war—whether in the form of a declaration of war such as in 1917 and 1941, or the Gulf of Tonkin resolution in 1964, or simply military funding—there has been overwhelming bipartisan support. This time around will be no different.

What the working-class movement needs is space to organize a broad public discussion of the connection between the rulers' war policies at home and abroad; space to organize active opposition to those policies in the factories and through our unions; space to join with all those willing to debate the issues in a civil manner, and to take our protest to the streets; space to engage in politics in the class interests of workers, farmers, and our allies here and around the world.

This debate should be organized above all among the almost half-million citizen-soldiers sent to the Arabian desert by Frank Lorenzo's friends in Washington. Those who are going to have to fight and die in any war waged by the bipartisan rulers of this country should have the direct say over whether or not such a war is declared. On the face of it, that simply seems decent and just. But there's a lot more to it than that. It poses the biggest single problem facing the working class: the fact that we have no independent political organization, no political voice of our own, no policies that advance our class interests against those who are responsible for exploitation, oppression, and war.

THE WORKING CLASS has no foreign policy. The labor movement has no foreign policy. The labor *officialdom* faithfully pushes the foreign policy of the employers and does what the bosses tell them to do. But the labor *movement*—the workers, the ranks, who are the unions—has no foreign policy. The classes who die in the wars waged by the bosses' parties and government—and who are pitted in those wars against working people like ourselves in other countries—have no foreign policy.

Many workers agree that it's unacceptable for the bosses to have a monopoly over setting all sorts of other policies: the policies that govern our unions; health and safety conditions in the mines and factories; work rules on the job; the right to slash our wages or throw us out of work; the right to bust our unions and keep up production with scab labor. But when it comes to foreign policy, the monopoly by the bosses is still largely accepted as almost a fact of life. The spectrum of valid choices is set by their two political parties. What's more, their foreign policy is viewed as "ours," the foreign policy of "our" country. But countries don't have policies. Countries are divided into classes, and classes have foreign policies. The foreign policy of the capitalist class in this country—and in every other capitalist country, everywhere in the world—is not "ours," it's "theirs." As Malcolm X taught us, working people in this country are not "Americans," we're the *victims* of this kind of Americanism.

Workers have no military policy, either. The labor movement has no military policy. Only the ruling class has a military policy. It begins with the hired thugs and the cops they use to bust up our strikes, to ride in scab trucks in West Virginia or in Bayside, Queens. And it goes right on through the organization of massive imperialist armed forces.

But the working class needs our own military policy as well as our own foreign policy. And there are layers of workers in recent years who have learned why, even if they haven't yet drawn this conclusion or thought of it this way. The *Daily News* strikers who have been victims of the goon squads brought in by management are learning about the military policy of the bosses; so are the coal miners, paperworkers, meat-packers, and others whose picket lines have been attacked by cops, whether "private" or "public." Also learning about it today are the workers and farmers in uniform—the cannon fodder (a term that has horrible concrete meaning in face of today's march toward a desert war of heavily armored armies) who make up the armed forces used by the imperialists to fight *their* wars to advance *their* class interests.

As long as capitalism and imperialism exist, there will be no peace. As long as the working class has no political party of our own—no labor party based on the unions, and independent of the imperialist Democratic and Republican parties—we will have no effective mass political organization to resist the war policies of the employing class by counterposing and fighting for our own foreign policies and military policies. And we will have no political party of our own to organize a fight against the bosses' war on our rights, our living standards, and our unions here at home, either. Instead, we will always be facing the framework of political choices set by *their* parties.

For the same reasons, communists are raising as part of our working-class campaign against the imperialist war that the people in this country should have the right to vote on war. The point here is not to divert the energies of workers, farmers, and other opponents of the war into electoral channels—there will be plenty of referenda and ballot initiatives to do that. The point is just the opposite. Our demand is that the question of war and peace be taken out of the hands of the Democratic and Republican politicians, out of the hands of Congress and the White House, and be taken into the factories and into the streets.

We know the imperialists always seek to tighten and restrict the space to organize and practice politics when they go to war. That's what happened during the first and second world wars, during the Korean War, and during the Vietnam War. And it will happen again. Many of us remember the so-called Cointelpro spying, disruption, and harassment operations organized by the FBI, CIA, local police "red squads," and other government cop agencies during the period of the Vietnam War. The Socialist Workers Party was a direct victim of those assaults, along with others involved in the fight against the war, in the struggle for Black liberation, and in other social and political struggles. Recognizing this reality puts a special premium on vanguard workers treasuring and fighting for every inch of space we can.[20]

That's why thinking workers pay special attention to any group of individuals and organizations who want to reach out and use democratic rights to publicly oppose the war drive—to discuss, to debate, to march; to initiate public protests, rallies, teach-ins, demonstrations. Those activities help create greater space for discussion and action around the war, greater space for the working class to get involved in politics.

This is the opposite of the terrain to which the capitalist rulers always seek to restrict the discussions and decisions on war. We are told that a great debate is taking place on Capitol Hill today—but it's a debate that involves at tops 535 people (536 if you include Vice President Quayle, president of the Senate)—most of them millionaires, and all of them (Democrats, Republicans, and their "socialist" subspecies alike) opponents of independent political action by the working-class movement. These are the same people who have led workers and farmers into every bloody war in this century.

THE FIGHT AGAINST the war and the fight to defend democratic rights necessitates the broadest forum for public debate and exchange of views, as well. The bourgeois politicians will try to block such discussion. As in the past, the union bureaucrats, petty-bourgeois pacifists, Stalinists, and social democrats will often join them in this reactionary effort—usually in the name of supporting this or that proposal or election campaign by a capitalist politician.

The working class, on the other hand, has every interest in promoting such discussion. Political clarity becomes more important than ever, and such clarity can be advanced only through *political differentiation*. That's why we advocate the norms of civil discussion—of the right to express your point of view, to argue for it without fear of verbal abuse or physical recriminations—inside the workers' movement. This also means having the courage to clarify differences—which often reflect conflicting class outlooks and interests—rather than paper them over.

At the same time, proponents of a wide range of different views can and will join together to act, to organize, and to participate in antiwar demonstrations and other public protest actions. Communist workers are the most energetic advocates of such united action for common goals, and the staunchest opponents of efforts to exclude individuals or organizations from such efforts because of their political views.

We seek to draw more workers, more soldiers, more farmers into these activities, so that those who have been struggling against the employers' offensive in this country can become part of the debate and a growing component of the fight against the war drive.

## A WORKING-CLASS CAMPAIGN

THE SWP is campaigning to reach out from vanguard unionists to broad layers of the working class and its allies in the United States and around the world, to draw them into activity to demand: Bring the troops home now! End the criminal blockade of Kuwait and Iraq, including the embargo on food and medicine! Foreign troops out of the Mideast!

A campaign by a revolutionary workers' party against imperialist war preparations is a time to turn more deeply than ever to the workers and farmers we are fighting alongside in struggles here at home. As war approaches, more of these working people—including some in the communist movement—end up in the armed forces as well. It is above all the workers and farmers, in and out of uniform, whom we seek to inform about the war drive and its reactionary goals, and to mobilize in action against it.

The SWP's campaign against the war is a political campaign of a workers' party structured along dual lines: through party branches in many cities, and through units of its members active in various industrial unions. It is not a campaign of frenetic activity based on the illusion there is something we as a party can do to stop the imperialists' course toward war. Instead, it is a campaign to involve the party more deeply in the life, struggles, activity, and politics of the only class that—when its organizations are mobilized in action in its own interests—can and will affect the course of history, including decisions on war and peace.

As a party of industrial workers, the SWP's campaign against the imperialist war drive will take us more deeply into the working class and the labor movement itself. It is through our co-workers and our unions that we will find our way to the broadest layers of GIs—to other unionists, to friends and family members of young co-workers serving a few years in the armed forces. Through such campaigning a workers' party forges its firmest links with layers of fighting farmers and agricultural laborers.

This campaign will be carried out through the party's existing structures, through our established lines of leadership development, with our fundamental propaganda instruments and institutions, and through our collaboration with the Young Socialist Alliance. That's why the single most important Pathfinder book that needs to be read, reread, and studied as part of this campaign is *The Changing Face of U.S. Politics: The Proletarian Party and the Trade Unions.* This book contains reports and resolutions adopted by SWP conventions and elected leadership bodies outlining the fundamental elements of the party's strategy for carrying out communist political work in the labor movement and building a revolutionary workers' party and world movement.

The SWP campaign against the war drive will be carried out by expanding the readership above all of the weekly *Militant,* as well as *Perspectiva Mundial, L'internationaliste, New International, Nouvelle Internationale, Nueva Internacional,* and other publications of the world communist movement. The same Eastern strikers, coal miners, and other workers and farmers who have become readers and supporters of the *Militant* because it is the best regular source of information about key working-class struggles in this country will discover that the *Militant* is also the only source of accurate information and analysis about Washington's march toward war. Some who have already lent their names and made promotional comments for weekly subscription advertisements in the *Militant* will now have an additional reason to do so once again.

Socialist workers and members of the Young Socialist Alliance are getting the *Militant* and other publications into the hands of unionists, GIs, veterans, reservists, farmers, and other working people. They are circulating it to young people, students, and others demonstrating against the U.S. war drive, organizing solidarity with the struggle against apartheid in South Africa, and participating in fights for Black rights and women's equality.

## Discipline, democracy, and leadership
Central to the success of this campaign will be the activity of communist workers who are members of ten industrial unions in the United States and Canada: the Amalgamated Clothing and Textile Workers Union; the International Association of Machinists; the International Ladies' Garment Workers' Union; the International Union of Electronic Workers; the Oil, Chemical and Atomic Workers; the United Auto Workers; the United Food and Commercial Workers; the United Mine Workers of America; the United Steelworkers of America; and the United Transportation Union.

These workers meet together to collectively discuss and decide their political work and priorities on both a local and national level. In launching the party campaign, national meetings of the SWP members and supporters active in each of these ten unions have been held in November and December. As the short article in the *Militant* announcing these meetings explained, the workers participating in them "will discuss [the] ten-year offensive by the employers against the labor movement, the resistance to it, and the deepening economic crisis at home for working people, and how this is intertwined with the fight against Washington's accelerating steps toward a slaughter in the Mideast."

Thinking workers sense that a war in the Middle East will reinforce every reactionary assault in this country on our democratic rights and our living and working conditions. It will exert pressure on the fight for full equality and against racist attacks on Blacks, other oppressed nationalities, and immigrant workers, including immigrants from the Middle East in particular in this case. It will encourage probes to roll back women's rights and will make the defense of past gains more difficult. It will reinforce the employers' union busting assaults aimed at continuing to drive down wages and benefits, extend the workday, intensify speedup, take back gains for health and safety on the job, and increase snooping on workers—at work and elsewhere.

The outbreak of an imperialist war is always a moment at which a revolutionary workers' party finds out whether what it has done beforehand has adequately prepared it for the most decisive experiences and biggest political questions confronting the working class and the labor movement. War puts revolutionary organizations to the test. If you are not fundamentally ready beforehand, there is nothing much an organization can do about it under the pressures of wartime. We are convinced that what the cadres of the SWP have accomplished over the past decade—by building a proletarian organization of the kind I have described—has prepared us to meet whatever test may come.

But a party campaign against imperialist war *does* mean that we have to look at our basic party institutions and make whatever adjustments are called for to best prepare us for the tasks and opportunities we will face. And we do so openly in front of fellow workers and supporters, both to solicit their views and to give them the confidence of knowing what we can be counted on for.

The stakes are much bigger, as are the opportunities for building the communist movement and the political consequences of errors. Thus the party's work becomes more centralized, more organized, and more disciplined.

Now is not the time for the party units to set up antiwar committees or other ad hoc structures, but for the branch executive committees and union fraction leaderships to take in hand the party campaign against the war drive and lead every aspect of the work. This includes joint efforts with others who agree that organizing protests in the streets is vital to reaching out to the broadest layers of working people and increasing the confidence to act.

Disciplined functioning can only be assured if at the same time the party becomes more *democratic* in all of its work. The communist workers active in the industrial unions must meet more regularly, both locally and nationally. They need to elect their leadership structures from among those communist workers who step forward in this situation—those who have shown how to lead in resisting the employers' offensive, and shown how to lead a campaign against the war. This must come through the activity of the workers actually carrying out the campaign on the job and through their unions, reaching out to farmers and GIs in broader action formations. In the process we go through common experiences and draw collective lessons.

IN THE FACE of the rulers' tightening wartime pressures on democratic rights, the greatest protection for communists and other vanguard fighters in the working class is to go deeper into our class and its organizations and to press to the furthest limits possible the space for political organization and activity—from the factory floor through all the institutions of capitalist society. We need to encourage debate and discussion. We need to encourage co-workers and other unionists to join with us—and with other opponents of the war—in protests, public meetings, and demonstrations.

When the bosses framed up Mark Curtis, we recognized that they went after him because he was a representative of other workers like him who were resisting the intensifying assaults of the packinghouse bosses; fighting for the rights of immigrant workers; and joining in struggles against racism, against U.S. intervention in Central America, and for women's rights.[21] They picked out Mark as one among other vanguard fighters in our class, and they went after him. With the outbreak of an imperialist war, the bosses, the cops, and the government will have an eagle eye out more than ever for the other Mark Curtises, outside or inside the SWP, who are explaining and organizing opposition to the slaughter. That is what's happened at the outset of every imperialist war.

At such times, it is more important than ever for revolutionary-minded workers to reaffirm the truth explained in the founding program of our movement, *The Communist Manifesto*, that communists "disdain to conceal their views and aims." We explain and advocate the same things to our co-workers and to the broader working-class public as we do to our members and supporters.

Party members will wear antiwar buttons to work and to union gatherings, prompting discussions and catching the attention of other workers interested in joining with us in campaigning against the war. We will promote the *Militant* and other communist publications that speak from the point of view of the working class about the war. We will sell *U.S. Hands Off the Mideast!* and other Pathfinder books and pamphlets that are invaluable weapons for working people in this fight, and that recount experiences and lessons from previous working-class opposition to war and to attacks by the employers and their government on unions and democratic rights.

When a war breaks out, when massive struggles erupt, that's when fighters read the most—just at the time when they're the busiest. They read more because they need to, because they want to arm themselves politically for the tasks and challenges they are facing, because they want to discuss with others. That's always when it's most valuable to read, when its most valuable to study. That's when you learn the most. That's how our class reconquers its true history, its best traditions, its lessons from previous struggles, its revolutionary political continuity.

Institutions such as the weekly Militant Labor Forum become more important. These forums need to be organized to advance this campaign against imperialist war along a working-class axis. What we need most of all are forums that provide a platform for unionists, farmers, and soldiers to discuss the war drive, to debate their differing views of it—how it relates to other battles they are involved in, what they face, what needs to be done.

Socialist election campaigns, and fights for ballot status, take on special importance when the capitalist rulers are marching working people into a war. These election efforts are not only a means to take the campaign against the war drive to a broader working-class audience by taking advantage of the additional platforms and broader press opportunities available to socialists at such times. They are also an important battlefront in our fight for political space, to assert the legitimacy of working-class political parties, to use the space that has been won previously.

With this in mind, the SWP is launching municipal election campaigns in more than twenty-five cities and towns across the United States in 1991. The Chicago Socialist Workers Party has already announced a major effort to get on the ballot there for the spring mayoral election. Socialist election campaigns will also be run in Austin, Minneapolis, and St. Paul, Minnesota; Boston and Lynn, Massachusetts; Baltimore; Birmingham; Charleston and Morgantown, West Virginia; Cleveland; Des Moines, Iowa; Detroit; Greensboro, North Carolina; Houston; Los Angeles; Miami, Miami Beach, and Miami Shores; Newark; New York; Omaha, Nebraska; Phoenix; Price and Salt Lake City, Utah; San Francisco; and Seattle, Washington.

Socialist workers are taking the fight against the war into meetings of their unions and other labor gatherings; to plant gates, airports, and mine portals; to farmers' conferences; to military bases and departure points; to high school and college campuses; and to street corners across the country. They are working with members of the Young Socialist Alliance to draw young workers, soldiers, and students into political discussions and debates in order to win them to this fight. They are helping to build protest picket lines and demonstrations such as the upcoming January 26 march on Washington, and participating in committees and coalitions organizing these actions.[22]

### Development of antiwar opposition

Vocal and organized opposition to a drawn-out war by Washington against Iraq will develop much faster and with more working-class and union involvement from the outset than during the Vietnam War or other U.S.-organized wars in this century. This is because of the weakening of U.S. imperialism, the legacy in the working class of the massive, organized opposition to the Vietnam War, the deepening social crisis in this country, and labor resistance to the employers' offensive at home.

At the same time, communists need to be clear-eyed about the pressures that will inevitably come down in the initial period of any war. Given the opposition to the war drive that we already find among many—although far from all—of our co-workers and other people we know, we can unconsciously fall into the error of thinking that imperialist preparations for previous wars in this century were substantially more popular among working people. That's not true. Going to war has never been broadly popular.

Prior to U.S. entry into World War II there was a large movement against the military preparations. It was centered in the working class and reflected the deep opposition to going to war among workers and farmers. It had a strong base of organized support in the CIO industrial union movement. It was interlinked with sections of the rising movement for Black rights. The opening chapters of *Teamster Bureaucracy: The Trade Union Campaign against World War II* by Farrell Dobbs provide a good feel for the depth of the opposition. It was strong. But during the opening two years of the war there was little evidence of that previous opposition.

Labor struggles against Washington's war at home and abroad began to open up again in 1943, however, with the coal miners' strike, a resumption of Black rights struggles, and then in 1944 a renewed and growing interest among workers in communist ideas reflected in expanding subscriptions to the *Militant* and recruitment to our movement.

Communists above all must have no illusion that antiwar sentiment can prevent an imperialist war. It never has. The rulers don't care what working people think or feel, so long as they are convinced they can get away with what they need to do to defend their profits and class interests. Modern history has taught the rulers that actually starting a war always results in dampening antiwar sentiment for a while. But only for a while.

The army in Saudi Arabia will fight. Other workers and farmers will give grudging support initially, even many who currently oppose going to war. Especially given the living memory of Vietnam, this fatalism will often take the form of just wanting to get it over as quickly as possible—to minimize the deaths of buddies and family members, so that life can get back to normal. That's especially the case among GIs, among workers and farmers in uniform, of course. Bush and the bipartisan gang from Congress who accompanied him to Saudi Arabia in November knew what they were doing when they embraced the slogan "No more Vietnams" as their own. They assured the soldiers that if "we" have to do it, we'll throw in everything we have and get it over with fast.

Fatalism among layers of working people, in and out of uniform, in the initial stage of a war is normal—but it is quite different from wanting to go to war. And as wars drag on, they always become increasingly unpopular and give rise to mounting working-class resistance. World War I culminated in the formation of revolutionary councils of soldiers, workers, and peasants in Russia, Germany, and elsewhere in eastern and Central Europe. In Russia, the workers and peasants took power. Similar revolutionary developments began to take place in the closing stages of World War II, many of them crushed and demobilized by the joint efforts of the Stalinists, social democrats, and bourgeois forces throughout Europe. And we've explained the rise of workers' struggles that took place here in the United States.

That process of polarization and differentiation will have to be gone through again if war is unleashed in the Middle East. We're convinced that it will be fought through more quickly this time. Opposition during war can develop very rapidly. That's what we are getting ready for. That's what we have our eyes on in this working-class campaign against the war.

IF WE'RE SERIOUS about this campaign, then we must pay close attention to the place where a large section of our class is organized. The men and women in the U.S. armed forces become decisive in a period leading up to a war. Don't simply call them "marines," or some other term. There is something more fundamental that defines them. They are workers in uniform. They are fellow workers, part of our class.

The labor movement must stand in complete solidarity with these workers in their fight to exercise their rights as *citizen-soldiers*—the right to say what they want, read what they choose, and participate in organized political life.

These rights are already under assault. The U.S. armed forces have slapped restrictions on the kinds of reading materials GIs can receive in the mail; even newspaper clippings are screened and sometimes returned to the sender. Washington has placed the troops in virtual desert quarantine, not even allowing press correspondents to say where in Saudi Arabia they are reporting from when they visit the bases—something that was not even done during the Vietnam War or World War II. And the big-business press hasn't uttered a peep of protest—not UPI, AP, the *New York Times,* ABC, CBS, NBC, CNN; none of them.

This is one of the reasons why the Pentagon has decided to halt any rotation of the troops. The rulers want to keep to a minimum the GIs' exposure to any information, discussion, or debate on the war. The rulers don't want to have workers and farmers going back and forth from Saudi Arabia to the United States, back and forth to discussions and debates with friends, fellow workers, and family members.

Workers and youth who are opposed to this war drive can still reach tens of thousands of GIs in this country, including some who will soon be on their way to the Gulf. I'm sure they will set up literature tables near military bases, at transportation centers, wherever they can think of. They will have debates, and their views will get a hearing.

Communists are opposed to individual resistance to serving in the armed forces. We're opposed to any clear-thinking worker in the army or the reserves not going with the rest of the working people in his or her unit to wherever they are sent.

Class-conscious workers go with the rest of their class, and they are "good soldiers" in the sense Farrell Dobbs, Fred Halstead, and other leaders of the communist movement have taught us to understand that term. Good soldiers are those who keep their buddies from getting killed, who keep them out of harm's way. But that means insisting on your full democratic and political rights to read, speak, and organize. As GIs have learned throughout this century, the officer corps is not concerned about a citizen-soldier's rights—or life—any more than foremen or management personnel in a packinghouse care about a worker's rights, health, or safety on the job.

At the same time, communists have always called on the workers' movement to defend unconditionally the democratic rights of any individual who refuses to serve, of any individual resister or conscientious objector. We reject their being jailed, repressed, or penalized by the imperialist government in any way. During World War II, Jim Cannon, Farrell Dobbs, and other SWP and former Teamsters union leaders who opposed the war landed in the same federal prison with a good number of members of religious, nationalist, and other groups who refused to serve. Cannon wrote about this in the book *Letters from Prison: The Communist Campaign against Wartime Repression.*

But we must not confuse our human solidarity with these individuals and our support for their democratic rights with support for their political course—which points away from the fight to organize and advance the rights of the hundreds of thousands of workers and farmers who are in the armed forces and who will fight and die if a war is unleashed.

It is the workers in uniform who are already feeling most directly the crackdown on democratic rights that accompanies every imperialist war drive, just as workers in so-called defense industries in this country will also begin to see their rights restricted. And the fight for political space for the entire working class will be advanced or pushed back by how much the rulers get away with in denying the rights of workers, in uniform or out, today.

Soldiers will go through wrenching experiences, and their attitudes and views will change. Their confidence in what they can accomplish, and must accomplish, will change. And that will be a decisive part of the transformation of the working class as a whole in the course of any war. It will be central to organizing and mobilizing working-class opposition to an imperialist war.

## Revolutionary-minded young people
It's in a period such as this that a youth organization like the Young Socialist Alliance faces the greatest challenges, as well as the greatest opportunities to win young workers, soldiers, and students to the communist movement. It is always among young people that the greatest reservoirs of energy, commitment, and sacrifice for organized resistance to imperialist war will be found.

This is not simply, or even primarily, because young people have to do the fighting. That's true. The young people who have to do the fighting will discuss and debate the war, and in growing numbers they will get involved in organizing opposition to it.

But there's more to it than that. Young people are the least ground down by the pressures of bourgeois society, less tied down by family, financial, and other obligations. They are less cynical, on the whole, less routinized, and more sensitive to the contradictions they see between what is and what's supposed to be. Regardless of how much or how little they understand politically, they are more alert to the flagrant inequalities and prejudices rife in capitalist society, the hypocrisy of the bourgeois politicians and their apologists, the brutalities of imperialist exploitation, racism, aggression, and wars.

THE U.S. RULERS are marching working people toward war and depression. But if they launch that war, there will be nothing about its consequences that will remain in their control. There will be resistance to the imperialist slaughter—throughout the Middle East and countries with large Muslim populations; in both Western *and* Eastern Europe; in many parts of the Third World; and right here in the United States. The emerging opposition to the war in this country will combine with fights against the employers' offensive here at home, which will increase in the period of recession and greater economic and social crisis that we have already entered.

It is not antiwar sentiment but the *mobilization* of these powerful social forces—the working people of this country—that can ultimately stay the hand of the imperialist war makers.

In the course of these fights, more and more workers, farmers, soldiers, and young people will draw revolutionary conclusions and recognize both the need and the advantages of being members of a communist organization, of joining the Young Socialist Alliance and the Socialist Workers Party.

We should know what it is that a revolutionary workers' party has to offer people who join our ranks as imperialism is marching toward war. Above all, the party offers fighters a way of working together democratically, collectively, and effectively at a time when what is shaping up in world politics is so important that the dissipation of our energies as individuals—no matter how committed—is unthinkable.

Up until now, the characteristic above all that has marked even the most conscious and committed of the rank-and-file fighters in the labor movement is that they have found no sustained, disciplined, collective way of functioning. They have stood up against big odds to take on the packinghouse bosses, Eastern Airlines, the coal operators, and many others—to fight their way around obstacles thrown up by the labor officialdom. They have registered important achievements and emerged as better and more class-conscious fighters.

But they remain individual fighters. They may have gone

through one, two, or more battles. But whatever they and other workers accomplish in any one battle, against any single employer, they end up back as individual militants.

The Socialist Workers Party has something important to offer fellow workers and young people who look for the forces in society that can change it. We offer a disciplined, democratic party of workers that can give them a way to be part of fights on many fronts against the employers and their wars against working people at home and abroad. We offer them the only road to advance the fight to build a powerful, revolutionary social and political movement of working people—a movement that can take the power to exploit and to wage war out of the hands of the capitalists by establishing a government of workers and farmers in this country.

# NOTES

1. The UN Security Council declared partial economic sanctions against the white-minority regime ruling Southern Rhodesia (today Zimbabwe) in December 1966. In May 1968, the UN body issued a resolution decreeing a trade blockade against Rhodesia. No enforcement measures were provided, however, and the measure was widely and publicly ignored, including by Washington. In November 1977 the Security Council decreed an arms embargo against South Africa that has also been widely ignored.

2. In the "Cuban missile crisis," as it was called in the U.S. media, President John F. Kennedy demanded the removal of Soviet nuclear missiles installed in Cuba at the request of the revolutionary government for defense against U.S. attack. Washington ordered a total blockade of Cuba, threatened an invasion of the island, and placed U.S. forces throughout the world on nuclear alert. Without consulting the Cuban government, Soviet premier Nikita Khrushchev decided to remove the missiles following a commitment by Kennedy that Washington would not invade Cuba. An exchange of cables between Cuban prime minister Fidel Castro and Khrushchev, documenting the sequence of events, was published in 1990. See *Granma Weekly Review*, December 2, 1990.

3. For the text of Alarcón's rebuttal to this and other U.S.-spon-

sored war resolutions in the UN Security Council, see Fidel Castro and Ricardo Alarcón, *U.S. Hands Off the Mideast! Cuba Speaks Out at the United Nations* (New York: Pathfinder, 1990). This book is also available from Pathfinder in Spanish under the title *¡EE.UU. fuera del Oriente Medio! Cuba habla en Naciones Unidas.*

4. For an account of the accomplishments of the Grenadian revolution and its counterrevolutionary overthrow from within, see Steve Clark, "The Second Assassination of Maurice Bishop," in *New International,* no. 6, pp. 11-96.

5. For more information on what led to the downfall of the workers' and farmers' government in Nicaragua, see "Defend Revolutionary Nicaragua: The Eroding Foundations of the Workers' and Farmers' Government." This resolution was adopted by the National Committee of the Socialist Workers Party in July 1989. Following its adoption in August 1990 by a convention of the SWP it was published in the *International Socialist Review* supplement to the September 7, 1990, issue of the *Militant.*

6. For an account of the U.S. assault on Panama in December 1989, see Cindy Jaquith et al., *Panama: The Truth about the U.S. Invasion* (New York: Pathfinder, 1990).

7. Fidel Castro, Ricardo Alarcón, *U.S. Hands Off the Mideast!,* pp. 10-11.

8. On July 24, 1990, as the Iraqi regime prepared to invade Kuwait, statements issued by the White House, State Department, and Pentagon made a point of noting that Washington had no formal military or defense treaties with Kuwait.

U.S. ambassador to Iraq April Glaspie met with President Saddam Hussein the next day to convey Washington's views directly. An account of the July 25 meeting subsequently released by the Iraqi government quoted Glaspie as telling Hussein, "We have no opinion on the Arab-Arab conflicts, like your border disagreement with Kuwait." The Iraqi account of the meeting was not challenged until March 20, 1991, nearly a month after the cease-fire, when the State Department allowed Glaspie to appear before a Senate committee and denounce the Iraqi transcript as "disinformation."

Three months prior to the invasion of Kuwait, Washington signaled warming relations with the Iraqi regime by sending a bipartisan team of six U.S. senators, headed by Republican leader Robert Dole, to Baghdad April 12, 1990, to pay a courtesy call.

9. Syngman Rhee was named president of South Korea in July 1948 by a National Assembly imposed two months earlier under U.S. occupation. In the opening hours of the U.S. invasion of Panama in December 1989, Guillermo Endara was sworn in as the

country's new president at Fort Clayton, a U.S. military base in the canal zone.

10.  Fascist regimes that crushed the organized workers' movement were installed in Italy in 1922 under Mussolini, in Germany in 1933 under Hitler. In Japan fascist movements, closely linked to the army officer corps, backed the semimilitary regime installed in 1932 that crushed the unions and workers' parties.

11.  Originating in a period of social crisis, a Bonapartist regime tends to concentrate executive power in the hands of an individual "strong man" who seeks to present himself as standing above the contending class forces, and to acquire a certain independence of action, in order to maintain the power of the dominant social layer. Gorbachev's Bonapartist course seeks to preserve the social privileges and monopoly of power of the bureaucratic caste in the USSR.

12.  In early 1991 the Soviet government began military assaults in the Baltic republics as well. Troops opened fire on independence supporters in Lithuania and Latvia in January, leaving twenty dead and hundreds wounded.

13.  See Mary-Alice Waters, "1945: When U.S. Troops Said 'No!'" elsewhere in this issue.

14.  The full text of Malmierca's speech is printed in the December 14, 1990, issue of the *Militant*.

15.  See "War, Revolution, and the Fight for a Workers' and Peasants' Government in Iran," printed elsewhere in this issue.

16.  The *Daily News* strike ended March 21, 1991, after mounting financial losses forced the Tribune Company to sell the paper to a new owner. The new contract called for dismissal of nonunion "replacement workers" hired by the Tribune management to try to break the strike. However, it also eliminated 800 jobs, one-third of the prestrike work force, and imposed wage concessions of $70 million.

17.  For an account of the packinghouse workers' strike, see Fred Halstead, *The 1985-86 Hormel Meat-Packers Strike in Austin, Minnesota* (New York: Pathfinder, 1986).

18.  In February 1990 the Pittston Coal Group signed a new contract with more than 1,900 miners in Virginia, West Virginia, and Kentucky following an eleven-month strike that began in April 1989. Over the course of the Pittston strike more than 40,000 members of the United Mine Workers in the eastern coalfields walked out in support of the action. More than 50,000 supporters from across the United States and around the world visited the union's strike center, Camp Solidarity, in southwest Virginia.

19. Eastern Airlines ceased operations January 18, 1991. For an account of the twenty-two month Machinists' strike that defeated the attempt to turn Eastern into a profitable nonunion carrier, see Ernie Mailhot and others, *The Eastern Airlines Strike: Accomplishments of the Rank-and-File Machinists* (New York: Pathfinder, 1991).

20. For an account of the fight by U.S. communists against government spying and disruption, see Larry Seigle, "Washington's Fifty-Year Domestic Contra Operation," in *New International*, no. 6; Margaret Jayko, *FBI on Trial* (New York: Pathfinder, 1988); and Nelson Blackstock, *Cointelpro: The FBI's Secret War on Political Freedom* (New York: Anchor Foundation, a Pathfinder book, 1988).

21. Mark Curtis, a packinghouse worker and member of the Socialist Workers Party, is serving a twenty-five-year sentence in Iowa on frame-up rape and burglary charges. His fight for justice has won widespread support around the world. Facts in the case are detailed in Margaret Jayko, *The Frame-Up of Mark Curtis* (New York: Pathfinder, 1989).

22. On January 26, 1991, more than 125,000 marched in Washington, 80,000 demonstrated in San Francisco, and 30,000 took part in actions in cities across Canada. The previous week, on January 19, more than 50,000 people marched in an antiwar protest in San Francisco and another 25,000 marched in Washington, D.C. The following month, on February 21, thousands of students on more than 250 U.S. campuses and high schools took part in teach-ins and rallies, part of an international day of actions that included protests in Canada, France, Japan, and the Philippines.

# WAR AND THE COMMUNIST MOVEMENT

## by Jack Barnes

**M**ORE THAN any event other than a mass revolutionary contest for power by the workers and peasants, wars have the biggest political impact on the working class, on its vanguard layers, and on union and political leaderships that claim to speak and act in the interests of working people.

Wars concentrate and accelerate every political trend and development. They intensify pressure at every vulnerable point and put every strong point to the maximum test. They hasten the defection of the weak and bring out unexpected abilities in the strong to shoulder new responsibilities.

There is a deep interconnection between how a political party goes into a war and how it comes out. The history of the twentieth century proves that if political clarity, courage, and determination are marshaled by vanguard workers, then the wars inflicted on us by the imperialist rulers can be turned against them, as more and more workers turn against the war.

The communist movement in this century was built, more than anything else, around the struggle for a working-class political orientation in the face of imperialist war:

- Why communists don't have a revolutionary policy for peacetime and a peace policy for wartime;
- How the working class must be organized to use the fight against imperialist war to deepen the revolutionary struggle to overturn the capitalist system responsible for these slaughters.

Modern communism, the communism of the twentieth century, passed its first decisive test when the Bolsheviks, under the leadership of V.I. Lenin, showed their capacity throughout World War I to chart a revolutionary course that culminated in the triumph of the Soviet workers' and peasants' republic in

---

*This article is excerpted from a speech given December 1, 1990, in New York City.*

October 1917. That victory rapidly brought that bloody war to an end on the Russian front and hastened the end of the broader slaughter.

The Bolsheviks championed the uprisings of oppressed nations throughout Europe, Asia, and the Middle East that were given a mighty impulse during the war and its aftermath. The Bolsheviks organized and agitated against the war among the soldiers—the peasants and workers conscripted into the tsarist army. No matter how deeply underground they were forced to operate as a result of tsarist repression, the Bolsheviks never stopped carrying out consistent revolutionary work in the factories, mines, and mills. They never stopped mobilizing support for the peasants' struggle for land. They never stopped advocating the defeat of the tsarist and capitalist war plans, abroad and at home, and seeking ways to transform the war into a revolutionary struggle to overturn the imperialist tyranny and bring to power a government of workers and peasants.

Following the outbreak of the war in August 1914, the big majority of those in all the imperialist countries who had previously been looked to as leaders of the revolutionary workers' movement lined up—often very "critically" and "reluctantly"—behind "their" national capitalists and governments in that war. The international Marxist movement collapsed in disarray, with most of its former leaders applauding the massacre of workers on "the other side."

Out of the many-million-strong international socialist movement that had existed prior to August 1914, only a handful initially emerged who were determined under wartime conditions to keep on doing everything in their power to ensure that their own ruling class was defeated—just as before the war they had always fought to defeat the exploiters and their governments in every strike, peasant uprising, and political battle.

The Russian revolutionary leader Leon Trotsky reports in his autobiography, *My Life,* that those former leaders of the bankrupt Socialist International who remained revolutionists and internationalists joked in the war's opening years that when they held a conference in Switzerland, they could all fit in four taxis to go to the meeting site.[1] It was a joke, but not that much of an exaggeration.

The communists sought every opportunity to turn the bloody

war—and the growing resistance by workers, peasants, and soldiers to its devastating effects—into a revolutionary struggle to wrest the *power to make war* out of the hands of the capitalists and landlords once and for all.[2]

Then, following the revolution that toppled the tsar in February 1917, Lenin and the Bolsheviks were responsible for one of the greatest gales of laughter ever to shake the soviets. (The soviets were councils of representatives from various workers' and peasants' organizations that had emerged in the course of the revolution.) Initially, the majority of these representatives were from the wing of the prewar socialist movement that had rejected the Bolsheviks' revolutionary course.

During a nationwide congress of the soviets in June, a leader of these organizations said that whatever other differences might exist among the delegates, no party represented there was so foolish as to say it was ready to take power away from the new liberal bourgeois government.

Lenin shouted from the floor: "There is!"

Most other delegates laughed. But four months later the Bolsheviks led the toilers in the establishment of the world's first workers' and peasants' republic. That revolutionary victory encouraged other working people the world over to try to emulate the Bolsheviks and deepen the international struggle for national liberation and socialism.

D URING EACH WAR since then, the workers' movement has paid a big price for misleadership by those who claimed to be communists but who in practice either diverted the revolutionary struggle against capitalism into pacifist byways, or who directly and openly aided the capitalist rulers in waging war and propping up their bloody system of exploitation and oppression.

During World War II, leaders of the Stalinized Communist parties in many countries joined with those in the regrouped Socialist International to impose this treachery on the vast ma-

*ENDNOTES FOR THIS ARTICLE BEGIN ON PAGE 223.*

jority of workers' organizations and national liberation movements. The leadership of the Socialist Workers Party, however, along with small groups of communists in other countries, refused to break from the revolutionary proletarian course charted by the Bolsheviks.

During the very week in December 1941 that Washington declared its entry into World War II, eighteen leaders and cadres of the SWP—most of whom had been class-struggle leaders of the Teamsters union and its antiwar wing in the Midwest—were sentenced to federal prison. They had been framed up on charges aimed at silencing the working-class campaign they were waging in the labor movement against the coming imperialist war.

During the opening period of the war, the *Militant*, the weekly communist newspaper that campaigned week in and week out against the bosses' war, their racist policies, and their repression, was assaulted by U.S. postal authorities. The FBI increased its spying on the party and its members and supporters. SWP members working in industry and functioning in the unions came under increasing pressure from the bosses, the cops, and those in the union officialdom and in the Stalinist and social democratic parties who helped marshal support for the war.

But less than two years later, by 1943, the coal miners organized in the United Mine Workers of America had begun resisting the wage freeze and no-strike pledge imposed on them in the name of patriotic unity. Black workers and other opponents of racist discrimination opened a new stage of the fight for equality in employment and on the job in the burgeoning war industries, as well as in the still–Jim Crow U.S. armed forces; mass rallies for these demands were organized by the March on Washington movement as early as June 1942.

The newspaper that U.S. postal authorities had tried to gag exploded in the greatest subscription campaigns in its history, gaining a readership of more than 30,000 by the summer of 1945. GIs in the Pacific mobilized mass demonstrations following the armistice, demanding to be brought home now instead of being used—as Washington had been planning—to hold back national liberation struggles breaking out in China, Vietnam, and elsewhere in the wake of the war.

In fact, the years at the close of and just after the war saw the most rapid increase in the size of the SWP in our history. This explosive growth came on the crest of the potential that existed for a year or so to recapture the momentum of the social movement that had built the CIO industrial union movement in the mid-1930s and to open a new stage in the fight for Black liberation. That potential was not to be realized, due to international political and economic factors beyond the control of the revolutionary workers' movement, as well as the class-collaborationist misleadership and betrayals of workers' interests by the union officialdom, Stalinists, and social democrats in the United States, Europe, and elsewhere. As part of fighting the imperialist war drive, we should be going back to the lessons of how communist workers waged a working-class campaign against an earlier war.[3]

# NOTES

1. Leon Trotsky, *My Life* (New York: Pathfinder, 1970), p. 249.

2. For more on how communists campaigned against World War I, see *Lenin's Struggle for a Revolutionary International,* John Riddell, ed. (New York: Anchor Foundation, a Pathfinder book, 1984), which is part of the series titled The Communist International in Lenin's Time.

3. Four books that tell how communist workers campaigned against World War II are: Farrell Dobbs, *Teamster Bureaucracy: The Trade Union Campaign against World War II* (New York: Anchor Foundation, a Pathfinder book, 1977); James P. Cannon, *Letters from Prison: The Communist Campaign against Wartime Repression* (New York: Pathfinder, 1973); C.L.R. James and others, *Fighting Racism in World War II* (New York: Pathfinder, 1980); and James P. Cannon, *The Socialist Workers Party in World War II* (New York: Pathfinder, 1975).

# Basic works of
# CHE GUEVARA

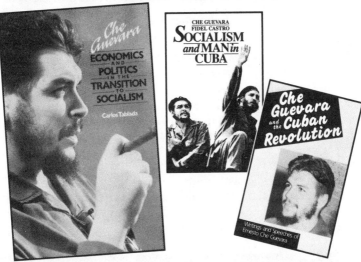

## Che Guevara and the Cuban Revolution
WRITINGS AND SPEECHES OF ERNESTO CHE GUEVARA
The definitive collection in English. 413 pp., $20.95

## Che Guevara: Economics and Politics in the Transition to Socialism
*by Carlos Tablada*

Examines Guevara's contributions to building socialism—in theory and in practice. 286 pp., $16.95

## Socialism and Man in Cuba
*by Ernesto Che Guevara and Fidel Castro*

Guevara's classic discussion of economics, politics, and consciousness in the transition to socialism. Includes Castro's speech on the 20th anniversary of Guevara's death. 44 pp., $2.50

## Che Guevara Speaks
Includes writings and speeches not available elsewhere in English. 159 pp., $11.95

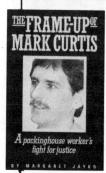

# COMMUNISTS DON'T HAVE A REVOLUTIONARY POLICY FOR PEACETIME AND A PEACE POLICY FOR WARTIME

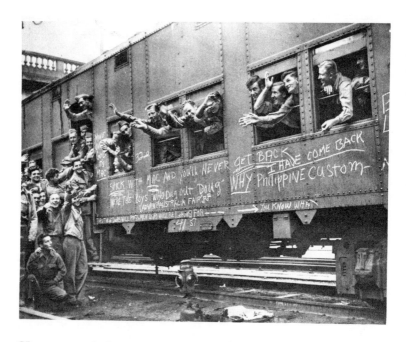

GIs protest redeployment to the Pacific in October 1945. Following World War II, U.S. troops rejected Washington's efforts to keep them in Asia to be used to crush anticolonial struggles in the Philippines, China, and elsewhere. Actions organized by soldiers' committees and backed by sections of the labor movement forced the demobilization of more than nine million troops by mid-1946.

# INTRODUCTION

C OMMUNISTS aren't communists in peacetime, only to become pacifists in wartime. They aren't proletarian revolutionists in peacetime, only to become middle-class radicals in wartime.

The working class must have its own antiwar program to answer the militarization and war policies of the capitalist rulers. It must have its own campaign against imperialism and war.

The articles that make up this section of *New International* document how the vanguard of the working class in the United States has responded to the political challenges posed by the three imperialist militarization drives that have marked the last fifty years.

In "Washington's Third Militarization Drive," Mary-Alice Waters explains the accelerated preparations for war that began in the last year of the Democratic administration of James Carter. The two preceding U.S. imperialist war drives, from 1937 through the end of World War II, and from 1947 to the defeat of U.S. imperialism in Vietnam, are reviewed in light of the war buildup we face today.

"Washington's Third Militarization Drive" was a report adopted in August 1985 by a convention of the Socialist Workers Party. It was published later that year in an *Information Bulletin* for members of the party. In editing it for circulation to the wider audience of *New International,* a number of points have been developed more fully.

The 1985 convention of the Socialist Workers Party also adopted a resolution, "The Revolutionary Perspective and Leninist Continuity in the United States." That resolution, published in *New International* no. 4, outlines the broad international relationship of class forces and political dynamics to which "Washington's Third Militarization Drive" refers.

In August 1985 the U.S.-financed and -organized contra war against the Nicaraguan government was still escalating. The Sandinista People's Army had not yet militarily defeated the contra forces but the tide was turning. The U.S. government was preparing for the direct use of U.S. military forces in Central America, if necessary, to bring down the government led by the Sandinista National Liberation Front. While there was bipartisan agreement in Washington that no accommodation was possible with the workers' and farmers' government in Nicaragua, there were sharp tactical divisions over how to bring about a change. Influential voices within ruling-class circles were convinced that alternative ways to bring the Nicaraguan people to their knees should be used before paying the high political price that would be exacted—above all throughout the Americas—if U.S. troops and murderous air power were directly unleashed against Nicaragua.

Because of these accelerating war preparations and the tactical debate over the wisdom of sending U.S. troops into battle in Central America, there was political space for opponents of U.S. policy to build sizable actions against U.S. military intervention, and to win significant support for them among working people, including in and through the organized labor movement. These possibilities had been confirmed by the April 20, 1985, marches in Washington, D.C., San Francisco, and a number of other U.S. cities, involving more than 100,000 people; these actions demanded a halt both to U.S. support for the contra army and to the apartheid regime in South Africa.

The report also assessed the fact that since 1980 the U.S. ruling class had succeeded in demobilizing opposition to renewed draft registration. Under those concrete conditions, the report projected a course of action for working-class forces opposed to conscription for the imperialist army. The discussion of the draft and of a revolutionary program for millions of working-class men and women in uniform led to renewed interest in what had happened to workers—in uniform as well as out—during the Vietnam War and World War II.

"The Communist Antiwar Program of the Socialist Workers Party, 1940 to 1969," printed here, was the second part of a resolution entitled "The Fight against the Vietnam War" adopted by the 1969 convention of the SWP. Based on a memorandum drafted by SWP national secretary Farrell Dobbs in June of that year, the resolution outlines the proletarian military policy adopted by the SWP on the eve of World War II, which called for military training of the working class under trade union control. The resolution explains how changes in the relationship of class forces in the 1950s and 1960s dictated different demands to accomplish the same revolutionary aims.

The resolution oriented a new generation of communists then joining the Socialist Workers Party and Young Socialist Alliance toward the most important political development taking place in the U.S. armed forces during the Vietnam War— the fight by GIs to defend their constitutional rights as citizen-soldiers to have the space to engage in political activity. The struggle against all forms of racial discrimination was deepening and becoming more militant, and opposition to the war was spreading. In this context, GIs demanded the right to read the literature of their choice; to express their views on the war, racism, and other political questions; and to organize themselves and participate in antiwar and Black rights actions when they were off duty.

Over time the antiwar movement was increasingly won to an appreciation of the importance of actions that maximized the participation of active-duty military personnel. This working-class orientation adopted by a political vanguard of the movement against the Vietnam War ultimately had a palpable impact on the ability of the U.S. rulers to continue prosecuting the war.

The story of how this was accomplished is told by one of its leaders, Fred Halstead, in *Out Now! A Participant's Account of the Movement in the United States against the Vietnam War*, (New York: Anchor Foundation, a Pathfinder book, 1978 and 1991).

Halstead was also the SWP candidate for president of the United States in 1968, and traveled to Vietnam to talk with GIs. During the campaign he drafted a widely distributed "Letter to GIs on the '68 Elections" explaining this perspective. Halstead wrote:

> No one has a better right to oppose the war than a combat GI. And while I understand that GIs are in a tight

spot, I also know that there is no law that says GIs have to be brainwashed, or that they do not have the right to think for themselves, or to read different points of view on the war, or to discuss the war.

I also believe they ought to have the right to demonstrate against the war. Actually, this has happened before in the U.S. armed services. Just after the end of World War II, there were huge demonstrations of GIs overseas demanding to be brought home instead of being left in the Pacific area and involved in the Chinese civil war that was then developing. I know about these demonstrations because I participated in them.

These actions by the GIs, and the support for them at home, actually forced a demobilization.

All this happened without any codes, orders, or regulations being violated, or any serious legal trouble. The movement was just too widespread and popular for anyone to stop it.

"1945: When U.S. Troops Said 'No!'" by Mary-Alice Waters tells the story of this hidden chapter in U.S. history. First published in the *Young Socialist* magazine in 1965—as the war in Vietnam was escalating and the antiwar movement was beginning to grow—the article was reprinted as a Young Socialist pamphlet. During the 1960s and early 1970s, thousands of copies were sold by the Young Socialist Alliance as its members campaigned to build an antiwar movement capable of reaching out to and mobilizing the power of the millions of young workers, including those in uniform. Unearthing a chapter of history that the employers and their war-making government would like to keep buried was part of a new generation's learning to fight effectively against imperialism and war.

At the time the article was written, Waters was editor of the *Young Socialist.* She later edited the *Militant* for a number of years and is currently editor of *New International.*

Long out of print, this article is being made available once again through the pages of *New International.* The "going home" movement of U.S. soldiers and sailors at the end of World War II altered the course of history. It will happen again.

# The Communist Manifesto

by Karl Marx and Frederick Engels
The founding program of the revolutionary
working-class movement. 48 pp., $2.50

## Socialism: Utopian and Scientific

by Frederick Engels
Explains the origins of the materialist world
outlook of the modern communist workers'
movement. 63 pp., $3.00

### Marx and Engels on the United States

Articles and correspondence on
the Civil War and other key
questions in the U.S. class
struggle from the 1840s to 1890s.
391 pp., $8.95

### Imperialism: The Highest Stage of Capitalism

by V.I. Lenin
Outlines the nature of imperialism
and the imperialist epoch — the
twentieth century.
$2.95

### Challenge of the Left Opposition

by Leon Trotsky
Documents the fight of the
communist opposition in the
1920s against the reactionary
political and economic policies of
the rising bureaucratic caste in
the Soviet Union led by Stalin.
Three volumes, vols. 1 and 3,
$26.95 each, vol. 2, $29.95

### The Revolution Betrayed

*What Is the Soviet Union
and Where Is It Going?*
by Leon Trotsky
Classic study of the bureaucratic
degeneration of the Soviet Union
under Stalin. Explains the roots of
the social and political crisis
shaking the Soviet Union today.
314 pp., $18.95

### For a Workers' and Farmers' Government in the United States

by Jack Barnes
Strategic questions facing working
people in the transition from
capitalism to socialism. 61 pp.,
8½-by-11 format, $7.00

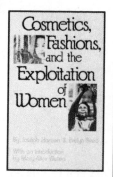

# WASHINGTON'S THIRD
# MILITARIZATION DRIVE

*by Mary-Alice Waters*

**M**ILITARIST propaganda—wrapped in patriotic bunting—
is a permanent feature of our epoch. Imperialist powers are always preparing for war.

In the United States, the emergence of modern militarism
goes back to the period following the defeat of Radical Reconstruction and is intertwined with the growing domination of
industrial and banking capital.[1] This period culminated in
Washington's assault on Hawaii in 1893 and then on Cuba,
Puerto Rico, and the Philippines in 1898 in the Spanish-Ameri-
can War—the first imperialist war waged by the North American colossus.

Within the imperialist epoch there are also particular militarization drives, and today, in 1985, we are in the midst of one.
Because we have now been living with it, and fighting against it,
for more than half a decade, it is easy to forget that this current
militarization drive had a well-defined beginning. We need to
look at it concretely so we can see what the ruling class has
accomplished, and what it hasn't.

### Shift in ruling-class policy

The current militarization campaign was initiated at the beginning of 1980. In his State of the Union message in January 1980,
President James Carter announced the decision to reinstate
draft registration. At the time, we pointed to this as "the first
real war speech of the Carter administration."

---

*This article is based on a report adopted by the August 1985 convention
of the Socialist Workers Party. Mary-Alice Waters is editor of* New
International.

*ENDNOTES FOR THIS ARTICLE BEGIN ON PAGE 265.*

The president's pronouncement, and the political offensive it was part of, signaled a shift in ruling-class policy. It marked the end of the retreat following the 1973 defeat in Vietnam and the fallout from the Watergate crisis at home.[2] It took the rulers the better part of a decade after they began withdrawing U.S. forces from Vietnam in 1971 to get themselves back into position for a militarization offensive.

Between 1973 and 1980 toilers around the world dealt body blows to imperialism on several battlefronts. These included the revolutionary overthrow of the landlord-based monarchy in Ethiopia in 1974; the defeat of Portuguese colonial rule in Africa in 1974-75; the defeat of the capitalist-landlord regime of South Vietnam and reunification of the country in 1975-76, and the fall of U.S.-backed forces in Kampuchea [Cambodia] and Laos; the defeat of the South African invasion of Angola by Cuban and Angolan troops in 1976, and the impulse that gave to a new upsurge of struggles throughout southern Africa, including against the apartheid regime in South Africa itself; the defeat in 1977 of the U.S.-backed Somalian invasion aimed at reversing the trajectory of the Ethiopian revolution; Zimbabwe's attainment of independence in 1980; the Iranian revolution of 1978-79; and the 1979 revolutions that led to the establishment of workers' and farmers' governments in Grenada and Nicaragua, along with the massive upsurge in El Salvador, advances in Guatemala, and the revolutionary boost these events gave to the fighting people of Cuba.

The 1980 Carter speech and draft registration announcement were timed to take advantage of two developments: in November 1979 U.S. embassy employees were taken hostage in Tehran; and in December 1979 Soviet military forces went into Afghanistan in the midst of an escalating civil war.[3] The U.S. ruling class seized on these events to beat the drums for their opening militarization moves with an outpouring of patriotic flag-waving and anticommunist propaganda.

The steps taken by the Carter administration were part of the systematic effort to counter the retreat imposed on Washington by its defeat in Vietnam and the erosion of public belief in the truthfulness of those who spoke for the institutions of capitalist government (broadly referred to as the Watergate crisis). These moves were aimed at reducing obstacles in the way of the U.S.

rulers using their overwhelming military might to defend their class rule on a world scale. At the same time, Carter's actions were directed—as are all capitalist militarization measures— against working people, the oppressed nationalities, women pressing to extend their rights, and the youth of this country— the mass candidates for cannon fodder. The militarization campaign was an integral part of a stepped-up offensive to weaken our struggles against the employing class, erode our democratic rights, diminish our effective political space, and deepen divisions among us—the better to increase profits and strengthen the U.S. capitalists vis-à-vis their competitors in other countries.

This was summed up accurately in a Political Committee report presented by Andrea Morell that was adopted by the Socialist Workers Party National Committee in May 1980.

The current imperialist militarization drive, the report explained, is a "drive by the U.S. rulers to regain the political ability to use their military might as they deem necessary against the world revolution." That is exactly what was, and is, involved.

This current militarization drive is the third such campaign the U.S. rulers have undertaken since the late 1930s.

The first began with President Franklin Roosevelt's "quarantine the aggressor" speech in October 1937 in preparation for entry into the European war that was coming. This militarization drive lasted roughly eight years, until the massive demobilization following U.S. imperialism's defeat of Japan in 1945.

The second began in the spring of 1947 with President Truman's executive order launching the loyalty-oath program and witch-hunt. On the international front, Truman's "aid" program to Greece announced the accelerated war drive cloaked in anticommunist rhetoric.[4] The second militarization drive continued through the Korean War and the first decade of the Cuban revolution, and ended only with the defeat of Washington in Vietnam. The early part of this period has become known—somewhat inaccurately—as the "Cold War."

The third militarization drive is the one we are discussing, which began in early 1980.

### A communist policy in wartime as in peacetime

When the capitalist class is organizing for war, and when it takes the decision to go to war, the working class must have its own policies to defend its interests and advance its struggles within those conditions imposed by the rulers. It is not enough to say that we reject imperialist militarism. Until the workers are strong enough to break through that framework—that is, to reject it *in struggle*—we also have to chart our own proletarian course in face of that reality.

The communist answer to imperialist militarism is straightforward and simple. It has been established and tested in struggle over decades. In fact, the communist movement of the twentieth century was born in struggle against those who led millions of workers into World War I by betraying the principle "Not one penny, not one person for the imperialist war machine!" That is our guidepost; without it we would be hopelessly lost.

But that slogan doesn't give us all the answers as we confront concrete propaganda and actions by the ruling class, as it drives forward its militarization and as it wages war. We are opposed to the imperialist draft. But if the working class is not strong enough to prevent a draft from being imposed, then we need a policy toward it. We need a policy on military training for working people. We need a policy for workers and farmers in the armed forces—an approach aimed at deepening working-class consciousness and advancing the fight of workers and farmers to defend their constitutional rights and class interests as they face the class brutalities of the officer corps, racism, and restrictions on political dissent. These policies must advance the struggle of our class and its allies to break from political dependence on the exploiters, the bosses' twin parties—Democrats and Republicans—and representatives, and the petty-bourgeois politicians of all varieties. Our policies must advance our class toward taking political power and establishing a workers' and farmers' government. Success in moving along that line of march is the true measure of any antiwar policy.

This is what the Socialist Workers Party has always referred to as our proletarian military policy, a perspective for the working class in response to the militarization policies of the capitalist rulers in the imperialist epoch. It begins not with military questions but with the proletariat. It presents a line of action to defend the class interests of workers and farmers in face of the militarization drives and imperialist wars that continued capitalist rule will inevitably bring. It begins with the concrete conditions in the class struggle, the level of consciousness and organization of the working class, and the relationship of forces between the exploited and exploiting classes. It begins with the intertwining of imperialism and war, not war in the abstract. It begins with the reality of class struggle, not the utopian search for class peace. It begins with "we," the workers and our toiling allies, counterposed to "them," the employers, their political representatives, and their aggression abroad.

The section of the Transitional Program entitled "The Picket Line, Defense Guards, Workers' Militia, the Arming of the Proletariat" summarizes the trajectory.[5] This section of the 1938 program of the SWP describes the necessary development of the workers' movement that begins with the organization of picket lines to enforce strike action; proceeds to the creation of workers' groups for self-defense against the antilabor, fascist, and racist gangs the employers will resort to as the class confrontation intensifies; and goes from there to the preparation for a workers' militia, which will be "the one serious guarantee for the inviolability of workers' organizations, meetings, and press" under sharpening conditions of class warfare.

This line of march culminates in the arming of the workers and farmers in the battle to defend themselves against the counterrevolutionary onslaughts and fascist terror that the capitalist class will unleash to defend its rule.

A proletarian military policy—a policy of the working class to confront imperialist militarism—is thus an integral part of working-class strategy as workers and farmers move toward establishing their own government.

IN 1969, as the size and scope of actions against the Vietnam War were growing rapidly and we were playing an increasingly weighty role in their leadership, a convention of the Socialist Workers Party adopted a resolution outlining the party's policy toward that movement and within it. The resolution discussed the application of the party's proletarian military policy before, during, and after World War II and compared objective conditions then to those we faced at the outbreak of the Vietnam War in the mid-1960s. The resolution noted that our political orientation and response to imperialist wars has little in common with the antimilitarism of the pacifists, or with the "socialist" antimilitarism promoted by Stalinists and social democrats as the "peace" component of their class-collaborationist policies.

"Military policy is an essential part of any transitional program of the revolutionary party in the imperialist epoch with its monstrous growth of capitalist militarism," the 1969 resolution notes. "The naive outlook of the early socialist movement, which disregarded the military aspects of the class struggle, has long since become outmoded. The actual relations between nations, peoples, and classes compel every political tendency to take a position and work out a policy toward both imperialist and class warfare."

The concrete military policy adopted by the SWP in 1940, on the eve of U.S. entry into the Second World War, was part of our communist continuity and part of a revolutionary perspective designed to promote the struggles of workers and farmers against the capitalists under the given wartime conditions.

The resolution explains that young workers and farmers drafted to fight in the U.S. imperialist army in World War II were "imbued with a mixture of anti-Hitler, antifascist, defensist, democratic, and patriotic sentiments." U.S. involvement in World War II was almost universally—if often grudgingly—accepted among working people, under the illusion that it was a progressive fight against fascism. Many workers and farmers felt that the fight for union rights, for farmers' needs, and against Jim Crow segregation and lynch-law terror against Blacks in the South would be advanced by the war against the Nazi regime in Germany and its allies.

Under these conditions, with U.S. entry into World War II approaching, the party unconditionally opposed the capitalist draft that went into effect in 1940—the first peacetime draft in U.S. history. This was simply a continuation of the long-standing communist policy against imperialist conscription. But we also took into account that antifascist, as well as patriotic, sentiments of workers and farmers led them to favor organized universal military service. The SWP therefore counterposed to the capitalist draft the demand for conscription by workers' organizations; we advocated military training and officer selection under trade union control, financed by the government.

Members of the party who were drafted went into the army. They learned military skills and sought to conduct themselves as soldiers in a manner that would win the political confidence of fellow workers and farmers in uniform. "Their participation as socialists in the military machine," the 1969 resolution says, "was viewed as a prerequisite for revolutionary action if a favorable turn of events made it possible to gain a majority to the idea of transforming the imperialist war into a struggle for workers' power and socialism."

## World War II: several wars in one

Contrary to popular belief both then and now, World War II was not a war to stop fascism. It was much more complex than that; it was at least "three wars in one," as the SWP explained at the time.

• It was an interimperialist war in which the defeat by Washington and its allies of Germany, Japan, and Italy did nothing to eliminate the economic and social roots of fascism nor the causes of imperialist oppression. Fascism, the most virulent form of maintaining imperialist rule, will again attempt to raise its head in any period of deep capitalist crisis and accelerating class polarization and combat.

• It was a war to roll back the Russian revolution and reestablish capitalism in the Soviet Union. With enormous sacrifice the workers and peasants of the first—and at that time only—workers' state turned the tide against German imperialism's invading armies. They prevented the imperialist powers from realizing this historic objective, which none of them have ever abandoned from October 1917 to this day.

• It was a multifront war for national liberation in which the colonized and oppressed nations of the world took good advantage of the interimperialist conflict to advance their interests—from India to China, Vietnam, Indonesia, Korea, the Mideast, Ireland, and Québec.

A fourth war also took shape as the imperialist bloodletting continued: the war carried out by resistance forces—many organized by the workers' movement—in the occupied countries of Europe. That was a war against the fascist dictatorships imposed by Hitler's National Socialist movement. It was also a war by the workers to create the most favorable possible conditions for the working classes in Europe to emerge victorious over their own bourgeoisies, whether fascist or "democratic imperialist," as the conflict unfolded.

### The Cold War: rebuilding the U.S. military machine

After Japan's surrender in August 1945, the U.S. rulers, who came out on top of the pile in 1945, found themselves confronted with a disintegrating army. Workers and farmers in uniform, particularly those in the Pacific theater, demanded to be brought home immediately. They saw no reason to stay in uniform once the war *they* were fighting, the war against fascism, had been won.

The rulers in Washington, however, wanted to reap the harvest of victory over their rivals by taking control of Asia. In particular, they aimed at keeping China under imperialist control. As GIs throughout Asia started demonstrating by the thousands, the Democrats and Republicans in Washington howled, "But we are losing China!"

The GIs answered, "*You* may be losing China. *We* are going home!" They simply refused to continue under arms. Demobilization was accelerated and go home they did, by the millions. The U.S. armed forces had ceased to be an effective fighting force for imperialist interests.

That's how the postwar period began in the United States: with a GI going-home movement that no class on earth could have stopped, as well as a massive strike wave that brought nearly two million workers—many of them newly returned vets—onto the picket lines demanding an immediate end to the wartime wage controls.

In response to the victory of the Soviet Union in World War II, the advance of the colonial revolution as the imperialist powers warred against each other, and the resulting shift in the international relationship of forces to the detriment of imperialism, Washington had to take steps to put back together a military force to use against struggles by workers and peasants around the world. With World War II barely over, the U.S. rulers needed a new militarization drive.

At the same time, the employers still had to housebreak the labor movement that had been born in the giant struggles of the rise of the CIO industrial union movement in the second half of the 1930s. They also had to try to prevent a massive movement for Black equality from arising on the basis of the civil rights militancy that had emerged during the war. The witch-hunt and anticommunist reaction of the end of the 1940s and the 1950s were aimed at accomplishing these goals.

The wartime conscription law was allowed to lapse in 1947, but the draft machinery was kept intact and the Selective Service Act was pushed through in 1948 as the new militarization drive began to roll. A "peacetime" draft was institutionalized for the first time in U.S. history. With the growing use of deferment loopholes by bourgeois and middle-class youth, the postwar army became even more working-class in composition. Military spending soared, as Washington accelerated the nuclear arms race following the Soviet Union's development of an atomic bomb in 1949. When the U.S. rulers held a monopoly on atomic weapons, they used the bomb on Hiroshima and Nagasaki, sacrificing the lives of more than 200,000 civilians in Japan. Their political aim in doing so was to demonstrate to the toilers of the world that Washington would not hesitate to unleash this weapon of mass horror to protect its empire.

The Korean War was launched in the midst of the witch-hunt at the end of the 1940s and early 1950s, but it was greeted in the United States with a marked decline in patriotic fervor compared with World War II. By no measure did it ever become a popular war. But there was little active opposition to the war aside from some socialist and pacifist organizations, which were rapidly declining in size and influence. (The social democrats at the time outspokenly supported the U.S. war against Korea.)

The housebreaking of the organized labor movement and its political retreat brought changed conditions that altered some elements of the SWP's response to the government's military policies. The party dropped the demand for military training under trade union control as a counterposition to the capitalist draft. Given the state of the union movement, this perspective no longer rang true to vanguard workers as a realistic way forward. At the same time, of course, the party continued to oppose capitalist conscription. Individual party members continued to serve if drafted, and we fought against victimization of GIs for their antifascist, antiwar, antiracist, or socialist views.

We were part of the defensive battles in the labor movement

against steps by the employers and the government to use the militarization drive to undermine the power of the unions in the war industries. In particular, we fought the introduction of the system of "security clearances,"[6] aimed at victimizing union activists and other militant workers and weakening union protection and safety conditions. The party also continued to defend the right of workers on picket lines to protect themselves against bosses' thugs, and especially the right of Blacks to defend themselves against racist violence and terror.

### Vietnam, the Black struggle, and the antiwar movement

As the Vietnam War accelerated, almost a decade and a half after the Korean fighting, a historic change occurred. Popular support for the imperialist war eroded in the late 1960s and this was reflected in the attitudes of working people, including, in the final years of the war, those in the ranks of the armed forces.

Revulsion against the U.S.-organized carnage in Vietnam became intertwined with the economic and social changes wrought by twenty-five years of capitalist economic expansion that began in 1941. These changes and the heightened expectations they gave birth to were registered above all by the powerful mass actions of the civil rights movement that brought Jim Crow segregation to its knees by the mid-1960s.

When the U.S. government began to escalate the war against Vietnam, the decade of mass civil rights battles that destroyed the system of legal segregation in the South was coming to an end. The movement that began with the Montgomery bus boycott in 1955-56 took on new energy with the student-led sit-ins that began in 1960, followed by the Freedom Rides initiated in 1961. Throughout the early 1960s a growing campaign of mass demonstrations made the names of cities like Selma, Birmingham, and Montgomery famous around the world. The 250,000-strong March on Washington in the summer of 1963 was followed by the 1964 Civil Rights Act that outlawed discrimination in public accommodations and employment. In 1965 the Voting Rights Act was passed, eliminating most of the state laws that had been used for decades to disenfranchise Blacks in the South.

As the battle for voting rights in the South was pressed forward through continuing mass actions, the spontaneous uprisings in the northern ghettos began, simultaneous with the first escalation of the Vietnam War. Harlem exploded in the summer of 1964, only a few weeks before the Gulf of Tonkin incident was staged and President Lyndon Johnson ordered the first bombing raids against North Vietnam.[7] In February 1965 Malcolm X was assassinated. Then came Watts in August 1965. The summers of 1966 and 1967 brought rebellions in dozens of U.S. cities culminating in the uprisings in Newark and Detroit, which were put down by National Guard troops at the cost of more than sixty lives. In April 1968, outrage over the assassination of Martin Luther King, Jr., and widespread conviction that the government was responsible, boiled into rebellions that swept the cities of the country.

Throughout the second half of the 1960s, opposition to the escalating war in Vietnam paralleled and intertwined with the radicalization of the Black movement. "Black Power" became the rallying cry in U.S. cities and the Caribbean. The struggle for Black rights became the central axis of politics inside the armed forces in Vietnam—the source of the class energy fueling dissent. Growing doubts about the war among tens of millions of soldiers and civilians alike were reinforced. The lingering vestiges of the witch-hunt were submerged by the deepening radicalization that expressed itself in numerous mass phenomena, such as the rise of the women's liberation movement, the first gay rights actions, growing support for Puerto Rican independence, and the Chicano Moratorium.[8]

The U.S. rulers, alarmed by growing fissures in the bourgeois social consensus, escalated the scope and brutality of police operations at home as well, systematically targeting the leaders of Black organizations, the antiwar movement, and working-class political parties. Although the details were not known until later, the fact that the government was conducting its Cointelpro operations was widely suspected and contributed to the decline in public respect for U.S. government institutions—especially those supposedly dispensing justice.[9]

The relationship between the struggle for Black rights, the broader social radicalization, and opposition to the Vietnam War in both the civilian population and among the U.S. troops sent to fight and die in Vietnam is important. Neither the depth of the working-class opposition to the war nor the dynamics of the antiwar movement and what happened inside the U.S. armed forces is understandable without that political context.

What happened during the Vietnam War had no precedent in the modern history of the United States and represented an enduring political shift in the popular attitude toward imperialist wars. An antiwar movement grew up in the middle of an ongoing "hot" war. This contrasted to the largely pacifist-led and petty-bourgeois-dominated peace movements that appeared before World War I and World War II. These earlier movements collapsed when the shooting started, as the vast majority of their leaders wound up supporting the imperialist war effort.

During the Vietnam War, the working class showed little readiness to sacrifice for the war effort. This attitude was even more pronounced in the Black population, as well as among Chicanos, Puerto Ricans, and other oppressed nationalities. Defeatist moods developed, as well as overt sympathy for the Vietnamese patriots and widespread revulsion at the immoral, racist, dirty war that Washington was waging.

Conscription became increasingly unpopular and the target of growing protest. The SWP and Young Socialist Alliance joined with others in making the demand to end the draft part of the fight against the war. At the same time, we continued to oppose making it the center of that fight and to reject the political course of individual draft refusal advocated by many petty-bourgeois currents in the antiwar movement. This approach to the draft was a fundamental aspect of a proletarian military policy under the conditions that existed.

Members called up for military service submitted to the law, as did millions of other youth. At the same time SWP and YSA members insisted on and fought for their constitutional rights, and the rights of all other citizen-soldiers, to organize and speak out against the war, racism, and inequality. The SWP and YSA fought to organize and orient the entire antiwar movement to carry out activities aimed at encouraging GIs to participate as an active component of the antiwar action movement. This proletarian orientation set an example for the entire antiwar movement and helped to broaden its impact among working people in and out of uniform.

The organized labor movement was virtually absent from the

anti–Vietnam War movement to the end. Local 1199 of the hospital workers' union and District 65 of the Retail, Wholesale and Department Store Union, both based in New York City, did bring substantial contingents to antiwar demonstrations toward the end of the war, including a high percentage of workers who were Black. Some individual labor movement figures and local unions endorsed a few of the final actions. But this was very much the exception. The norm in the labor officialdom was support for the U.S. rulers' war.

The antiwar movement that grew up under these conditions gave decisive aid to the Vietnamese people who, with unexcelled tenacity and heroism, won their national liberation by politically defeating the massive imperialist intervention of the United States. One result of the retrenchment this setback imposed on the U.S. rulers was a direct victory for the workers and farmers of the United States: in 1973 the capitalist draft was halted. In 1976 draft registration itself was terminated.

### New militarization drive needed
The political repercussions of the defeat in Vietnam set the framework within which the U.S. rulers had to operate throughout the 1970s. By the end of the decade the need for a new militarization drive was posed with growing urgency.

Carter's announcement of the intention to reinstate draft registration was one of the first shots in this campaign. It coincided with a deepening assault on the rights and living standards of working people at home. This combination marked the beginning of a shift to the right of the whole framework of capitalist politics, which became increasingly bipartisan in domestic policy (it had been bipartisan in foreign policy since 1942). This shift continued and accelerated with the rulers' choice of Ronald Reagan in the November 1980 presidential election.

The large-scale expansion of military spending began not with Reagan but late in the Carter administration and has continued since then. The U.S. rulers campaigned to win placement of cruise and Pershing II missiles in the capitalist countries of Europe despite broad popular opposition. They organized and funded the contras to try to bring down the workers' and farmers' government of Nicaragua.[10] Military maneuvers in the Caribbean and Central America were escalated to unprecedented size and frequency, combined with a massive expansion of military aid to the murderously repressive governments of El Salvador, Honduras, and Guatemala, as well as Costa Rica. Cuba once again became a target of escalating threats.

U.S. "peacekeeping" troops were sent to the Middle East in 1982,[11] the first time since the Vietnam War that U.S. soldiers abroad were sent into combat situations. In a carefully calculated move, the United States government collaborated with and in fact made possible the British rulers' war against Argentina and invasion of the Malvinas Islands the same year.[12] In 1983 U.S. invasion forces landed in Grenada and installed a proimperialist regime on that island.[13]

Each of these steps has been part of the calculated militarization campaign of the ruling class—the implementation of a policy of propaganda combined, whenever they can get away with it, with direct military action and other, "covert" measures.

There has been a simultaneous drive on the domestic front against working people in the United States. The employers have deepened attacks on the living standards, rights, and organizations of the working class and its allies. The latest among these include the current expansion of "spy trials," aimed at intimidating political opposition within the ranks of the armed forces and restricting democratic rights.[14] The employers and the cops are stepping up their use of the "security clearance" weapon against the labor movement in industries involved in production of military goods.

### Reaction to Carter's 1980 registration plan

This is the context in which we need to go back and look more closely at the response to the rulers' decision at the beginning of 1980 to reestablish draft registration. Their purpose was to make reinstatement of the draft itself easier, if they later deemed that to be necessary. The goal was to have all the legal mechanisms in place and a pool of men ready to draw on when they decided to make that move.

But Carter's 1980 State of the Union speech triggered an immediate and large-scale reaction in this country—it was still too soon after the Vietnam slaughter. It is easy half a decade later to lose sight of how big and how significant that reaction was. Action coalitions emerged in most major cities and on hundreds of college campuses. A national Committee Against Registration and the Draft (CARD) was formed. Sizable demonstrations were organized, several thousand strong, in many cities. In March 1980, just two months after the initial announcement, twenty-five thousand marched on Washington in a demonstration organized by a coalition of forces taking the name National Mobilization Against the Draft.

Opposition to the draft registration plan became part of virtually every progressive political action taking place anywhere in the country, month after month. It was an important feature of the demonstrations against nuclear power and weapons in April of that year.[15] It became part of a Washington, D.C., march for jobs and peace organized by Operation PUSH in May.[16]

There was also a significant reaction in the working class, which was reflected even in the officialdom of the labor movement. William Winpisinger, president of the International Association of Machinists, and George Hardy, president of the Service Employees International Union, both members of the AFL-CIO Executive Council, opposed a resolution in the council endorsing Carter's proposal to reestablish draft registration. The IAM also gave space in its Washington, D.C., office to organizers of the national march against registration and the draft in the capital.

This was the kind of initial response the proposed draft registration evoked.

One reason for the strong reaction was the general assumption that if draft registration were instituted, the draft itself would not be far behind. At the time, the SWP pointed out (more accurately than we knew) that what was involved was not reestablishing the draft, but the rulers' attempt to reestablish *draft registration*. We emphasized that we should not confuse the two things, or telescope the two battles into one. It was not yet determined, we said, how fast they would be able to get even the registration plan implemented. There would be real confrontations and tests of strength before reinstatement of the draft itself was attempted—and a strong reaction to the registration proposal could help push the rulers back.

In the face of the large-scale opposition, the ruling class itself began to divide tactically on the timing and character of the implementation of the registration plan. Within a matter of months influential voices of capitalist opinion such as the *New York Times* switched positions. The *Times*'s editors had originally supported the registration plan. But they soon came out against it, arguing that it was untimely and unnecessary at the moment. They feared it was going to cause more problems than it was worth.

In June 1980 the draft registration law was adopted by both houses of Congress, but without Carter's original proposal to include the registration of young women as well. This led to an immediate court challenge of the law. As a result, a federal judge declared the law unconstitutional even before the first registration period opened.

When the initial two-week registration period did begin, hundreds of thousands of young people simply declined to sign up. They decided to wait it out, let it slide. They chose not to place themselves in the front line of those complying with a law that they didn't like, that many were demonstrating opposition to, and that had been declared unconstitutional anyway.

According to published estimates, as many as 40 percent of draft-age men in some cities failed to register. These might be exaggerated, but nobody knows the exact figures.

What took place was not individual resistance by a handful but the mass refusal to sign up—perhaps "neglect" is more accurate—by a broad layer of young people.

At that point, the outcome of this battle over draft registration remained an open question. All one could say is that it would be resolved in the course of the struggle against registration and in the context of the overall militarization drive itself. It also remained to be seen how quickly there would be a decision to try to move from draft registration to imposition of the draft itself. Everything remained unresolved, including such important questions for the draft-age youth themselves as how successful the government would be in turning up the heat on those who failed to register, and whether or not the nine robed justices of the ruling rich on the Supreme Court could be forced to declare the law itself, or any indictments under it, unconstitutional.

As the Political Committee of the Socialist Workers Party noted in a report adopted on June 14, 1985, "In this context, as part of our proletarian military policy, including our opposition to imperialist military conscription, our movement wholeheartedly identified with and supported the initial mass nonregistration by young people in response to the unconstitutional law passed by Congress."

The Young Socialist Alliance took the lead in this. The August 8, 1980, *Militant* featured an interview with John Wood, a member of the Young Socialist Alliance who was working on the docks in Baltimore, explaining "Why I'm not registering for the draft."

Wood said, "As the time for registration approached, it was clear to us in the YSA that something new and important was happening.

"It's clear that very large numbers of young people, young working people and others, see this as an effective way to oppose the whole thing.

"I know it was clear to me, when I went to the May 17 [1980] Washington jobs demonstration called by Jesse Jackson, that many young Black people would not be barging over to the post office to register. And it's a lot more widespread than that." The *Militant* added, "Many young white workers are saying no, too. Not a select few."

Wood said, "So I think it's not a matter of a relatively few people taking this stand and inviting the government to come after them. I think a lot of working-class people—the backbone of the country—are behind us on this."

The protests continued, along with large-scale nonregistration, through 1980 and into 1981. This was a setback to the rulers' plans—at least to their timing.

**Debate over women and the draft**

At the same time another important, and countervailing, political development occurred. The original Carter proposal included women among those who would be required to register. Many in various women's rights organizations and other liberal forces swallowed the bait and began to insist that women had a "right" to be drafted into the imperialist murder machine. It was essential to fight for this "right," they argued. In doing so, they helped divert the debate away from registration and the draft, and from the war drive that this was a component of. The forces opposed to draft registration were divided. The success of this diversionary move was the Carter administration's first victory in its effort to reinstitute registration for the draft.

A campaign was organized by middle-class leaders of the women's movement, especially those of the National Organization for Women. They said they were opposed to the draft and to draft registration. But if registration is going to be the law, they argued, then women have the "right" to be part of it too. All their energies went into trying to assure that women would be required to register if the law was adopted. Many other liberals, both male and female, took the same position.

This did a double disservice. First, it reinforced the militarization drive by arguing that registration of women could be a step forward—as if drafting and killing women along with men to maintain the domination of imperialism is a step toward women's equality in the United States or anywhere else in the world! Second, it was used as the final argument to kill the Equal Rights Amendment to the U.S. Constitution, which at that time was wounded but still alive. By linking the fight for the ERA with extending draft registration and the draft to women, figures in NOW and other women's rights organizations gave the kiss of death to the ERA. The idea that ratification of the Equal Rights Amendment might bring closer the conscription of young women was used demagogically by the enemies of the ERA. Many women and men who had been inclined toward it, or undecided about it, turned against the amendment. It was enough to kill the ERA.

Shifting the debate onto the ground of how to make the registration law and a future draft more "fair" and "equitable" derailed and demobilized a significant section of the opposition to draft registration.

In June 1981, one year after the registration law went into effect, the Supreme Court ruled it constitutional.

### Reaction to first indictments of nonregistrants
That didn't settle the matter, however, even from a legal point of view. There were other challenges in the courts to the law and to its enforcement. It wasn't until another year had passed, in June 1982, that the first indictments were issued for failure to register. By the time these indictments were announced, the mass campaign against registration had long been demobilized.

There were some protest demonstrations, but they were significantly smaller than those that had occurred earlier. This was at a time when U.S. marines were already in Lebanon, the forces of the crumbling British empire had just occupied the Malvinas Islands, and the contra war against Nicaragua was escalating rapidly.

An important factor in the muted response to the first indictments was that it now appeared much less likely that draft registration would be followed by reintroduction of conscription itself. Two and a half years after the announcement of the new registration law, there was still no draft nor any substantial wing of the ruling class proposing to introduce one. Fear of the consequences of registration was reduced as a result.

This cut two ways. Separating out the registration law from the actual reintroduction of the draft made it easier for the government to get the registration machinery established. But the U.S. rulers also paid a price. The battle over reinstating draft registration had been won, but the battle over reinstating the draft itself was still going to have to be fought out at some future date. It had definitely not been won.

A second factor in the decrease in protests over the registration law was the government's selection of those to be indicted, which it thought out very politically. To date, only eighteen young men have been charged. Eighteen in five years. All but one has been an outspoken opponent of the registration law who has publicly stated that he was refusing to register as a matter of individual conscience or religious principle. The government made sure that the ones they put in the dock did not constitute a representative cross-section of the working people of this country. For example, not a single Black youth—to my knowledge—has been indicted for nonregistration. Nor a single Chicano youth, nor a single Puerto Rican. A good number have been religiously-motivated pacifists from middle-class homes, individuals who choose jail rather than conscription under any circumstances. It has been the opposite of a cross-section of the GIs who will have to die in imperialist adventures.

These eighteen themselves were indicted only after repeated letters, FBI visits, and other official moves by the government—giving them repeated chances to register, even after being indicted. This is what the government and courts have generally described as the "beg policy."

After the indictments finally began in 1982, there was another round of court battles. Opponents of registration challenged the indictments on the grounds that they violated the constitutionally protected right of free speech by selecting people for prosecution on the basis of their publicly expressed opinions. It was only in March 1985 that the Supreme Court finally ruled that the indictments had not unduly abridged constitutional rights. The judges argued that the government's "beg policy" made it clear that the individuals were indicted not for their opinions but for their refusal to register. Only in April 1985—five and a half years after Carter's announcement of the new registration law—did the first nonregistrant begin serving a prison sentence.

On September 10, 1985, David Wayte, one of the convicted nonregistrants, was sentenced to six months' "house arrest" at his grandmother's home. This is consistent with the government's pattern from the outset of singling out only publicly proclaimed nonregistrants from middle-class social backgrounds and handing down minimal sentences. Few Black, Puerto Rican, or other working-class young people have any illusion that they would end up with half a year at grandma's if they were to face prosecution even for shoplifting! The government thereby cranks up another notch the pressure to register, without having to resort to harsh sentences that could become a political liability.

**Tightening the legal net**

In the meantime, of course, the screws have been tightened on the tens of thousands of nonregistrants. The government is gradually drawing the legal net around those who had hoped simply to slip through. The so-called Solomon amendment, for example, bars federal college loans for those who haven't registered. This amendment—tacked on to another bill and adopted in 1982—was implemented, challenged in court and, in July 1984, declared constitutional by the Supreme Court. Numerous states have adopted similar laws. The Selective Service has instituted computer cross-checking of driver's licenses, voter registration lists, and other forms of identification to locate nonregistrants. The government has announced plans to extend these computer checks to college-loan applications, drawing the U.S. Department of Education into enforcement of the registration law.

The result of such measures has been an undeniable increase in the percentage of those registering. This reflects the shift in the opinion and response of young working people in face of stiffening enforcement of the registration law.

When we discussed the newly adopted registration law in 1980, we posed a number of questions for ourselves. The answers, we said, should guide our tactical stance toward the initial registration period. What were young workers thinking, and what were they going to do? What was the response of the young people we work with? Those we live next to? Those we are involved with in our unions? Were they going down to sign up? Or were they more likely to say, "Wait a minute, let's see what's happening on this. This whole thing isn't even constitutional yet." Once we posed it this way, we had no difficulty seeing that a large layer of our co-workers were saying, "Let's wait and see. Let it slide awhile."

And, of course, that is still the case for a good number. There are hundreds of thousands of young people who still haven't registered. They are hoping to just get lost in the bureaucratic shuffle, or to continue to be ignored by the federal cops and prosecutors. Some figure it's wiser to temporarily forgo applying for a driver's license, or better to use a slightly different name for a while, than to deal directly with registration.

But as the cops close in on them and they start getting letters from the Justice Department and then visits from the FBI, most young workers come to the reluctant conclusion that they had better sign that registration card. Not signing can lead to all kinds of hassles, while, who knows, registering may never lead to anything.

Many young men are like a friend Joe Swanson told me about. Joe's friend hadn't registered. He got some letters from the Justice Department, and he still didn't register. But when the FBI finally came around looking for him, he said, "I don't like this registration, and I'm against the draft. But I really don't want to go to jail for this. Not now. Not for this." So he filled out his card and mailed it in. But he did it under protest. Paraphrasing Eugene V. Debs he wrote on the form, "The only war I want to fight is the class war." The computer in Washington sent the card back to him, saying, "This card has been mutilated. This registration is invalid." So after giving them as much trouble as he thought he could get away with, he sent in his registration.

I'm not sure if this person is a member of the YSA today. If he isn't, he ought to be. We agree with his decision to register—and with his hatred for imperialist war and all mechanisms connected with it. As working-class fighters we're not interested in individual acts of moral witness. We don't advocate breaking capitalist laws, and we don't willfully break them. The stakes are much higher than this law or that law. What we're after is changing the class that makes the laws. And that can't be accomplished by individual acts, no matter how courageous or self-sacrificing they may be. It is not a question of individual stands by ones or twos, or even by hundreds or thousands, but of mobilizing the millions. That is why revolutionary working-class fighters never by their own choice end up in jail for long stays.

**Party and YSA policy on draft registration**
Since the registration law went into effect, young members of the SWP and the YSA have taken the same approach as other working people. Some of them have registered, many probably have not. There has been no party or YSA decision determining what young men in the movement should do about registering. We have had a political stance of solidarity and identification with those who were part of the initial mass nonregistration. But it was left to each individual comrade to make up his own mind about how this affected him.

Now, however, we have to shift in light of the evolution of the concrete situation. Opposition to draft registration, as a visible and public campaign, has declined. As far as the capitalist courts are concerned, the constitutionality of the law is no longer in doubt. Nor is there a legal cloud over the ability of the government to continue its selective prosecution of nonregistrants. That was settled a couple of months ago.

The registration question, moreover, has become—for now—separated not just from the question of the draft, but also from the developing movement against the U.S. drive toward war in Central America and the Caribbean. Nowhere on April 20 was the question of draft registration a prominent feature of the protests. As we have seen, this is in large part a product of the strength of the initial mobilizations that forced the ruling class to back off on the draft itself, as the price for establishing registration. Nonetheless, the retreat from a fight against registration is part of the reality we face today, and it has to be taken into account in connection with adopting a policy.

These factors are decisive. They are more important, it should be added, than the question of how many individuals aren't registering. By itself that doesn't mean much. There have always been substantial numbers of young men in the United States who didn't register for the draft—in the time of the Civil War, during World War I, in World War II, in the Korean War, throughout the fifties, and into the Vietnam War years. We can assume there will continue to be large numbers, in absolute terms, who will find ways to avoid registering.

But that is not our starting point. What we have to look at are not the actions of individuals, even a lot of individuals, but the evolution of the political battle, the class relationship of forces on this question, at this stage of the fight. There has been a significant shift in this relationship of forces from what existed in the first few years after the draft registration law was adopted. Therefore, we have to adjust our response.

The National Committee proposes that we adopt as party policy that every member who is required by law to register do so. We will recommend to the YSA that it follow the same course.[17]

OUR POLICY, then, can be summed up as follows:

1. We will continue to work with others to organize the broadest possible political opposition to capitalist conscription, and to all the laws and machinery that are being established to prepare for it and that will eventually be used to implement it. This is part of our opposition to the militarization drive of the rulers and their preparations for the use of U.S. troops to invade Nicaragua. That is our political stance.

2. Party members of registration age submit to the legal requirements of draft registration. They comply with the law—nothing more, nothing less.

3. We continue to seek to orient coalitions organizing actions

to advance the involvement of workers and farmers—including those in the armed forces. This means encouraging soldiers to exercise their constitutionally guaranteed rights to speak out and demonstrate against the war preparations of the rulers. Above all, it means selling them material that tells the truth about imperialism and war, and workers' stake in the fight to change the class that rules.

Who in this country has a greater stake in acting to halt the drive toward war than the young workers and farmers who face being sent into combat against the armed and organized workers and farmers of Nicaragua? And who has a greater right to speak out, to organize, to march, to rally against the preparations for that war?

### Bring the GIs into the developing antiwar movement!

This last point is worth taking a closer look at. It relates to what we and others accomplished in making the April 20 demonstrations so successful, and what that opens up for the future.

The April 20 demonstrations signaled the growing willingness of a range of political forces to unite in action against U.S. government policies in Central America. They were a turning point because of what they registered in terms of the possibilities that exist right now to deepen labor participation in the antiwar campaign and the anti-apartheid movement. The level of union development and political activity is far greater than at even the high point of the anti–Vietnam War actions. April 20 also registered an advance in the participation of layers of Black, Chicano, and Puerto Rican fighters, women, youth—all of the potential components of this movement that is beginning to be forged.

We don't know how this will develop, and we don't have to make predictions. *What we do have to do is to turn more deeply toward these openings.*

We also have to note one of the weaknesses of the April 20 actions, and one of the weaknesses of our participation in helping to organize them. No effort was made to draw in and highlight the participation of young workers and farmers who are in the armed forces—nor did we propose such an effort. Not a single active-duty GI was called to public attention as a participant in the April 20 actions. There were some GIs there— we know that—but involving them was not a conscious political goal of the April 20 coalition.

This was a default of the April 20 coalition. And it was especially a default of ours, because we more than anyone else ought to know better.

An orientation toward working people—including those in military uniform—is an essential part of a proletarian orientation for the antiwar movement. It is an essential part of the orientation and the activity of the forces that we are part of, the forces that are trying to lead the antiwar action movement forward. It is essential to deepening working-class sympathy and involvement.

We shouldn't have our eyes on some future army of draftees that has not yet been created. Our eyes should be on the hundreds of thousands of young working people in uniform *today*, who have a big stake in the fight against the war policies of the ruling class. It is an armed force made up of co-workers of ours, of brothers and sisters and sons and daughters of co-workers, and of working farmers. It is an armed force of young people, of Black and Puerto Rican and Chicano and Native American youth. It is a force that the antiwar action coalitions should turn toward, as they turn toward deepening the involvement of working people in the fight against the war drive of the rulers.

This is not a hard adjustment for us to make. It is part of our political training, our orientation. It is part of the tradition and experience of the SWP and YSA. And no one is in a better position to argue for it than us—workers active in our unions and in the movement against the drive toward war in Central America and the Caribbean.

But this will be a political battle. We will have to debate those who are against the war but do not share the perspective of taking this fight to the organizations of the working class.

We have no illusion about the character of the imperialist army and its role in the world and in this country. It is a reactionary world police force of millions. It is organized to spread murder and terror around the globe. It can't be reformed or "humanized" by adding more women to it, or anything else. Only when the victorious workers and farmers in this country take apart that military machine and put together a different one will the future survival of humanity be guaranteed.

But we also know that the ranks of the armed forces are different from those in the police forces. The army is made up of young workers and farmers who join the "volunteer" army for a couple of years to get off the streets and get some promised job training or money for future education. The overwhelming majority of these young people are not "lifers"; they don't plan to spend their lives in the army. They are not part of the officer caste. They do not see themselves as willing parts of a repressive machine. They do not identify with the ruling class. *Most important, they have not been declassed, as cops are.* When workers or farmers join the police force, they *abandon* their class. But young working people who sign up for the armed forces do so because of the economic situation they face; the last thing they want to do is to go fight and die to protect the profits of the ruling families.

What's more, these citizen-soldiers are constantly being subjected to attempts to deny them their constitutional rights. The high percentage who are members of oppressed nationalities face organized racist discrimination aimed, in part, at keeping soldiers divided among themselves and therefore more submissive to the demands of the military brass. At all times they confront the anti-working-class officer corps—Black as well as white.

As the preparations for war increase—and as the toll on life and limb turns out to be different from what they have been led to believe—more and more GIs will seek to express their views. They will reach out with both hands to anyone they can find in civilian life who will help them do so, and help defend their rights in the process.

Among these young workers and farmers who today find themselves in the military machine are individuals who will be won to a revolutionary perspective and will join the Young Socialist Alliance and the Socialist Workers Party.

## Working-class campaign against imperialism and war

As with every aspect of our communist antiwar program, our starting point is the working class, not some special focus on the armed forces. The challenge of organizing growing numbers of citizen-soldiers into the fight against imperialism and war is not a matter of getting antiwar action coalitions to pay more attention to a "GI sector." It is part of our effort to build the kind of movement that can mobilize the social forces, the class forces, necessary to stay the hand of the U.S. rulers.

The April 20 actions and the Peace, Jobs, and Justice Coalition that emerged out of them are important because of what they demonstrated about the growing opportunities in this country today to bring the working class and the labor movement more deeply into the struggle against apartheid and against Washington's drive toward war in Central America and the Caribbean. This opens the door to a more effective fight and better leadership.

The United Steelworkers union endorsed the April 20 demonstrations, along with eight other International unions. This confirms some of the arguments we have been making about the shift in the political situation in the United States over the past decade, and what that opens up for communist political work in the labor movement around the fight against the imperialist war drive in Central America. It brings new opportunities to deepen this work through the unions, and to draw them increasingly toward the center of this fight. It advances the overall politicization of the labor movement.

What developed this winter and spring enabled us to actually carry out—as a *nationwide* party, with *national* industrial union fractions[18]—the course of work in defense of the Nicaraguan revolution we decided on at our last convention, in August 1984.[19] There had been a limit to how effectively our branches and fractions could put this course into practice so long as there wasn't much *action* going on involving broader forces.

That was what changed with the call for the April 20 demonstrations against U.S. policy toward Central America. That opened up the biggest opportunity since the current militarization drive began in 1980 to do what the changes in U.S. politics convinced us it was now possible to do in the labor movement. And we will accomplish more along these lines this fall as we build the October 11 and October 19-26 actions, and prepare for the national demonstrations against the war drive, and in defense of abortion rights, already tentatively slated for spring 1986.[20]

## Capitalist militarization and the working class

With this orientation in mind, it is useful to return for a final look at the three ruling-class militarization drives outlined earlier in this report. This time, however, let's do so from the standpoint of the state of the labor movement at the time, and the position of the party in relation to the unions.

The first of these militarization drives—from late 1937 through the end of World War II—opened in the midst of the tumultuous battles that built the CIO. Our small forces were deeply involved in the rise of that social movement of our class and its allies. The founding SWP convention in 1938 adopted a turn to the industrial unions as national party policy, explaining that this was essential preparation for what the party—with its growing layer of new young recruits—and our class were confronting as Washington deepened its course toward war.[21]

The rulers used their war preparations, and above all the entry into World War II itself, to contain and push back this working-class radicalization. Farrell Dobbs's book *Teamster Bureaucracy*, the last of the four volumes in the series on the Teamsters, describes this militarization drive, the trade union campaign against it led by the class-struggle unionists in the Midwest Teamsters, and why our party leaders were targeted and railroaded to jail by the Roosevelt administration as part of the preparation for imperialist war.[22]

What the U.S. working class and its allies had conquered during the last half of the 1930s, however, set limits on how well the ruling class was able to maintain its antilabor course throughout World War II. By mid-1942 Black organizations were beginning to mount opposition to segregation and inequality in the war industries, the government, and the armed forces. A march on Washington was called for July 1, 1942, by leaders of the Brotherhood of Sleeping Car Porters, the NAACP, and the Urban League, before being canceled under government pressure. The following year the coal miners' strikes challenged the wartime "labor peace" that the rulers sought to impose on the unions, with active collaboration from the big majority of the officialdom.[23]

The next three years saw the "Bring us home" movement, a massive strike wave in this country, and further battles for civil rights. These struggles then bumped up against the onset of the postwar economic expansion and political reaction.

The next ruling-class militarization drive, beginning in 1947 and continuing through the withdrawal of U.S. ground troops from Vietnam in 1973, was marked by the political retreat of the CIO industrial unions. The strengthened position of U.S. capitalism coming out of World War II made possible economic concessions by the bosses to broad layers of organized industrial workers. This tended to mask the degree to which the unions were being progressively weakened by the consolidation of the bureaucracy and the class-collaborationist course it was fastening on them.

Many socialists and other militants were hounded and witchhunted out of the unions. Opportunities to carry out political work in the unions sharply declined. The one major workingclass movement that did arise in the late 1950s, the mass struggle to defeat Jim Crow segregation, originated and developed largely outside the unions, although involving many veterans of the labor battles of the previous two decades.

In contrast to our situation during the militarization drive of the late 1930s, the SWP was shrinking. Even though a substantial percentage of our members were still working in industry and remained union members, the party was sharply restricted in its ability to carry out any organized, ongoing political work through rank-and-file local and national industrial union fractions. We had lost our national trade-union fraction structure.

THE STATE OF the U.S. labor movement throughout the Vietnam War determined the character and limits of our revolutionary working-class antiwar policy. Our goal from the outset was to build the kind of movement that would mobilize growing numbers of working people, but our opportunities to do this through the unions, from a base within the labor movement, were scant. We fought to orient the antiwar movement toward involving GIs and winning the active support of organizations of Blacks, Chicanos, and Puerto Ricans. We took advantage of the few openings that did develop to get union endorsement and involvement on any level possible, and such opportunities did increase as opposition to the war mounted at the end of the 1960s and early 1970s.

Even at the high point of organized protests against the Vietnam War, however, nothing comparable to endorsement of a demonstration by the United Steelworkers or any other major International union ever occurred. There were no union-sponsored tours to Vietnam, such as those that do take place, even if modest in scale, to Nicaragua and El Salvador today. Vietnamese trade union leaders were never invited to speak before meetings of U.S. unions and labor federations. There was nothing like the kind of involvement by farmers and farm organizations that has begun to develop even at this stage in the fight against the U.S. war drive in Central America and the Caribbean.

That brings us to the changes in the working class, the labor movement, and the SWP in face of the current militarization drive of the ruling class.

## Offensive at home and abroad

From the beginning, the war preparations of the U.S. ruling class have been part and parcel of a mounting assault on the rights and living standards of workers and farmers in this country as deepening competition abroad and economic shocks continue to be felt by the employers. The capitalists are increasingly taking aim at the U.S. labor movement, including the industrial unions. As our 1985 political resolution puts it, "This onslaught, its effects, and the emerging resistance to it by the ranks have moved the industrial working class and its unions to the center of politics in the United States for the first time in almost four decades."

As a result, working people are more open to recognizing the interconnections between the bosses' war drive and the offensive against the unions and working conditions, wages, job rights, and social services. The parallels between the brutal pressures on working farmers in this country and what the rulers are doing to the working people of Central America, South Africa, and the Middle East are more easily seen.

Although there are guerrilla battles and resistance by the ranks, the weakening of the unions over the past decades is being demonstrated by the unrelenting blows our class is sustaining in the absence so far of any organized fightback by the labor movement. Especially since the blows of the 1981-82 recession, the bosses have succeeded in organizing a rout of the unions.

At the same time, we are finding greater opportunities right now to carry out political work in the unions—against the imperialist war drive in Central America, and around other social and political questions—than at any time since the opening of the capitalist offensive in the mid-1970s. We do not see large-scale anti-imperialist consciousness developing in the ranks, let alone rising revolutionary class consciousness. But there is greater interest and more willingness to take action. That is what has changed, and it is having an impact inside the unions.

Another important thing has changed since the Vietnam War period. A big majority of party members today hold industrial union jobs, as do a good number of members of the YSA. We are building nine national industrial union fractions. We're gaining experience as worker-bolsheviks and as revolutionary union politicians. We're making progress in strengthening our national fractions. This is improving our branch institutions and our effectiveness as a nationwide campaign party.

For these reasons, our orientation in the fight against imperialist war today is as different from that of the anti–Vietnam War period as our orientation during the Vietnam War was from that leading up to and during World War II. Although there are no struggles comparable to the rise of the CIO, the period we have entered has more in common with the late 1920s and early 1930s than with the late 1960s.

# NOTES

1. Following the U.S. Civil War, Radical Reconstruction regimes were established in the southern states, authorized by the U.S. Congress and backed by the Union army. These legislatures, led for the first time by both Black and white elected representatives, repealed forced-labor laws and established universal male suffrage. Social reforms were carried out by these legislatures—the most far-reaching in South Carolina and Mississippi—and by local governments in other states. Ambitious literacy drives were organized in many areas. Public schools were established for the first time throughout the South. Apprenticeship and training programs were launched.

The aspiration for land and the wherewithal to till it among the freed slaves and landless white farmers was central to the class struggles that marked the radical thrust of the Reconstruction regimes during the decade following 1867. Only with "forty acres and a mule" could the mass of Black laborers have escaped the agricultural work gangs that replaced the slave-based plantation economy and have moved forward, together with poor whites, as free farmers.

The U.S. Congress, however, refused to institute a thorough-going land reform. While a few state legislatures made some land available at low cost (the most advanced case being South Carolina, which also provided cheap credit), the Radical Reconstruction regimes did not expropriate the land of the big plantation owners and distribute it to the freed slaves or landless whites. This failure above all allowed the exploiting classes in the South to rebuild their power and launch a campaign of legal and extralegal terror against Blacks and other working people.

By 1877 northern capitalists sought to block the growing alliance of Black and white farmers and workers in the South. Congress withdrew Union soldiers and gave free reign to armed reaction. This opened the road during the years that followed for Jim Crow, the system of legal segregation, to be imposed to divide working people along skin-color lines. Racism and anti-working-class reaction were given a powerful boost throughout the United States. The Black population was transformed into an oppressed national-ity. The resurgent racism during the closing decades of the century was intertwined with the rising imperialist militarism and was used to justify the assault on the people of Hawaii and the Philippines especially.

The defeat of Radical Reconstruction marked the most serious setback to the U.S. working class, North and South, in its history. (For a discussion of the place of Radical Reconstruction in the history of the class struggle in the United States, see Jack Barnes, "The Fight for a Workers' and Farmers' Government in the United States," in *New International*, no. 4, pp. 168-72.)

2.  U.S. forces, first sent to Vietnam in 1950 as "advisers," eventu-ally numbered 536,000 at their high point. In January 1973, after long negotiations, peace accords were signed in Paris. By March 1973 U.S. combat forces had been withdrawn. The Watergate crisis that erupted later that year began with the public exposure of the fact that the White House under President Richard Nixon had utilized burglaries and wiretaps and authorized FBI operations against even Democratic Party political competitors. Such methods had long been used against working-class organizations and the

Black movement. The ensuing political crisis, rooted in deep divisions within the ruling class over Washington's defeat in Vietnam, led to the forced resignation of Nixon in 1974. Widely publicized congressional hearings in 1975-76—during which many more facts became known about the murderous operations of the FBI, CIA, and other political police agencies, both in the United States and abroad—further undermined public confidence in the truthfulness of those who spoke for U.S. government institutions.

3. Students, with the backing of the Iranian government, occupied the U.S. embassy in Tehran in November 1979 to protest Washington's decision to invite the deposed shah to the United States. Soviet troops—eventually numbering more than one hundred thousand—intervened in Afghanistan in late December 1979.

4. Executive Order 9835, issued by Truman in March 1947, made "disloyalty" grounds for dismissal from government employment. The order defined disloyalty as association with any organization deemed "subversive" by the attorney general. That same month the White House sent military advisers to bolster the reactionary government of Greece, then fighting a civil war against Communist Party–led partisans, and announced plans to send $300 million in arms and economic aid.

5. The Transitional Program was one of the founding documents of the Socialist Workers Party. Written by Leon Trotsky in Mexico City after discussions with SWP leaders, it was adopted by the SWP in 1938 following extensive discussion. For the section cited here, see Leon Trotsky, *The Transitional Program for Socialist Revolution* (New York: Pathfinder, 1977), pp. 123-26.

6. "Security clearances" often include a police "check" on an individual's background, associates, political views, and personal life. They remain a condition of employment at many U.S. plants with government contracts.

7. On August 2, 1964, two U.S. destroyers patrolling near the coast of North Vietnam were allegedly fired upon by North Vietnamese torpedo boats. President Lyndon Johnson used this staged incident as the pretext to launch the first U.S. bombing raids on North Vietnam and to press through Congress the infamous Gulf of Tonkin resolution, later used as the authority for massive escalation of the war. It was subsequently revealed that a draft of the resolution had been prepared nearly two months before the incident.

8. A broad coalition of forces, based on organizations of the oppressed nationality of Mexican origin, organized protests against the Vietnam War in 1970 under the name Chicano Moratorium.

Local demonstrations in California, Texas, New Mexico, and Colorado preceded a national Chicano Moratorium demonstration in Los Angeles, August 29, 1970. The action, which drew twenty-five thousand participants, was the largest protest against the war up to that time in Los Angeles and registered the confidence and political consciousness of a growing Chicano liberation movement.

9. Lawsuits in the 1970s by the Socialist Workers Party and Young Socialist Alliance, as well as by other organizations and individuals, forced the FBI to turn over hundreds of thousands of pages of previously secret documents detailing a political disruption program—code-named Cointelpro—aimed at communist groups, Black rights organizations, antiwar organizations, and their members and supporters. For more information on this more than decade-long political-police operation, see Nelson Blackstock, *Cointelpro: The FBI's Secret War on Political Freedom*, 3d ed. (New York: Anchor Foundation, a Pathfinder book, 1988); Margaret Jayko, *FBI on Trial* (New York: Pathfinder, 1988); Larry Seigle, "Washington's Fifty-Year Domestic Contra Operation," in *New International*, no. 6, pp. 157-203; and George Breitman, Herman Porter, and Baxter Smith, *The Assassination of Malcolm X*, 3d ed. (New York: Pathfinder, 1991).

10. Following the overthrow of the Somoza dictatorship in July 1979, Washington began to finance, train, and organize a mercenary army—the contras—to wage war against the new workers' and farmers' government in Nicaragua, led by the Sandinista National Liberation Front (FSLN). The contra forces were militarily defeated in a hard-fought and draining seven-year war that concluded in March 1988, but the political retreat of the Sandinista leadership led to the erosion and eventual downfall of the workers' and farmers' government. In March 1990 the FSLN lost the presidential and National Assembly election to the United National Opposition slate headed by Violeta Chamorro.

11. Washington sent marines to Beirut in August 1982, to help oversee the forced expulsion of more than seven thousand supporters of the Palestine Liberation Organization. At their peak, U.S. forces based in Lebanon and just off shore numbered three thousand marines, a naval task force of twelve ships, and ninety aircraft.

12. In April 1982, British government troops, backed by U.S. military intelligence and supply efforts, invaded the Malvinas, a group of islands off the coast of Argentina over which Buenos Aires

had sought to reestablish its sovereignty.

13.  U.S. troops invaded Grenada October 25-26, 1983. The invasion force, eventually numbering more than seven thousand, landed a week after the murder of Prime Minister Maurice Bishop and the overthrow of the workers' and farmers' government in a Stalinist coup led by Deputy Prime Minister Bernard Coard.

14.  More than twenty persons were indicted in U.S. courts on "espionage" charges in the early 1980s, including nine in 1984 alone.

15.  On April 26, 1980, more than twenty-five thousand marched in Washington, D.C., to protest nuclear power plants and weapons.

16.  More than five thousand marched in Washington May 17, 1980, to demand "jobs, not war." The demonstration was called by Operation PUSH, a Chicago-based organization founded by Jesse Jackson.

17.  The August 16, 1985, meeting of the YSA National Committee also discussed and adopted this policy.

18.  The term *fraction* refers to the percentage of members of the union who are members of the Socialist Workers Party. At the time this report was given the SWP had nine industrial union fractions, in the Amalgamated Clothing and Textile Workers (ACTWU); International Association of Machinists (IAM); International Ladies' Garment Workers' Union (ILGWU); Oil, Chemical and Atomic Workers (OCAW); International Union of Electronic Workers (IUE); United Auto Workers (UAW); United Mine Workers of America (UMWA); United Steelworkers of America (USWA); and United Transportation Union (UTU). A tenth national industrial union fraction was added in 1986, in the United Food and Commercial Workers (UFCW).

For an overview of the interconnection between the industrial fraction and other work in building a communist party, see Jack Barnes, *The Changing Face of U.S. Politics: The Proletarian Party and the Trade Unions* (New York: Pathfinder, 1981).

19.  The resolution discussed and approved in draft form at this convention, "The Revolutionary Perspective and Leninist Continuity in the United States," is published in *New International*, no. 4, pp. 7-97.

20.  Thousands took part in anti-apartheid protests in cities around the United States October 11-12, 1985, and in demonstrations October 25 and November 1 protesting U.S. intervention in Central America and Washington's ties to apartheid. Major actions the following spring included a demonstration of 100,000 in Washington, D.C., March 9, 1986, in defense of abortion rights; 25,000 in

San Francisco April 19 protesting the U.S.-organized war against Nicaragua; and 100,000 in New York City June 14 demanding an end to U.S. ties to apartheid.

21. See the resolution "The Trade Union Movement and the Socialist Workers Party," adopted at the SWP founding convention in January 1938. The resolution is contained in *The Founding of the Socialist Workers Party* (New York: Anchor Foundation, a Pathfinder book, 1982), pp. 111-28.

22. *Teamster Rebellion, Teamster Power, Teamster Politics,* and *Teamster Bureaucracy* make up a four-volume series on the 1930s strikes and organizing drive that transformed the Teamsters union in Minneapolis and the Midwest into a fighting industrial union movement. These Pathfinder books were written by Farrell Dobbs, a leader of these labor battles and later national secretary of the SWP.

23. The half-million-member United Mine Workers union, forced out on strike by soaring inflation and deteriorating safety conditions, shut down nationwide coal production four times in 1943, defying attempts to block them from acting on grounds of wartime "national unity." For an account of these strikes see "How the Miners Won," in Art Preis, *Labor's Giant Step* (New York: Pathfinder, 1972), pp. 174-97. A week-by-week account of the wartime struggles against segregation, taken from the pages of the *Militant,* is found in C.L.R. James et al., *Fighting Racism in World War II* (New York: Anchor Foundation, a Pathfinder book, 1980).

# THE COMMUNIST ANTIWAR PROGRAM
# OF THE SOCIALIST WORKERS PARTY
# 1940 TO 1969

**M**ILITARY POLICY is an essential part of any transitional program of the revolutionary party in the imperialist epoch with its monstrous growth of capitalist militarism. The naive outlook of the early socialist movement, which disregarded the military aspects of the class struggle, has long since become outmoded. The actual relations between nations, peoples, and classes compel every political tendency to take a position and work out a policy toward both imperialist and class warfare.

The position of the Socialist Workers Party in this field as in others has been derived from Marxist principles and the methods and traditions of bolshevism. This general line has been consistently followed from the beginning of our movement in this country.[1] But since 1940 the tactical application of this course has twice been modified because of changes in objective circumstances.

In 1940, on the eve of the impending U.S. entry into World War II, the SWP set forth its revolutionary socialist antiwar program in the form of the proletarian military policy. This represented a specific application of the methods of the Transitional Program adopted in 1938 to the working-class psychology and political conditions of the time.[2]

The program was based on the following concepts: (1) it continued our irreconcilable opposition to imperialist war and the capitalist system that breeds it; (2) it projected the perspec-

---

*The September 1969 convention of the Socialist Workers Party adopted a resolution entitled "The Fight against the Vietnam War." Published here is part 2 of that resolution.*

*ENDNOTES FOR THIS ARTICLE BEGIN ON PAGE 276.*

tive of a struggle to win leadership of the working class in order to carry through a fight for state power and establish a socialist society; and (3) it laid stress on the need to build a Leninist-type party to fulfill these objectives.

Our approach was categorically counterposed to the misleading ideas and political confusion sowed by the professional pacifists and the Stalinists and social democrats on the issues of militarism.

The pacifists proceed on the utopian premise that the laws of the class struggle and capitalist competition can be nullified by the cooperation of people of goodwill who can prevail upon the imperialists to refrain from war making. Pacifists oppose the development of the class struggle in favor of class peace at almost any price.

From their moral and religious opposition to violence as such, and not simply to reactionary violence, flows a rejection of the right of armed self-defense. They substitute individual "witness" for organized collective action. Their conscientious objection to military conscription and training leads to draft evasion or victimization by imprisonment, which further isolates antiwar elements from the masses.

Pacifist ideology is as pernicious and prostrating under wartime conditions as in times of sharp class conflict. It demoralizes and disorients antiwar activists and movements, deters mass mobilizations, and plays into the hands of the imperialists.

Pacifism as a policy may look plausible so long as peaceful relations prevail, but it collapses like a pricked balloon as soon as hostilities are declared. In previous periods many professional pacifists have turned into fanatical war supporters once the ruling class has plunged the nation into battle.

MARXISTS, on the other hand, have always recognized that under military conditions a military policy is mandatory.

In addition to their false line of class collaboration and supporting "peace" candidates who surrender to the warmongers, the Stalinists and social democrats take positions that are not essentially different from the simple antimilitarist attitudes of the pure pacifists and that prove to be equally impotent in the struggle against capitalism and its wars. Historically they too have capitulated to the warring state power after war has broken out, or else they have refrained from advancing or acting upon a program of struggle to take state power from the capitalist rulers—the only way that capitalist militarism and imperialist wars can be abolished.

The military policy adopted in 1940 was a revolutionary line designed to promote the anticapitalist struggles of the workers under the given wartime conditions.

It was anticipated that proletarian revolutions would emerge in the advanced capitalist countries directly out of the consequences of World War II and that the worker masses in the giant conscript armies would play the decisive role in them.

The transitional measures proposed in the program were to be a bridge from the revolutionary vanguard to the young worker-soldiers drafted into the U.S. armed forces, who were imbued with a mixture of anti-Hitler, antifascist, defensist, democratic, and patriotic sentiments. They aimed to develop an assertion of their class independence within the capitalist military machine, so that it would be possible to proceed step by step toward winning ideological and political hegemony among them in preparation for the anticipated revolutionary upsurge.

This undertaking was politically prepared and reinforced by the party's public opposition to the imperialist war, dramatized by the 1941 Smith Act trial and its documentation.[3]

As part of its program, the party continued its unconditional opposition to capitalist conscription. At the same time, it took cognizance of the fact that the antifascist and patriotic sentiments of the workers led them to favor compulsory military service. It therefore counterposed the concept of conscription by the workers' organizations to the capitalist military draft. It advocated military training under trade union control, financed by the capitalist government.

These proposals aimed to build class-conscious workers' military formations capable of defending labor's interests under conditions of capitalist militarism, imperialist war, and the threat of fascist counterrevolution.

Party members called up for military service submitted, as individuals, to capitalist conscription. In the armed forces they lent themselves to learning military skills and sought to win the political confidence of their fellow soldiers. Their participation as socialists in the military machine was viewed as a prerequisite for revolutionary action if a favorable turn of events made it possible to gain a majority to the idea of transforming the imperialist war into a struggle for workers' power and socialism.

This set of measures, presented in propaganda form at the outset of the war, did not become the basis for any substantial action during the conflict because the actual pattern of events took a different turn that did not coincide with our expectations.

The most radical development that took place in the army was the "We want to go home" movement of the GIs at the end of the war in the Pacific, which upset the plans of the Pentagon strategists by weakening their armed forces.

Although revolutionary situations erupted in Western Europe, no victorious revolutions occurred in the advanced capitalist countries.[4] The axis of the world revolution shifted to the colonial world.

THESE POSTWAR conditions created a world situation that was qualitatively different from that of the 1941-45 period. However important interimperialist rivalries remain, they have been subordinated to imperialism's Cold War against the workers' states and its military interventions against the colonial revolutions. The U.S. armed forces have become the principal instrument of world imperialist aggression.

These global developments have generated marked changes in the views of the American people toward the issues posed by Washington's armed interventions. U.S. involvement in World War II was almost unanimously accepted under the illusion that it was a progressive war waged against fascism.

While a noticeable and a significant decline in patriotic fervor was registered during the Korean War of the early 1950s, active and overt opposition was pretty much confined to circles on the left, which were then on the decline.

Vietnam has brought about a decisive shift in popular attitudes toward imperialist war. An unprecedented antiwar movement has emerged and continues to win more and more supporters in the midst of a shooting war. It is led by insurgent youth who belong to the post-witch-hunt generation and who have been radicalized by the colonial revolution and the Black liberation struggle.

Instead of urging on the government to victory at all costs, among large sections of the population defeatist moods have been gaining ground since 1965. This resistance to the imperialists expresses itself directly in sympathy for the Vietnamese revolution and indirectly through condemnation of the war as illegal, immoral, and unjust, and in the reluctance of organized workers and Blacks to make any material sacrifices for the war effort.

This country's ruling class is having to pay the toll of its function as the chief guardian of world capitalism. In becoming the top dog of the imperialist pack, it has fallen prey to all the basic contradictions of international capitalism in its death agony. Washington is obliged to finance and provide the main military means required for increasingly massive measures to stem the tide of the anti-imperialist and anticapitalist mass struggles throughout the world.

The heavy costs of this course are being levied upon the people in the form of conscription and sizable military casualties; mounting taxes and inflationary pressures on real wages;[5] and gross neglect of urgent social needs. These consequences of imperialist militarism have caused more and more Americans to question the Vietnam conflict and the official rationale for its prosecution. The official demagogy and barefaced deceit employed by the government to justify U.S. intervention have generated widespread suspicion. The growing criticism of imperialist policy and resentment against the war keeps adding to the number of Americans who want to bring it to a speedy halt.

The pacifist sentiments of the masses have a different significance than the ideology and policies of the professional pacifists. They grow out of distrust of the foreign policy imposed by the monopolists and militarists and revulsion against their aggression that have a revolutionary potential. If these healthy instincts can be deepened, politically developed, and properly directed, they can become the basis and point of departure for the creation of a mass anticapitalist consciousness that can pass beyond the narrow political limits set up by the professional pacifists and their fellow class-collaborationists who have dominated previous "peace" movements.

The task of our party is to direct this antiwar protest into class-struggle channels. To make its military policy fit the new international and domestic conditions, the party has introduced the following changes in its tactics:

The slogan of military training under trade union control has been laid aside, along with the advocacy of conscription into workers' military organizations.

More emphasis is placed upon opposing capitalist conscription, which is becoming increasingly unpopular.

As in the past, party members called up for military service submit to the draft.

In doing so, they refuse to sign the unconstitutional loyalty oath now made part of the conscription procedure.

Although the main weight of the antiwar movement continues to center in the civilian population, the opposition to the war that has developed within the present conscript army has added a new and extremely important dimension to the forces involved in the fight against the imperialist war makers. Revolutionary socialists within the armed forces focus their political activity on the assertion and defense of their constitutional right to express their views as citizens upon the war and other issues of government policy, using sound tactical judgment in exercising that right and avoiding disciplinary hang-ups and penalties over routine military matters and orders.[6]

The basic aim of our current transitional approach is the same as its predecessor. It seeks to promote a struggle for power and socialism by the workers and their allies and to build a strong, democratically disciplined combat party capable of leading that struggle to the end.

# NOTES

1. The Socialist Workers Party traces its continuity to the founding of the Communist Party in the United States in 1919. Revolutionary workers and other fighters inspired by and seeking to learn

from the Bolshevik leadership of the victorious October 1917 revolution in Russia came together in a political party that was part of the newly founded Communist International (Comintern). For an account of this, see Farrell Dobbs, *Revolutionary Continuity: Birth of the Communist Movement, 1918-1922* (New York: Anchor Foundation, a Pathfinder book, 1983).

Following the degeneration of the Communist International under Stalin, a small minority of the U.S. Communist Party—including some of its central leaders and delegates to Comintern congresses—rejected the party's and the Comintern's anti-Leninist course and continued to fight for a communist perspective. Expelled in 1928, they began publishing the *Militant* newspaper and founded the Communist League of America. Reinforced by new layers of revolutionary workers, the communist cadres formed the Socialist Workers Party in 1938. For further information, see James P. Cannon, *The History of American Trotskyism* (New York: Pathfinder, 1972).

2. For more on the SWP's revolutionary socialist antiwar policy during World War II, see "Military Policy of the Proletariat" and "Summary Speech on the Proletarian Military Policy," in James P. Cannon, *The Socialist Workers Party in World War II* (New York: Pathfinder, 1975), pp. 66-83, 93-103. Also see "The Manifesto of the Fourth International on the Imperialist War and the Proletarian World Revolution," in *Writings of Leon Trotsky (1939-40)* (New York: Pathfinder, 1973), pp. 183-222.

3. Enacted in June 1940 as part of the militarization drive that prepared U.S. entry into World War II, the Smith Act was intended and used to break the organized class-struggle vanguard of the labor movement that was leading opposition to Washington's imperialist war preparations. The law provided stiff jail terms for advocacy of views deemed seditious. First to be convicted under the new law were eighteen leaders of General Drivers Local 544 in Minnesota and the Socialist Workers Party. On December 8, 1941, the day after the bombing of Pearl Harbor, the Minneapolis defendants were given sentences ranging from twelve to eighteen months in prison. Following World War II the Smith Act was also used to railroad leaders of the Communist Party to jail. In 1958 the most important provisions of the thought-control law were declared unconstitutional. See James P. Cannon, *Socialism on Trial* (New York: Pathfinder, 1973); Farrell Dobbs, *Teamster Bureaucracy* (New York: Anchor Foundation, a Pathfinder book, 1977).

4. Toward the end of the Second World War, massive working-class upsurges occurred in a number of Western European coun-

tries as the Nazi occupation came to an end. In some areas, armed partisan units led by the Communist Party were the dominant force as the German troops withdrew. However, on the basis of the deal struck by Roosevelt, Churchill, and Stalin at Yalta, for a division of European spheres of influence, the Communist parties in Western Europe backed the reimposition of capitalist governments and ordered workers to surrender their arms.

5. By the late 1960s, large-scale military spending to finance the Vietnam War had begun to fuel an inflationary spiral. This halted what had been a steady rise in real wages since the end of the Second World War.

6. During the Vietnam War numerous attempts were made by the military command to intimidate, victimize, and silence GIs who insisted on their constitutional rights to freedom of expression and freedom of association. The most significant fight on this issue was the 1969 case of the Fort Jackson 8. After up to sixty days in the stockade at Fort Jackson on charges that included disrespect, holding an illegal demonstration, and disobeying an order for getting together to listen to tapes of Malcolm X and discuss the war, the army brass decided to drop the charges rather than court-martial them. Andrew Pulley, one of the Fort Jackson 8 defendants and an organizer of GIs United Against the War, ran for president of the United States in 1980 on the Socialist Workers Party ticket. See Fred Halstead, *GIs Speak Out against the War: The Case of the Fort Jackson 8* (New York: Pathfinder, 1970); and Andrew Pulley, *How I Became a Socialist* (New York: Pathfinder, 1981).

# 1945: WHEN U.S. TROOPS SAID 'NO!'

## A hidden chapter in the fight against war

*by Mary-Alice Waters*

THE WAR IN VIETNAM has had profound effects on the entire American population. As the war continues to escalate step by step toward a massive land war in Asia, the opposition among the U.S. population also rises steadily.

This opposition is reflected among the troops themselves, who are more and more voicing their hesitations about fighting in Vietnam. It is in this context that the post–World War II troop demonstrations in the U.S. Army take on special historical significance.

It is accurate to call this a "hidden chapter in the fight against war," because the vast majority of our generation is unaware that the greatest troop revolt that has ever occurred in a victorious army took place at the end of 1945 and the beginning of 1946. The central issue was whether U.S. troops would be demobilized, or whether they would be kept in the Pacific to protect Western interests from the growing colonial revolution.

The typical American college textbook makes at best a passing reference to the "Bring us home" movement. A good example is found in *The American Republic* by Hofstadter, Miller, and Aaron (p. 641): "At the end of the war, strong pressure arose within the army and among civilians for the return of American soldiers from overseas. The government responded so quickly that for a time it seemed that we might be incapable of even occupying the countries we had defeated." The text then goes on to state that this "impaired the United States position in

---

*This article first appeared in the November-December 1965 issue of the* Young Socialist, *published by the Young Socialist Alliance. It was later published as a Young Socialist pamphlet and widely distributed throughout the years of the anti–Vietnam War movement.*

international affairs."

This is the officially endorsed interpretation of the troop revolts and their consequences. American military officials said the same thing in order to defend themselves against the angry demands of the troops and their supporters in the United States. But the GIs had another point of view on demobilization. A pamphlet issued by the Soldiers' Committee in Manila during the height of the demonstrations declared:

> According to a War Department spokesman, demobilization is proceeding at alarming rapidity. Alarming from whose point of view? Alarming to generals and colonels who want to go on playing war and who do not want to go back to being captains and majors? Alarming to businessmen who stand to make money having their investments rebuilt at army expense? Alarming to the State Department, which wants an army to back its imperialism in the Far East?

The conflicting interests expressed in these two quotations generated a mass movement that changed the entire course of postwar history.

### Resentment among troops explodes

When V-J Day brought an end to the war in the Pacific,[1] the American troops expected to be speedily returned to the United States. Quite naturally, they felt there was no longer any need for fifteen million men in arms and that they should be released.

Contrary to their expectations, however, the army command started transferring combat troops from Europe to the Pacific. The official explanation was that troops were needed for occupation duty. Congress was immediately flooded with petitions and letters from the GIs protesting this action. Even the White House announced on August 21, 1945, that it had received a protest telegram from 580 members of the Ninety-fifth Division stationed at Camp Shelby, Mississippi.

The Ninety-seventh Infantry Division, which had already

*ENDNOTES FOR THIS ARTICLE BEGIN ON PAGE 299.*

spent five and a half months in Europe, was ordered to the Pacific. En route across the United States the soldiers displayed signs from the train windows saying, "Shanghaied for the Pacific," "We're being sold down the river while Congress vacations," and "Why do we go from here?" Two reporters who tried to interview soldiers on the train were arrested by military police under the pretext that troop movements were still classified information. The reporters were released several hours later, after the Twin Cities military security officer reprimanded the troops' commanding officers for exceeding their authority.

Throughout the fall of 1945 the campaign to bring the men home increased as families and friends held mass meetings across the country, and as resentment among the troops grew stronger. Columnist Drew Pearson reported on September 15, "Gen. Harry Lewis Twaddle, commander of the Ninety-fifth Division, Camp Shelby, Mississippi [the same group that had earlier protested to the White House] assembled his troops to explain occupation duty in Japan. The boos from the soldiers were so prolonged and frequent, it took him forty minutes to deliver a fifteen-minute speech."

By December, the resentment among the troops had reached explosive proportions. On Christmas day in Manila 4,000 troops marched on the Twenty-first Replacement Depot headquarters carrying banners demanding, "We want ships." The demonstration, touched off by the cancellation of a troop transport scheduled to return men to the United States, lasted only ten minutes. But the high point of the day occurred when the enraged depot commander, Col. J.C. Campbell, thundered, "You men forget you're not working for General Motors. You're still in the army." At that time there were 225,000 workers on strike against General Motors at plants across the United States. Since the GI demonstrations coincided with the greatest labor upsurge in U.S. history, the obvious similarities between the actions of the soldiers and the actions of the striking workers back home drew comments from many quarters.

The New York newspaper *PM* carried a January 13, 1946, dispatch from Nuremberg, Germany, saying:

The fact is the GIs have strike fever. Almost every

> soldier you talk to is full of resentment, humiliation, and
> anger. . . . The GIs now feel they have a legitimate gripe
> against their employers. If the gripe does not include a
> wage scale, that is purely a minor consideration. They
> don't like their conditions of work, they don't like the
> length of their contract, they don't like their bosses.

On December 26, the day after the large demonstration in
Manila, Colonel Krieger, an army personnel officer in the Philippines, assured 15,000 men in the replacement depots that
they would be swiftly returned to the United States. On January
4 Lt. Gen. Lawton Collins, director of Army Information, admit-
ted that shipping was available to bring back all eligible men
overseas in three months.

Within days, however, *Stars and Stripes,* the widely read army
newspaper, carried an announcement by the War Department
that Pacific demobilizations would be *cut* from 800,000 to
300,000 per month due to the difficulties in obtaining replacements.

The GIs were infuriated. Their mood was well expressed by a
soldier whose letter was read into the *Congressional Record* on
January 23, 1946. He wrote, "First it is no ships, now no replacements; are we going to sit by and let them blackmail our families
and hold us hostages to push through their compulsory military
training program?"[2]

On January 6, 1946, thousands of these "hostages" demonstrated at different points in Manila. One group was dispersed
at Quezon Bridge and another broken up by military police as it
approached Lt. Gen. William D. Styer's headquarters.

The demonstrations continued on January 7. More than
2,500 men marched four abreast to the general's headquarters
carrying banners reading, "What does eligible mean?" "Service
yes, but serfdom never," and "We're tired of false promises,
double-talk, and double-crossing." They distributed mimeo-
graphed leaflets saying, "Redeployment has been deliberately
slowed down to force compulsory military training. . . . The
State Department wants the army to back up its imperialism."

That night, according to various reports, between 12,000 and
20,000 soldiers jammed into the bombed-out shell of the Philip-
pine Hall of Congress to continue the demonstration and listen

to speakers angrily denounce U.S. aggression in north China and the Netherlands Indies (Indonesia), and demand that the Philippines be allowed to settle its own internal problems.[3] A UPI dispatch from Manila on January 7 described the capital as "tense."

## The demonstrations spread

As news of these mass protests spread, the wave of GI protests began to sweep around the world. On January 7, the second day of demonstrating in Manila, 2,000 GIs staged a mass meeting at Camp Boston, France, demanding a speedup in European demobilization. That same day, 6,000 soldiers on the Pacific island of Saipan wired protests against the slowdown in demobilization, and on Guam 3,500 enlisted men of the 315th Bombing Wing of the Twentieth Air Force staged a hunger strike. The following day on Guam, 18,000 men took part in two giant protest meetings. From Hawaii, Alaska, and Japan, thousands of cablegrams flooded into the United States. Directed at friends, families, Congress, churches, veterans' groups, and unions, the message demanded that pressure be put on the War Department to bring the troops home.

In Yokohama, Japan, 500 GIs met to plan for larger demonstrations. In Reims, France, 1,500 gathered to protest "illogical explanations" of the demobilization slowdown. In Paris, posters reading, "Don't let our Manila buddies down. Meeting, Arc de Triomphe, 8:30," drew over a thousand GIs who paraded down the Champs-Élysées to the American embassy. In Germany a telegram signed by one hundred GIs demanded:

> Are Brass Hats to be permitted to build empires? Why?. . . The evident lack of faith of our friends and neighbors is causing bitter resentment and deterioration of morale of men in this theater. It is to be hoped that our faith in democratic procedure is not finally lost.

From London, 1,800 enlisted men and officers of the Eighth Air Force demanded in a telegram:

> We want an explanation of delayed return. . . . *New York Times* says all U.S. troops who have not been redeployed have venereal disease or have volunteered. Ambiguous

> replies from congressmen and three canceled shipping
> dates do not help. We are tired, homesick, disgusted men
> . . . eligible for discharge December 1, 1945. In the
> European theater over thirty months.

At Andrews Field, Maryland, 1,000 soldiers and WACs[4] booed down their commanding officer when he tried to explain the delay in discharging them.

On January 9 the protests continued to spread. In Frankfurt, Germany, a demonstration of 5,000 was met at bayonet point by a small group of guards and some twenty were arrested. Five thousand soldiers demonstrated in Calcutta, India, and 15,000 at Hickam Field in Honolulu. In Seoul, Korea, several thousand soldiers issued a resolution stating, "We cannot understand the War Department's insistence on keeping an oversized peacetime army overseas under present conditions."

At Batangas, Philippines, 4,000 soldiers voted funds for full-page ads in U.S. papers demanding the removal of Secretary of War Robert Patterson. Simultaneously, a service newspaper issued in Hawaii bore the headline: "Patterson Public Enemy No. 1."

As the GI demonstrations developed greater organization and militancy, the protest within the United States deepened too. For months the troops had been rubber-stamping the mail sent to the United States with slogans such as: "Write your congressman—get us home" and "No boats, no votes." They had been carrying on a vigorous letter-writing campaign themselves, writing Congress, families, friends, and newspapers demanding they be released and asking others to write letters too. In the midst of the GI revolt, Sen. Elbert D. Thomas, head of the Military Affairs Committee, complained to the press: "Constituents are on [the congressmen's] necks day and night. The pressure is unbelievable. Mail from wives, mothers, and sweethearts demanding that their men be brought home is running to almost 100,000 letters daily." And that figure did not include direct appeals from the servicemen!

As the wave of mass demonstrations began to subside, the issues became broader and the soldiers protested against other abuses. On January 13, 1946, 500 GIs in Paris adopted a set of demands that a UPI dispatch characterized as "a revolutionary program of army reform."

The Enlisted Man's Magna Charta, as this program was called, demanded:

1. Abolition of officers' messes, with all rations to be served in a common mess on a first-come, first-served basis.

2. Opening of all officers' clubs at all posts, camps, and stations to officers and men alike.

3. Abolition of reserved sections for officers at recreational events.

4. Abolition of all special officers' quarters; requirement that all officers serve one year as enlisted men, except in time of war.

5. Reform of army court-martial boards to include enlisted men.

In addition, these soldiers demanded the removal of Secretary of War Patterson and elected a committee to present the Magna Charta to a Senate investigating committee scheduled to come to Paris two weeks later. Their final action was to establish the "GI Liberation Committee" and urge everyone to return to their units and organize for further actions.

## Officers unable to curb revolt

The administration of Democratic Party President Harry Truman was well aware that this massive GI revolt represented a serious challenge to the American military system. The army of World War II was not designed to permit criticism from the ranks. GIs who protested to their congressmen or participated in similar actions left themselves open to severe reprisals. But the massive character of the GI protests after World War II did not give the authorities much leeway. They could not victimize the leaders without stirring up even larger protests; at the same time, it was difficult to crack down on hundreds of thousands of men at once. Yet from the military's point of view, the situation was critical and the rapidly dissolving discipline had to be halted somehow. When privates and sergeants started requisitioning planes and jeeps to carry elected GI representatives to meetings with congressional investigating committees to talk about arranging transportation home, the officers knew they were in trouble.

The military used a soft hand at first. It merely "requested" that all complaints go through normal channels and imposed greater censorship on service newspapers. On January 11 the staff of the *Daily Pacifican,* an army newspaper in Manila, printed a statement that "new restrictions on freedom of expression imposed from above no longer enable us to bring full news and full truth to our GI readers."

Demonstrations spread geographically and broadened in scope, however, as indicated by the Paris meeting where the Magna Charta was proclaimed. Furthermore, the military had no intention of immediately living up to the promises it had made to pacify the soldiers. A UPI dispatch on January 16 announced, "The U.S.S. *Cecil,* carrying veterans to the United States, left Manila one-third empty, the Navy disclosed today." The Manila Soldiers' Committee on that same day, January 16, announced plans for another mass demonstration.

At this point the army decided things had gone too far. On January 17, Chief of Staff Gen. Dwight Eisenhower issued an order banning further soldier demonstrations. A similar order was issued by Gen. Joseph McNarney, commander of U.S. forces in the European theater, who stated that "further meetings may prejudice the prestige of the occupation forces."

Lt. Gen. Robert Richardson, Jr., ordered a court-martial for any soldier or officer in the mid-Pacific who continued to agitate for speedy demobilization, and confined to quarters three leaders of the Honolulu protests while the army "investigated" their remarks about the demobilization policy. Other minor reprisals followed, primarily in the form of transfers and threats of disciplinary action. Two men were removed from the staff of *Stars and Stripes* and sent to the island of Okinawa—considered the "Siberia of the American army"—for signing a joint protest against official muzzling of the paper.

Leaders of the Manila Soldiers' Committee were also transferred to Okinawa. One of these leaders was Sgt. Emil Mazey, former president of the militant Briggs Local 212 of the CIO United Auto Workers. Mazey had led the fight at the 1943 UAW convention to revoke the no-strike pledge and introduced a resolution to form a labor party. Although his recent history hasn't been so inspiring—Mazey is now secretary-treasurer of the UAW and UAW president Walter Reuther's right-hand man—the leading role he played in the "Bring us home" movement was indicative of the close interrelationship between the militant labor movement and the GI revolt at the end of the war.

## Workers in army and unions unite in struggle

A conscript army of millions depends on workers and farmers for its human raw material. Many of the men who served in the U.S. forces during World War II had been part of the great labor battles of the late 1930s and had been deeply affected by them. Thousands upon thousands of them had taken part in the CIO organizing drives that had transformed the labor movement, and they had learned the methods and tactics of mass struggle from their experiences. They had gained organizational ability and knew the power of united action. These lessons and the abilities of men like Emil Mazey were used with great effectiveness by the rebelling troops.

At almost every base where soldiers demonstrated, they also began to organize themselves. One news item after another reported that "the soldiers elected representatives to present their demands" or "the GIs chose a committee to plan further action." The highest point of organization was reached by the Manila Soldiers' Committee. On January 10, 1946, 156 delegates—each elected by different outfits in the Manila area, and representing 139,000 soldiers—held their first meeting. The delegates unanimously elected a chairman and adopted a program. The chairman appointed a central committee of eight, which according to the *New York Times* (January 11) included "two officers and is widely representative of creeds and backgrounds." In addition to Emil Mazey, the group was composed of a Black soldier from North Carolina, a white soldier from Alabama, a Jewish soldier, another of Italian background, and regional representatives from different sections of the United States.

The protesting soldiers were as conscious of their allies in the unions as Colonel Campbell had been when he reminded the soldiers that they were not working for General Motors. The outfit stationed at Batangas, Philippines, headed by Mazey, sent an appeal to the United Auto Workers asking for support. The cablegram was immediately made public by the union, and R.J. Thomas, then president of the UAW, issued a statement saying:

> I have the utmost sympathy for the outraged feelings
> of these GIs. The War Department having made a public
> commitment on the rate of discharge, that commitment
> should be carried out in full at least in nonhostile

countries. What soldiers and sailors do we need to occupy the Philippines? To ask the question is to expose how ridiculous it is.

The CIO council of Los Angeles called a demonstration in front of City Hall and then marched to picket the Chinese consulate on January 5 in order to show their support for the GIs' demands.[5] Many unions passed resolutions similar to the one passed by the Akron CIO council, which stated, in part:

> WHEREAS committees of soldiers on Manila and other fields of occupation have requested the aid of the labor movement in speeding their return to their homes and families;
>
> THEREFORE BE IT RESOLVED that the Akron Industrial Union Council joins in the soldiers' protests against the slowdown in demobilization and gives support to the millions of workers in uniform who long for peace, for home, and for a return to normal life; and
>
> BE IT FURTHER RESOLVED that the Akron Industrial Union Council is in full accord with the demonstrating soldiers who protest against being used to protect the wealth and foreign properties of such antilabor corporations as Standard Oil and General Motors.

These would be surprising words to hear from the U.S. labor movement today. But in 1946, while the troops were demonstrating abroad, the unions on the home front were engaged in a struggle for their very existence. These two fights were really twin battles in the same war.

From 1941 to 1945 the labor movement in the United States operated under severe restrictions imposed by the Roosevelt government with the assistance of the labor bureaucracy. A War Labor Board was established that settled all disputes by compulsory arbitration. Hours were lengthened and wages were frozen at the prewar level. A War Manpower Commission was established with control over some 2.3 million federal employees, in addition to workers in many of the industries classified as "essential." Civil liberties were severely curtailed and outspoken opponents of the war, such as leaders of General Drivers Local 544 in Minneapolis and members of the Socialist Workers Party, were jailed under the Smith Act.

All sizable political forces in the country—including both capitalist parties and the Stalinist and social democratic tendencies in the workers' movement—united in support of the war drive and in denouncing any attempts by workers and Blacks to protect their rights. The leadership of both the AFL and the CIO enthusiastically pledged to enforce a no-strike policy for the duration of the war. The field was wide open for the employers to launch an all-out attack on the gains made by the unions during the thirties. They were not long in taking advantage of this opportunity. As Adm. Ben Moreell, chief of the U.S. Bureau of Yards and Docks, told an October 1942 meeting of the AFL Building and Construction Trades Department in Toronto:

> I will admit that no one can live without labor, but they certainly can live without labor unions. They are living without them in Germany, and in Italy and in Japan, and they seem to be doing right well—at least for the moment—and, in my opinion, they will damn well live without them here if all of us don't get in there and pitch.

As the war drew to a close, the bitterness of the workers over wartime restrictions on their rights and the attempts to prevent them from using their organizations to fight effectively to defend themselves against speedup and safety violations reached explosive proportions. Within six months after V-J Day, there were more than 1.7 million men and women on the picket lines in the United States demanding shorter hours and wage increases to compensate for the soaring cost of living.

The employers, remembering the post–World War I era, hoped that the millions thrown out of jobs by the cutback in war production plus the millions of returning veterans could be used to break the unions. But the labor situation in 1945 was far different from that of 1919. The industrial union organizing battles of the 1930s had transformed the U.S. labor movement and begun to break down divisions from Jim Crow segregation within the unions, especially the CIO. Consciousness of the need for labor solidarity was qualitatively greater than following World War I.

Also during the war the unions had fought for and won job guarantees, full seniority rights, and other benefits for their members in the armed forces. Union consciousness among the leaders of the troop demonstrations helped to assure that veterans would be sympathetic to organized labor. As a result, returning veterans could not be mobilized as a strikebreaking force. They joined the picket lines instead, and fought with the unions for pay raises and a decent standard of living. It was a common sight to see men marching under banners that read: "This entire group—veterans of World War II," and "Veterans demand 18½ cents an hour."

## American troops refuse to crush colonial revolts

One of the most important results of the "Bring us home" movement was that it served notice that the U.S. troops would not allow themselves to be used against their brothers, either at home or abroad. The resolutions, letters, and telegrams written by the GIs give a clear indication of their mood. They protested being used to back what they themselves labeled American imperialism in the Far East and resented the role of protecting business interests abroad. What was behind these accusations? What were the American troops being used for that created such bitter resentment?

The events in Indochina are an excellent example. At the Potsdam conference it was decided that northern Indochina—what is today North Vietnam—would be awarded to Chiang Kai-shek's government as a sphere of influence, and that southern Indochina would be given to the British.[6]

Immediately following V-J Day, throughout all of Vietnam the anti-Japanese guerrilla forces led by the Viet Minh rode to power on the wave of a popular revolution and established the Democratic Republic of Vietnam.[7]

When the British occupation forces arrived in the south in September 1945, the Ho Chi Minh government welcomed them with open arms, only to find that the British had no intention of allowing Vietnam to become an independent nation. As the British were having their own troubles in India, Burma, and elsewhere, they returned control of the former French colony to Paris. French troops, collaborating with the Japanese officer corps that had only weeks before been "the enemy," launched a military campaign to wipe out the Vietnamese liberation army.

U.S. troops stationed in the Far East were well aware that Washington was aiding the effort to subjugate the Vietnamese people and reimpose French colonial rule. In addition to other material aid, many U.S. troopships, instead of bringing American soldiers home, were used to transport French reinforcements to Indochina. The New York newspaper *PM* carried the following story on November 12, 1945:

> Victory ships *Taos* and *Pauchag* [left Marseilles] October 31, each carrying more than 1,000 troops to Indo-China. The crewmen of the *Taos* signed on in New York with the understanding that they were to proceed to India to bring American troops home. Upon their arrival [in Marseilles] they learned they were also to be used to carry French troops to the Orient.
>
> Prior to the sailing of the *Taos* and the *Pauchag*, three other [U.S] Victory ships left France bound for French Indo-China carrying French troops.

The Indochinese story was repeated in the Netherlands Indies (Indonesia). With the conclusion of the war against Japan, the Indonesian nationalist forces set up a government and proclaimed their independence. The Dutch launched a campaign of extermination against them that can easily be compared to the atrocities committed by the United States in Vietnam today. An AP dispatch on December 30, 1945, pointed out that American aid to the Dutch was considerable:

> Two thousand American-trained and -equipped Dutch marines arrived off Batavia [Indonesia] today. Trained at Quantico, Va., Camp Lejeune, N.C., and Camp Pendleton, Calif., and fully supplied with American equipment, the marines are considered among the finest troops in the Netherlands armed forces.

An extremely bitter U.S. marine stationed in China described how the soldiers felt about American aid to the Dutch in a letter to his father read into the *Congressional Record* by Rep. Charles W. Vursell of Illinois on December 3, 1945. The GI asked:

> Is our navy to be used for ferrying supplies to the Dutch in Java or for getting our troops home?. . . We have a great fleet, but when a group of ships carrying United States troops are stopped at Hollandia,[8] the

troops ordered off, and supplies for Java put aboard, then it is time to call a halt. That little story we got from our First Marine Division news sheet.

Why was the U.S. government so concerned with the situation in the Netherlands Indies? The December 28, 1945, *United States News* explained it by saying:

> If the Javanese people are successful in their challenge to Dutch rule, the effect may be felt through a large part of Asia. Already, in Sumatra, Malaya, Siam [Thailand], and French Indo-China, there are evidences of unrest. . . . [The outcome of the events in Java] may determine what happens to the white man's position in neighboring areas inhabited by hundreds of millions of people.

The U.S. government was vitally concerned that these hundreds of millions of people and their countries, rich in natural resources, should not be lost to American economic domination. Several months before the war was over, Senator Tunnel, in a speech to Congress on February 15, 1945, spelled it out very clearly: "It would be an anomalous position for the United States to occupy, after putting up the men, the money, and enduring all the sacrifices which these mean, to have our country precluded from the markets we have liberated."

Events similar to those in Indochina and Indonesia occurred all over the Pacific, causing no small amount of bewilderment among American troops. A *New York Times* editorial on November 25, 1945, summed up the situation by saying:

> After the war the fires of nationalism broke forth and the resulting violence produced the paradox of 500,000 or more Japanese troops in Southeast Asia being deliberately kept under arms. . . . A British spokesman described them as "good troops" who fought well.

Gen. John Reed Hodge, the commander of American forces in Korea, told newsmen, "We had to leave the Japanese some small arms as protection against the Koreans since it is our duty to maintain order." He went on to add, "As a matter of fact the Japanese are my most reliable source of information." The brutality of the thirty-five-year Japanese colonial enslavement of the Korean people was notorious. The collaboration of U.S. military commanders with the hated Japanese officer corps to "maintain order" subjected U.S. GIs, who thought of themselves as liberators, to growing hostility.

Is it any wonder the American soldiers began to ask what they were being used for in the Pacific? Their allies suddenly became their enemies, and the officer corps of their former enemy became an ally.

**American GIs in China**

The most blatant use of American troops to suppress the colonial revolution occurred in China. At the end of the war national liberation forces under the leadership of the Chinese Communist Party were supported by the vast majority of the population, but Chiang Kai-shek's troops still controlled part of south China. The United States immediately moved in American soldiers to support Chiang and try to defeat the Red Army and suppress the vast revolutionary tide that was sweeping China. China was *the* great prize market of the Pacific, and men like Senator Tunnel did not want the United States to be excluded. According to the U.S. *Foreign Policy Bulletin* of November 30, 1945, the strength of Nationalist [Chiang Kai-shek] troops "is reinforced by the presence in north China of over 50,000 United States marines, who have made possible the entrance of Chungking divisions by holding certain cities for them until their arrival,[9] jointly patrolling these centers with the central [government's] troops thereafter, and guarding stretches of railway in the Peiping-Tientsin [Beijing-Tianjin] area."

How did the American soldiers feel about being used this way? A pilot in the Army Air Force at Kunming, China, wrote a bitter letter printed in the New York newspaper *PM* on December 2, 1945:

> We hear news reports daily over the radio about the Chinese war and the United States intention of staying out. We know now that our own country lies even as German Nazism lied to the German people.

He then went on to explain how American pilots were ordered to paint over the insignias on their planes before they flew missions.

The marine who wrote the letter that was entered in the *Congressional Record* on December 3, by Representative Vursell (quoted earlier), complained:

> Today General Wedemeyer stated that the marines would remain in north China until the "unsettled affairs are settled." . . . That means we are protecting the Chinese Nationalists from the Communists. That is the truth. We are preventing the Communists from controlling this area until the Nationalists get here. In short, we're deciding what government China should have. We are doing exactly what we told Russia not to do. No wonder they don't trust us in Russia.

After asking why Wedemeyer and Truman were using repatriation of the Japanese forces as a pretext for intervening in the Chinese revolution, the marine went on to say, "Dad, if I could only impress you with the bitter hatred that exists among the marines over this, perhaps you could understand how we feel."

### Why did U.S. troops revolt?

Today, U.S. troops are again fighting in Asia. They are being used in a colonial war even more brutal and destructive than those that followed World War II. Their morale is low, and most do not like what they are doing. But their resentment has not yet reached the heights it did following the Second World War. Why did soldiers refuse to fight then?

First of all, they were just plain tired of fighting. They had had enough and wanted out. But this does not adequately explain their rebellion. Had they been convinced of the need to fight, and had they felt it was their duty to crush the growing colonial revolution, they might have done so. However, five years of wartime antifascist propaganda could not be wiped out in a matter of months. World War II had been described as a war to liberate subjugated people from the yoke of fascism, as a war to destroy a system that practiced genocide, as a war against Nazi totalitarian oppression of the working class and its organizations.

At the end of the war, when the Allied powers tried to reconquer their former colonies, the American soldiers simply said, "No, this is not what we fought and died for." In an open letter to President Truman, an army psychiatrist warned of a "psychological breakdown" among the troops as a result of "being used to stifle the very democratic elements they hoped to liberate." Another reason the soldiers refused to go on fighting was that "the great fear" of communism had not been ingrained in them yet. The Soviet Union had been an ally in the fight against fascism, and the American troops were not convinced of the need to fight their former friends.

Another significant aspect of the troop revolt was the racist character of U.S. foreign policy, as well as the completely racist organization of the army. The World War II army was still totally segregated, assuring that Black troops would get the hardest and dirtiest menial assignments. One result of this was that many of the construction battalions assigned to the Pacific after the war were all-Black units. This meant that delayed demobilization hit them hardest.

Throughout the war, strikes and demonstrations against the Jim Crow practices of the military had mounted, as Black troops refused to accept that the "fight for democracy" meant postponing the struggle against racist abuses.[10] In March 1945, the Thirty-fourth Seabee Construction Battalion went on a hunger strike. In another instance, a Black unit of the Women's Army Corps went on strike at Fort Devons against menial labor assignments. The women were all court-martialed and sentenced to one year at hard labor and dishonorable discharges.

The Port Chicago disaster has gone down in history as one of the most grisly consequences of Jim Crow practices in the armed forces. Port Chicago, California, was a major supply depot on the West Coast, and the navy crews that loaded ships were almost entirely Black. On July 17, 1944, one of the ammunition ships being loaded in the harbor exploded, and 327 men died, the majority of them Black sailors. When those who survived were ordered back to work, most of them refused because of the obviously unsafe working conditions. In retaliation, the navy shipped hundreds of them off to the Pacific. In the largest mass trial in naval history, fifty were court-martialed on charges of conspiracy to mutiny. Every single sailor court-martialed received a sentence of at least eight years at hard labor, and several received as many as fifteen years.

Such examples give an idea of the racism that was institutionalized in the U.S. armed forces and contributed to the fact that Black troops were less than enthusiastic about being used to subjugate Asia. They knew from long, bitter history the racist attitudes that made wholesale slaughter of nonwhite people "acceptable" to the military command.

## Historical consequences of troop revolt

The mass demonstrations by soldiers to "Bring us home," brief as they were, had far-reaching consequences in the post–World War II era.

First, *they did force the U.S. government to demobilize the troops.* More than 12 million men and women were serving in the armed forces at the end of the war, and by midsummer 1946 this had been reduced to 3 million. By June 1947 it was down to 1.5 million troops. The strength of the revolt, its size and depth, and the massive support it received within the United States brought about a near disintegration of the American military machine. The government had no choice but to disband the large draftee army.

Second, the revolt gave notice to the military that the entire concept of a permanent, disciplined, peacetime conscript army could not be easily foisted on the American population. It is hard for our generation to comprehend this fact, but a conscript army never existed, except during large-scale wars, prior to our lifetimes! The charges made by the soldiers that they were being used as hostages in the military's campaign to force universal military training made it evident that the people of the United States wanted no part of such a program; it was two years before Congress could safely pass a law instituting universal military training. Madison Avenue advertising techniques had to swing into high gear before Americans "bought" the idea.

Third, the "Bring us home" demonstrations made it clear to the U.S. ruling class that a new political propaganda campaign was needed and had to begin immediately if working people in the United States were to be convinced of the worldwide "communist menace" and a military force rebuilt adequate to play a counterrevolutionary role wherever needed. When American troops rebelled at fighting the Chinese Red Army and "Communist" guerrillas, it was time for antifascist slogans to be replaced by anticommunist propaganda; the struggles of the colonial people for independence had to be transformed into "Communist conspiracies." In 1947 the new militarization drive began.

Fourth, the troop revolt postponed the entire postwar time schedule as proposed by British prime minister Winston Churchill and U.S. president Harry Truman for the war against the Soviet Union. The U.S. troops served notice that they would no longer fight, and it took time to generate the Cold War witch-hunt campaign, that reactionary assault on democratic rights whose target was the U.S. labor movement. As a result the Soviet Union gained a breathing space to recover from the war, to begin to rebuild its industrial capacity, and to develop into a nuclear power. The colonial revolution was able to advance and the United States was prevented from trying to militarily crush the Chinese revolution in the last half of the 1940s. The victory of the Chinese revolution in 1949 and the fact that the United States no longer had a nuclear monopoly contributed to the stalemate in Korea in the opening years of the 1950s. The U.S. government was prevented from gaining a military victory in Korea; the workers' state in the northern part of the country was not rolled back.

The stalemate in Korea and the unpopularity of that war in turn made U.S. working people loath to enter the Indochinese war on the side of the French in 1954. This, and the French government's decision to turn down the offer, were the main factors that prevented U.S. president Dwight Eisenhower from asking Congress for permission to use nuclear weapons already en route to Vietnam at the time of Dien Bien Phu in 1954.[11]

Fifth, the close ties that existed between the "Bring us home" movement and organized labor made it evident that millions of returning soldiers would not be antiunion and could not be counted on to serve as strikebreakers. This gave a tremendous boost to the labor struggles occurring in the aftermath of the war. It meant that the CIO made significant gains in the immediate postwar period. Although, the Cold War red-baiting campaign served to split and seriously weaken the unions, and the class-collaborationist leadership left them hog-tied, the unions were not physically destroyed as were the working-class organizations of Germany, Italy, Spain, and Japan under fascism. Had such a defeat occurred in the postwar era, the working class would probably not yet have recovered. A case in point is Spain, where thirty years after the defeat of the Spanish workers, the unions are only now beginning to rise again.[12]

Sixth, the struggle for Black rights was given impetus by the "Bring us home" movement. The inclusion of Blacks on the soldiers' committees and the interracial solidarity against the most blatantly racist aspects of American foreign policy served to encourage the freedom struggle within the United States as well as abroad.

And seventh, the "Bring us home" movement is graphic proof that the working class in the United States is capable of mass action on political questions, that working people are not concerned only about their stomachs.

Finally, the postwar troop revolt has tremendous significance for those of us involved in the antiwar movement today. One of the most important questions being discussed by Americans who are opposed to the war in Vietnam is the challenge of how to reach the troops, of how to explain to them why we are opposed to the war and why they should not have to fight and die in a war that is not in their interests. The "Bring us home" movement provides some answers to that question.

"Bring the troops home" is the demand the GIs themselves will raise. It is the slogan that will mobilize the hundreds of thousands of men and women we must mobilize in order to stop the war. Demands to negotiate a settlement, or to call a cease-fire, or to send in the United Nations—which for the soldiers simply means exchanging a brown helmet for one that is UN blue—will be recognized by the troops as a subterfuge for continuing the war.

When the GIs have had enough, they will want out and nothing less. They will then organize and mobilize themselves. But this will not happen in isolation. It can occur only as an integral component of deepening class struggle at home—when the GIs know that their determination is matched by the action of millions at home to achieve the same end. Then, history has already shown us, GIs can unite in the kind of actions that will shake the very foundations of U.S. foreign policy and the U.S. military machine.

As the number of conscript troops in Vietnam grows, their response to the demand "Bring the troops home" will increase.

We should raise this demand continuously and settle for nothing less. Our uncompromising fight at home will let them know they are not alone in their dissatisfaction with the war in Vietnam. To every man, woman, and child, every soldier and civilian, the antiwar movement must say, "Bring the GIs home now!"

# NOTES

1. September 2, 1945, the day the Japanese government formally surrendered to the Allied powers, became known as V-J Day (for Victory in Japan). V-E Day (for Victory in Europe) was May 7, 1945.

2. Legislation authorizing compulsory military training (conscription) was enacted in September 1940 and expired in March 1947. After a lapse of a year, peacetime conscription was instituted with the passage of the Selective Service Act in June 1948.

3. Japanese forces occupying the Philippines were defeated by the U.S. armed forces in 1944-45. The Philippines, however, remained a U.S. colony, as it had been since 1898. The U.S. government immediately launched a military campaign to crush the Hukbalahap (People's Army against Japan) guerrilla forces, which had organized resistance to Japanese occupation throughout the war. The guerrilla movement was advocating a sweeping land reform in the countryside. The Philippines was granted independence on July 4, 1946. The U.S. Army, however, continued to conduct military actions against the rebel forces, who were dispersed and defeated by 1954.

4. The Women's Army Corps, known as WACs, was a U.S. Army organization created in 1942 to enlist women for duty in the military. It was formally dissolved in 1978.

5. The bourgeois Kuomintang government at the time, led by Chiang Kai-shek and backed by U.S. military forces, was conducting a war against the revolutionary upsurge sweeping China.

6. A meeting of the leaders of the main victorious Allied powers (Washington, London, and Moscow) was held in Potsdam, Germany, in July-August 1945 to carve up conquered territory and assign economic and political domination to one of the victors.

7. The Viet Minh, the League for the Independence of Vietnam, had waged a struggle against Japan to free the country from colo-

nial rule. In September 1945, an independent Vietnam was proclaimed, with Ho Chi Minh as president. When French troops began to return that same month, the Viet Minh resumed the struggle, driving out the French in 1954.

8. Hollandia, today Djajapura, is the capital of the Indonesian province of West Irian.

9. Chungking (Chongqing), a city in south central China, served as the capital of the Chiang Kai-shek government during World War II.

10. For a week-by-week account of this struggle, taken from the pages of the *Militant,* see C.L.R. James et al., *Fighting Racism in World War II* (New York: Anchor Foundation, a Pathfinder book, 1980).

11. In April 1954 U.S. rulers discussed ordering massive bombing to help lift the siege of Dien Bien Phu, a village in northwest Vietnam where freedom fighters were nearing a decisive victory over the occupying French forces. U.S. aircraft carriers armed with nuclear weapons were deployed off the Vietnamese coast, and the Republican administration of Dwight Eisenhower considered their use as a possible part of the operation.

12. Following a three-year civil war, fascist forces led by Francisco Franco had ousted Spain's republican government by March 1939. The Franco dictatorship remained in power for more than thirty years.

# COMMUNISM, THE WORKING CLASS, AND THE ANTI-IMPERIALIST STRUGGLE

## LESSONS FROM THE IRAN-IRAQ WAR

Tehran, February 1979. Soldiers, workers, and students celebrate victory in insurrection against the brutal U.S.-backed monarchy in Iran. Washington and other imperialist powers welcomed Baghdad's expansionist invasion of Iran the following year as a potential deathblow to the Iranian revolution.

# AN EXAMPLE FOR REVOLUTIONISTS

## Introduction to two documents

*by Samad Sharif*

**H**OW DO COMMUNISTS in the oppressed countries of the colonial and semicolonial world conduct themselves in the face of imperialist-inspired aggression? How do they join in the anti-imperialist struggle along a line of march that advances the fight by workers and peasants against their capitalist and landlord exploiters, those at home as well as abroad?

These questions of revolutionary working-class strategy have been increasingly central to the worldwide struggle for national liberation and socialism in the twentieth century. And they have been sharply posed once again by events in the Arab-Persian Gulf since August 1990. What course should revolutionary-minded workers and peasants in the Middle East, including those in Iraq, have followed in face of the murderous war unleashed by Washington and its allies? How should they have responded to the Iraqi capitalist regime's expansionist invasion and occupation of Kuwait in August 1990? What course would they chart to advance the interests of the Kurds and Shiites, and of other exploited and oppressed toilers in Iraq, in the aftermath of Washington's devastation of the country and Baghdad's ongoing repression?

There is today no organized revolutionary current among the workers, peasants, and youth of Iraq. The workers' movement there has faced decades of harsh repression at the hands of the bourgeois Baathist regime of Saddam Hussein and his predecessors. Moreover, the weight of Stalinist and various bourgeois and petty-bourgeois nationalist misleaderships has disoriented many revolutionary-minded fighters in Iraq over the past half century.

At the opening of the 1980s, however, the political course and activity of a communist organization in Iran—the Workers Unity Party (HVK—Hezb-e Vahdat-e Kargaran)—did point the way not only for revolutionary organizations in the Middle East, but for revolutionists, anti-imperialist fighters, and communists throughout the world. We are reprinting here two resolutions outlining that communist course; they were adopted by the HVK and distributed in Iran during the opening years of the Iraqi regime's expansionist war against Iran in the early 1980s.

In putting these working-class perspectives into practice in Iran, the HVK sought to base its cadres in the factories and in the factory committees (*shoras*) established during the revolutionary overturn of the U.S.-backed monarchy in 1979. The HVK saw this turn to the industrial working class in Iran as essential to building a proletarian party, including winning workers who are women and from various oppressed nationalities.

Together with other workers, HVK members were among the draftees and volunteers who fought and died to defend the revolution against the Iraqi invasion. Some HVK members were excluded by the authorities from serving at the front because of their political views. These revolutionary workers joined volunteer production brigades in the factories to meet pressing war needs.

As EXPLAINED in the two resolutions reprinted here, the HVK held that an effective defense of the revolution necessitated deepening the struggles by workers, peasants, and oppressed nationalities against Washington and other imperialist powers and against the capitalists and landlords whose interests were guarded by the Islamic Republic, the bourgeois regime that was consolidating power after the toppling of the shah. Communist workers in Iran explained the need to press forward those struggles with the goal of preparing the toilers to establish a workers' and peasants' government in Iran.

Many of the HVK's members and leaders had been won to the communist movement prior to the revolution while in exile in the United States. In the mid-1970s revolutionary-minded opponents of the shah's regime formed an organization in exile called the Sattar League (named after Sattar Khan, a central leader from the Azerbaijani region of the 1905-11 Constitutional Revolution in Iran). The Sattar League played a leading role in the United States in mobilizing support for victims of the repression of the Iranian capitalist-landlord regime and the hated jailers, torturers, and assassins of the SAVAK, the shah's secret police. It organized to translate into Farsi and circulate as widely as possible fundamental Marxist works such as *The Communist Manifesto* and works by V.I. Lenin, Leon Trotsky, and others. As part of a common world movement with the U.S. Socialist Workers Party and cothinkers in other countries, the Sattar League trained an initial cadre in communist politics and prepared them to return to Iran to participate in the class struggle there when conditions made that possible.

That opportunity came with the ascending mass movement of Iranian workers, peasants, and youth that challenged the shah's regime throughout most of 1978, culminating in the February 1979 revolutionary overturn of the monarchy. The cadres of the Sattar League returned to Iran in January 1979 and formed a communist organization together with other returning exiles from Europe. By late 1979 this organization had taken the name Revolutionary Workers Party (HKE—Hezb-e Kargaran-e Engelab).

Iraq's capitalist rulers had seen the overturn of the shah's regime and weakening of the old Iranian armed forces as an opportunity to seize oil-rich Khuzistan Province and the Shatt-al-Arab waterway and nearby port facilities just across Iraq's long eastern border with Iran. At the same time, they feared the political example of the Iranian revolution on workers and peasants in Iraq and its destabilizing impact on capitalist-landlord regimes throughout the region.

In October 1978, as the mobilizations in Iran to bring down the shah reached massive proportions, Baghdad had expelled Ayatollah Ruhollah Khomeini from Iraq, where this opponent of the Iranian monarchy had been living since his forced exile from Iran in 1964. Following the revolution, the Iraqi regime opened its doors to top officials of the shah's regime and members of the officer corps of the SAVAK and Iranian army; it helped them establish base camps from which to organize armed operations and coup attempts against the new government in Tehran.

While welcoming these counterrevolutionary forces from

Iran, in the spring and summer of 1980 the Iraqi regime up-rooted and expelled tens of thousands of Iraqis, alleging they were of Iranian origin. Those forced into exile were mostly from southern Iraq and were followers of the Shiite branch of Islam. (Although Shiites constitute a majority of the Iraqi population, they have historically faced systematic discrimination by the ruling capitalist and landlord layers in Iraq, the majority of whom are Sunni Muslims. In Iran the majority, both of the population and the ruling layers, are Shiite.)

O N SEPTEMBER 22, 1980, Baghdad launched an invasion of Iran. While Washington and its imperialist allies claimed official neutrality in the conflict, they in fact encouraged the Iraqi aggression against Iran. The world's wealthiest and most powerful capitalist rulers hoped the assault against Iran would deal a deathblow to the revolution and make possible the reimposition of a regime there directly subservient to imperialist interests. The U.S. rulers' approach was aptly described a few months prior to the opening of the war by the *Wall Street Journal:* "With revolutionary Iran creating so much tension in the Middle East, Washington would clearly welcome any role the Iraqis might play in stabilizing the Persian Gulf."

Baghdad was armed throughout the war by several imperialist governments—Paris in particular, as well as Rome, London, and others. Just on the eve of the invasion, Iraq signed a deal for some $4.5 billion in arms from the French and Italian governments.

The monarchies in Saudi Arabia, Kuwait, the other Gulf states, as well as virtually all other governments in the Arab League (except for Algeria, Libya, and Syria) backed Baghdad's war effort against Iran. Many provided substantial financial support to help Iraq sustain its military operations.

In the fall of 1980, Iraqi forces rapidly occupied more than 4,000 square miles of Iranian territory. They captured the strategically important southern town of Khorramshahr and several others, including the outskirts of Iran's main oil-refining and port city of Abadan. By the end of the year, however, the Iraqi advance had ground to a halt in the face of resistance by Iranian workers, peasants, and youth who volunteered in their hundreds of thousands to resist this imperialist-backed effort to crush the Iranian revolution and stop the toilers of Iran from defending and advancing their gains.

By May 1982 Iran's defending forces had recaptured Khorramshahr in a major battle and within a few months had driven the Iraqi army back across the border. Iranian troops themselves crossed into Iraqi territory.

It was in this political context that the two resolutions reprinted here were drafted and circulated in Iran. The first document, from December 1980, resulted from a split in the HKE under the pressures of the war. With the onset of the Iraqi invasion, the HKE had recognized the aggression as a danger to the revolution and had joined in the political and military mobilization to turn it back. As the toilers had no army of their own to organize the resistance, HKE members served in the armed forces of the Islamic Republic.

Toward the end of 1980, a majority of the HKE leadership began to retreat from a communist line of march. They turned away from an orientation toward building a revolutionary proletarian party in the working class and workers' shoras. They increasingly gave up the fight for independent working-class political action. These HKE leaders began to portray the capitalist government in Iran as a progressive regime that at least to some degree represented the interests of the oppressed and exploited working people—a course that rapidly led them to abandon the revolutionary perspective of replacing this regime with a workers' and peasants' government.

An important initial manifestation of this turn away from a revolutionary course was a reversal of the organization's previous position of unconditional support to the struggle for national self-determination by the oppressed Kurdish people in northwest Iran and opposition to the war being waged against them by Iranian government troops. A layer of HKE leaders began to argue that the Kurdish organizations were carrying out military provocations and the government was merely responding as part of its resistance to the Iraqi aggression.

Those in the HKE leadership who maintained a communist course responded that far from strengthening resistance to Baghdad's invasion, Tehran's war against the Kurdish people was actually weakening it. Since the Kurds had long faced brutal national oppression at the hands of the Iraqi regime as well, they were potentially a powerful ally—on both sides of the border—in the fight against Baghdad's aggression. Instead, the Iranian government was diverting troops and matériel to wage war against the Kurds and denying them their national rights.

By December 1980 all those in the HKE who remained on a communist line of march had been expelled. In January 1981 they joined with other former HKE members who opposed the majority leadership's retreat from a communist course to form a new organization, the HVK. The December 1980 resolution was one of the HVK's founding documents.

The second HVK document is from July 1982, shortly after the reconquest of Khorramshahr by Iranian troops. While supporting the entry onto Iraqi soil as a necessary defensive military measure in the war, the HVK stressed the importance of standing in complete solidarity with the Iraqi workers and peasants, clearly affirming respect for Iraq's national sovereignty, and giving uppermost consideration, with regard to each military move inside Iraq, to the political perceptions and class interests of the Iraqi toilers. The resolution also pointed to the mounting obstacles created by the Iranian government to an effective defense of the revolution against imperialism and its regional allies.

THE WAR GROUND on for six years following the Iranian victory at Khorramshahr, with the Iraqi regime eventually regaining the edge militarily. Hundreds of thousands lost their lives on both sides, as Baghdad launched air and missile attacks on cities in Iran; used chemical weapons in the fighting, including against Kurdish civilians living in Iraq; and sought to strangle Iran economically by attacking commercial shipping in the Arab-Persian Gulf. A U.S. naval armada intervened in the Gulf against Iranian defense efforts, under the cover of an invitation from the government of Kuwait.

The Iranian regime, for its part, retaliated by launching attacks on population centers in Iraq and relying on military tactics that resulted in the needless slaughter of tens of thousands of young Iranian workers and peasants who selflessly volunteered to go to the front to defend the revolution. On the home front, the pressures on working people increased as a result of the military, economic, and social policies of the capitalist regime. The government crackdown on the right to political expression and organization intensified, with mounting numbers of jailings and executions of political activists. The factory shoras were pushed back and dismantled. Attacks accelerated against women fighting for greater social and economic equality. The government rejected implementing an agrarian reform to meet the peasants' demands for land and the wherewithal to till it.

In August 1988 Tehran agreed to a cease-fire on terms favorable to the regime in Baghdad, leaving the entire Shatt-al-Arab waterway and some other Iranian territory in Iraqi control. Two years later, in mid-August 1990, the Saddam Hussein regime finally signed a permanent settlement with Iran in order to relieve military pressures on its eastern flank in face of the U.S.-organized buildup in Saudi Arabia and nearby waters. That agreement ceded back to Iran all the territory conquered by Baghdad in the course of the bloody eight-year-long war. In September 1990 the Iraqi and Iranian governments restored diplomatic relations.

## The Struggle Is My Life
### by Nelson Mandela

"My political beliefs have been explained . . . in my autobiography, *The Struggle Is My Life*."
— Nelson Mandela, July 1989

New expanded edition includes four speeches following Mandela's release from prison. 281 pp., $12.95

## Nelson Mandela: Speeches 1990
### *'Intensify the Struggle to Abolish Apartheid'*
Speeches in South Africa, Angola, and Britain highlighting the new stage in the struggle against apartheid. 74 pp., $5.00

## Thomas Sankara Speaks
### *The Burkina Faso Revolution 1983-87*
Speeches and writings by the assassinated president of Burkina Faso tell the story of the revolution that unfolded in this West African country. Internationalism and support for the struggles of peasants, workers, and women were hallmarks of Sankara's revolutionary leadership. 260 pp., $17.95

## Women's Liberation and the African Freedom Struggle
### by Thomas Sankara
Explains the origins of women's oppression and the struggle needed to end it, with special attention to women in Africa. 36 pp., $2.50

**PATHFINDER**  SEE PAGE 2 FOR DISTRIBUTORS

# WAR, REVOLUTION, AND THE FIGHT
# FOR A WORKERS' AND
# PEASANTS' GOVERNMENT

I N COLLUSION with U.S. imperialism, the government of Iraq
has launched a military attack against Iran aimed at over-
throwing the Islamic Republic. Imperialist attacks against the
Iranian revolution have thus entered a new stage. The aim is to
prevent further expansion of the revolution in the region; sever
the anti-imperialist dynamic of the Iranian revolution; regain
imperialism's lost positions; and reverse the trend of world
revolution, which the Iranian revolution has infused with new
strength.

A movement of mass resistance against this military attack is
shaping up.

1. Imperialism is seeking to reverse to its favor the world
relationship of forces, which the Iranian revolution altered to the
detriment of imperialist interests. This is the attempt of a declining power. The attacks take place from a position of weakness.

Iraqi president Saddam Hussein seeks to prevent the expansion of the Iranian revolution, a revolution that has inspired the
revolutionary spirit of the toiling masses of Iraq, who are moving toward the overthrow of his regime. The mass mobilizations
and anti-imperialist actions of the Iranian people have attracted
the attention of the toiling Arab masses. This is especially true
of the mobilization of millions on Jerusalem Day.[1] A reflection
of this process is the support given to Iran in the war against

---

*This resolution was drafted in December 1980 and adopted at the
January 22-24, 1981, convention of the Hezb-e Vahdat-e Kargaran
(Workers Unity Party). The English translation, originally published in
the April 20, 1981, issue of* Intercontinental Press, *has been checked
against the Farsi original and revised.*

ENDNOTES FOR THIS ARTICLE BEGIN ON PAGE 324.

Iraq by the governments of Libya, Syria, and Algeria (which are themselves under pressure from imperialism and the Israeli government). On the other hand, reactionary Arab governments that have no base among their own masses take refuge in imperialism's embrace, becoming more isolated from the people.

The hopes of all counterrevolutionaries in the area hinge upon U.S. imperialism, which has stepped up its military preparations for an attack against the revolution. From Turkey to Egypt, the U.S. military presence has increased, and U.S. warships are headed toward the Persian Gulf. The confrontation between the revolution and imperialism has reached the critical stage of war.

The Soviet Union and China, two large workers' states that could and should have supplied immediate and ample military, economic, and political aid to defend the revolution against Iraqi attack, have so far taken a "neutral" position. The Stalinist ruling bureaucracies in these countries have thus cowardly endangered the position of the workers' states vis-à-vis imperialism.

2. Because of the war, the Iranian revolution has entered a new stage. Contrary to the expectations of the leaders of the counterrevolution, the Iranian army met the challenge of the Iraqi attack. The Islamic Republic was not overthrown. The people rose to defend the revolution.

City toilers and the Arab masses of Khuzistan[2] fought the invaders alongside the Pasdaran[3] and the soldiers. They see their liberation intertwined with independence from the imperialist yoke and unity with the Iranian revolution.

Youth all across the country enlisted to be sent to the front. Groups of twenty-two formed by the Baseej-e Mustazafin[4] received military training sessions with the aid of community mosques.

At the initiative of the masses, centers of armed resistance are now being formed across the country—in factories, communities, villages, and schools. The army of twenty million is forming from the grass roots of society,[5] and the masses are exerting increasing control over activities in the factories, communities, and villages.

All across the country people are collecting necessary goods and sending them by truck to the front. To ensure fair distribution of goods, community *shoras* [neighborhood committees] are increasing their activities. Through the organization of the masses, the revolution is preparing itself for a long and cold winter.

Along with the formation of independent organizations of the masses, mass mobilizations—both political and military—are taking place. Millions are once again marching in the streets in defense of the revolution and against imperialism. Workers, peasants, women, oppressed nationalities, and tribal people view this war as their own; they see that safeguarding their gains and freedom is dependent on victory in the war.

O<small>N NOVEMBER</small> 4 students all across the country took part in a demonstration called by the Muslim Students Following the Imam's Line, displaying the revolutionary spirit of the young generation in defense of the revolution.[6] The participation of women in nationwide mobilizations and in mass organizations is particularly noteworthy. The vigilance of the masses and the determination of working people to defend the revolution have attracted segments of the wavering middle class and has neutralized other layers that were tending toward the counterrevolution.

The mass demonstration of armed men and women on October 25 in Esfahan and the demonstration in Tabriz during the October religious holiday—the Feast of Ghadir—are symbols to the world of the power and determination of the masses to defend the revolution. The great fighting spirit of the masses corresponds to the vital duty of victory in this war. For the first time since the February 1979 insurrection, the masses are once again arming themselves. The committees formed prior to the insurrection—with the new title of community shoras—are being reinstituted for the purpose of rationing food and other necessary goods.

Once again, mass mobilizations of millions are taking place. These actions are similar to those that took place after the occupation of the U.S. spy den, which inscribed the main enemy of the revolution in the consciousness of the masses. The experiences of the past stages of the revolution are thus coming together. At this stage, the workers' shoras are the only mass organizations from the past that have retained within them the continuity of the revolution.[7]

3. The war has accelerated class polarization—a polarization between those who want to carry the war against Iraq and imperialism through to the end and those who want to compromise. Workers consider this war their own and are prepared for death and sacrifices. Protection committees[8] and centers of resistance have been formed in the factories.

Workers are demanding mobilizations for military training and have declared their readiness to go to the front. Workers go to the front through a variety of channels, such as the groups of twenty-two organized by the Baseej-e Mustazafin. In many factories workers have voluntarily donated one or several days' wages for aiding the war effort and refugees from the war. Workers' shoras are being built and strengthened in this struggle. Thus the position of the working class in the revolution is being strengthened.

Immediately following the outbreak of war, the Federation of Islamic Shoras demanded that military mobilization and resistance centers be formed within the factories, villages, and communities. In addition, they demanded that action be taken to exercise complete control over the capitalists, middlemen, and hoarders who are profiteering off the distribution of foodstuffs and other vital goods. They also demanded control over distribution and sale of goods produced in the factories through the workers' Islamic shoras, and pointed to the need to create consumer cooperatives everywhere in order to prevent the counterrevolution from sabotaging distribution.

The Islamic Shoras of Workers declared in a statement: "The Islamic Shoras of Workers in Productive and Industrial Units must, with full force, implement their control of the factories and work energetically to prevent any conspiracies or disruption by agents of the previous regime, capitalists, and the counterrevolution; maximize production; and remain on the alert to nip in the bud any form of conspiracy."

The Federation of Islamic Shoras has created the Military-Ideological Mobilization staff and is demanding that centers for resistance and preparedness be formed in the factories. The federation has also demanded that war news be broadcast in different languages by the Iranian media, in order to neutralize the lying propaganda being spread by imperialist broadcasts and to bring news about the struggle of our oppressed people to the ears of toilers around the world.

A message issued by the workers of the oil industry appealed to workers of the world to defend the Iranian revolution against the Iraqi military invasion. They asked Iraqi oil workers to apply the lessons of the struggle against the deposed shah and to form strike committees against Saddam Hussein's regime.

The Federation of Eastern Shoras, which had been declared illegal prior to the war, has renewed its activity.[9] Despite the fact that the local *komiteh*[10] had prevented these shoras from being active, the federation—meeting in the mosques—has now renewed its activities involving the original representatives. In the factories it has distributed leaflets on the war and in defense of the revolution. Resistance units are being organized through the shoras, and Islamic Associations in the factories are being trained to be sent to the front.

THE REVOLUTIONARY SPIRIT of the toilers in time of war is the opposite of the idleness, cowardice, and sabotage of the capitalists and landowners. From the start of the war between Iran and Iraq, the class polarization has deepened and the camps of the antagonistic classes have become more clearly defined.

In contrast to the Arab toiling masses—who are defending the revolution—the reactionary sheikhs, tribal heads, and feudalists of Susangerd welcomed the Iraqi attack.[11] Capitalists and big landowners began hoarding goods and sabotaging production and distribution. From the very beginning they fled the war zones. The Friday Imam[12] of Tehran, in his first Friday prayer address after the war began, warned the capitalists who had fled the war zones that they should not expect to return to the homes and wealth the toilers had fought to defend. This statement reflects the deep sentiment of the masses against the capitalists.

The capitalists and factory managers have attacked the living standards of the workers, using the war as a pretext. In some factories they have issued directives abolishing workers' yearly vacations and housing loans. Using the pretext of the need for food and money for the front, they have canceled the noontime meal [that workers were provided with]. The capitalists are able to carry out these actions by exploiting workers' dedication. The bosses remain opposed to workers' shoras and seek to prevent them from expanding and carrying out activities. At the same time, the capitalists are also disrupting the national economy through hoarding and jacking up prices.

Workers have reacted with patience and self-sacrifice to the capitalists' economic austerity program, viewing the measures as required by the conditions of war. At the same time, however, the balance of forces has shifted to the workers' favor against the capitalists. Because while the capitalists and management disrupt production, the workers actively participate in both production and the mass resistance movement.

Workers protest the fact that management and those in charge create obstacles to prevent mobilizations and military training. In the situation of direct confrontation with imperialism created by the war, the toilers take these questions seriously. That is why they have shown patience concerning austerity measures but make clear their disapproval when management refuses to allow mobilizations, creates obstacles to military training, or creates obstacles with regard to other questions related to the war and disruption of the economy. Therefore, workers have begun their own independent mobilizations. This serves to strengthen the workers' shoras in the direction of transforming them into independent executive units of the workers.

In wartime, the crises and chaos of the capitalist economy weigh heavily on the shoulders of working people, their standard of living declines, and the capitalists try to solve the crisis of their system by imposing an austerity program on the workers. Under these conditions, the struggle for the demands of the Transitional Program continues.[13] This includes the struggle for an increase in wages to match the rate of inflation and for a reduction in working hours and the addition of new work shifts, with no reduction in pay. Workers are using their political and social weight in the struggle to defend their living standards, and they are doing so without being accused of disrupting production.

4. The allies of the working class—poor peasants, oppressed nationalities, women, and youth—have also risen against the attacks of the Iraqi regime. The quick reaction of the masses shows that the revolution is alive and the toilers are ready to defend the achievements of the insurrection.

An important sector of the participants in the October 25 armed demonstration in Esfahan were peasants from the villages around the city who participated carrying their tools. The peasants from around the city of Mashhad also demonstrated against the Iraqi aggression. The Arab masses from the cities and villages fought so heroically alongside their Pasdar and soldier brothers that they prevented the immediate fall of the cities of Khorramshahr, Abadan, Dezful, and Ahwaz. Although the Iraqi forces took over sections of Abadan and Khorramshahr, the people of those cities, especially the Arab population, played a decisive role in the heroic armed resistance.

THE PROPAGANDA of Saddam Hussein falsely claims to recognize the right of self-determination for the Arabs [in Khuzistan]. But this is simply a case of Saddam using bourgeois nationalism against the revolution. The oppressed Arab nationality in Khuzistan has shown that it ignores such demagogy. Instead they see their freedom as inseparable from their liberation from imperialism, in unity with the Iranian revolution as a whole. The struggle of the Arab masses has defused the effects of such propaganda even in the Arab countries of the region such as Syria and Libya, as well as in Palestine.

In Kurdistan, where the government has not halted its fratricidal war, the Kurdish people have nonetheless supported the Islamic Republic against the offensive by the Iraqi regime. Groups of Kurdish workers have donated one day's wages to the front, and in some Kurdish cities street demonstrations have taken place in defense of Iran and against Saddam Hussein's regime. Kurds in Iraq, who for years have suffered under the oppression of the Iraqi government, are decisively struggling against the military invasion of Iran by Iraq and are fighting against Hussein's regime.

In Tabriz, as a result of the casualties from the bombings of

318    *Workers Unity Party*

the oil refinery and other industrial centers, the workers and toilers of Azerbaijan have felt the need for mobilization and resistance against imperialism and the Iraqi regime. The 30,000 people at the funeral for the martyrs of the bombing of industrial and civilian centers in Tabriz showed their hatred toward the Iraqi regime and U.S. imperialism. It marked the first time in six months that the oppressed Azerbaijani nationality stood up decisively against imperialist attacks. This is an indication that despite the efforts of the bourgeoisie, the anti-imperialist movement in Azerbaijan has not been diverted. The street mobilizations of the Azerbaijani people during the [religious] days of Ghadir, Tasua, and Ashura, and the march by the armed forces of both the army and the Pasdaran, were even more extensive.

Also, the people of Sistan and Baluchistan, plus 6,000 tribesmen and border dwellers in Bushehr, organized demonstrations in defense of the revolution.

THE OPPRESSED NATIONALITIES, in solidarity with one another and with the Iranian revolution, are struggling for their liberation from the imperialist yoke. The perspective of strengthening their unity in order to further advance the anti-imperialist struggle has now become more of a reality.

The solidarity of women and their declared readiness to go to the front is widely raised. Women have participated in first-aid groups and in the collection of goods and money being sent to the front. Women have also announced their readiness to receive military training. In some factories women have actually participated both in military training and in other aid for the front. In the October 25 Esfahan demonstration, women participated armed with household utensils, such as forks and knives, declaring their readiness to go to the front. War has created the conditions for women to participate more in the activities of society and to see the perspectives for their liberation as tied to the victory of the anti-imperialist movement.

The youth whose term in the army ended in 1977—that is, those trained by the shah to fight in Dhofar[14]—and those slated to be drafted have widely declared their readiness to go to the front. In the first few days of the call for service of those youth whose enlistment had ended in 1977, more than 24,000 young men registered for the front.

Youth in Khuzistan gathered round the army barracks, especially in Ahwaz, and demanded to be armed. The youth in the trenches began making Molotov cocktails and other weapons, and in many border areas they have played a key role in military battles.

Neighborhood committees and community shoras have once again been formed with broad participation by young people. And just as during the [February 1979] insurrection, they are participating in guarding the communities and distributing necessary goods. The groups of twenty-two formed by the Baseej-e Mustazafin with the aid of local mosques—groups formed to provide military training—are mostly composed of and organized by the youth.

5. The limited political-military policy of the government in the face of the Iraqi invasion does not in the least measure up to the needs of safeguarding the revolution, or to the degree of dedication and sacrifice shown by the working masses.

The unprecedented determination and militancy shown by the people in defense of the Islamic Republic has not met with a positive reaction from the government. In some cases the government has even expressed its displeasure. For example, the neighborhood shoras that were formed in the throes of the revolution were pronounced illegal in a directive issued by the Ministry of State. The Ministry of Education and Welfare declared that classes were to be held on November 4.

The widespread slogan "Give us arms" is not welcomed by the government. At the same time, Ayatollah Montazari in his Friday speech in Qum reflected the masses' anxiety when he declared, "The army commanders are not moving ahead and acting decisively." The capitalist government fears the specter of the armed oppressed masses engaged in war with imperialism.

The divisive policies of the government of the Islamic Republic with regard to the oppressed nationalities have dealt a blow to the unity of the anti-imperialist bastions. The approach of the oppressed nationalities to this war is a sign of the revolution's depth and of the high level of consciousness of the toilers of the oppressed nationalities. This solidarity with defense of the Iranian revolution occurs despite many blows, constant attacks, and divisive moves by the regime. This is particularly true with regard to the civil war in Kurdistan, imposed on the Kurds by the regime of the Islamic Republic. The national rights of the Kurdish people are still being denied. And government leaders have insisted that the army and Pasdaran remain in Kurdistan for the war on the home front. Military units are collecting weapons and disarming the people. In a statement addressed to the peasants of Kurdistan, the army and the Pasdaran threatened severe punishment for those who are cooperating with Kurdish political groups by providing foodstuffs.

In Kurdistan, as in other parts of Iran, the guns must be aimed at imperialism and its junior partners. The fratricidal war in Kurdistan should be ended and a military unity formed between the Kurds and the armed forces (the army and Pasdaran), so all weapons are pointed at imperialism. Confronting imperialism and the Iraqi military offensive, the Kurdish people must be armed—not disarmed. And self-determination must be granted to Kurdistan. It is only by taking such steps that the real divide between the forces of the revolution and of the counterrevolution will be clearly defined.

The government's incapacity to solve the problems of war and revolution has been revealed before the masses. It has made no concerted effort to arm the people. It has failed to implement economic planning to counter high prices, unemployment, and hoarding, which are accelerating in face of the government's hesitation to monopolize foreign trade. The Komitehaye Haft Nafare have made no progress in distributing land to poor peasants or in improving conditions in the villages.[15] Steps have been taken to limit the activities of political parties and newspapers that support the revolution and to impose censorship.

The people ask, "Why are the Pasdaran not being armed with heavy weapons?" The Pasdaran in Kurdistan ask, "What are we doing in Kurdistan when the revolution is being attacked by the government of Iraq?" The obscure points surrounding the negotiations to free the hostages were posed in the same context.[16] Because of the lack of open diplomacy and the government's secret negotiations with foreign officials, the people are questioning the government's actions. The toilers ask, "When we are the ones who bear the heavy burden of war, why is it that scarcity and poverty are divided so inequitably and are imposed only on us, while the capitalists and big landowners continue to exploit and live in comfort?"

At this new stage of the revolution, the masses look to the leaders less and less. They more and more take solutions to problems into their own hands, carrying out their own mobilizations and building their own organizations. For a victory in the war, the masses are more open to listening to working-class and anti-imperialist solutions. There are tremendous possibilities for a revolutionary workers' party.

The people regard the government of the Islamic Republic as being in the same trench with them in this war. As long as the working class is not prepared to take on the command of the war, it defends the revolution under the military command of this government.

POLITICAL PREPARATIONS for creating a workers' and peasants' government are on the agenda today. These preparations include maintaining the political independence of the working class; presenting a proletarian program counterposed to the debilitating and divisive policies of the capitalist government; struggling for military and political mobilization of the masses; fighting for unification and expansion of workers' shoras; struggling for the right to self-determination of the oppressed nationalities, essential in strengthening the anti-imperialist barricades; struggling for land and better conditions for the poor peasants; and fighting against poverty.

6. The military offensive of Iraq and imperialism, aimed at beheading the Iranian revolution, has aroused mass resistance. This in turn has created immense possibilities for implementing the party's program, strengthening our links with the working class, and expanding our ranks by winning fighters from the working class and the youth. Our political analysis of the new stage of the revolution emanating from the war, and the program that we as revolutionary socialists put forward for a victory in this war, would be incomplete without specifying the next step in party building.

At the present stage of the class struggle, war and revolution have intertwined and found a joint destiny. The working class participates in this war to win victory for its own revolution, to implement its own demands, and to obtain leadership of the masses. The working class views this war as its own war and struggles to bring it to victory. The political preparations of the working class for the creation of a workers' and peasants' government are being carried out in the midst of this war and by participation in these struggles.

The conclusion from this reality is that our party, too, must mobilize along with our class. We must consciously and actively participate in the mass resistance movement and struggle toward achieving political leadership of this life-and-death battle. Consequently, now more than ever it is imperative that party cadres and militants of the Young Socialist Organization participate in all mass activities and struggles. This includes the political, economic, and military mobilizations and organizing efforts at the front, as well as participation in the front lines of battle. This would be a conscious decision by the party and the youth organization in consideration of all our possibilities. In this way, the most militant elements of our class will be attracted to the party, and our program will be presented to the entire class.

Therefore, at this conjuncture carrying through the turn toward the industrial centers and working-class neighborhoods, and participating in the resistance movement through the shoras and the workers' organizations, is a more pressing and vital task for our party than ever before. Our comrades should be in the heart of the working class—in the factories and in the front lines of their struggles. In this way our revolutionary link with the working class becomes a reality—a link, based on the program of socialist revolution, that creates the conditions for building a mass party. The party's success in the future depends on the bold implementation of this next step.

THE MOST IMPORTANT tasks of the proletariat under the conditions of the war with Iraq, and to promote a victory against imperialism, are concretely as follows:

• Unconditional material defense of the Islamic Republic

against the military intervention of the imperialists, the military offensive of the Iraqi regime, and the conspiracies of the internal and foreign allies of the Iraqi regime. Immediate military mobilization and combat training of all volunteers for the front through the Baseej-e Mustazafin, with the government providing whatever is needed. Building the liberation army of twenty million. Arming the workers' and peasants' shoras and community shoras. Creating and expanding workers' centers of resistance. Providing industrial centers with weapons for defense. Arming the Pasdaran with heavy military equipment. For democracy and shoras in the army and Pasdaran.

• Confiscating the wealth of the capitalists and landowners who, in the critical conditions of war, sabotage the economy through hoarding, swindling, and fraud. Immediate punishment of the hoarders and confiscation of their goods, under the exigencies of war conditions. Legislation and implementation of progressive taxation. A complete monopoly of foreign trade. Subordination of production to the needs of war. Nationalization of banks and insurance companies under the control of shoras of workers and employees. Production, distribution, and price controls under the supervision of workers' and peasants' shoras and community shoras. Rationing of basic foods, as well as of fuel oil, with distribution controlled by the community shoras in order to give priority to the toilers. Free housing and government financial aid to refugees from the war, along with military training and arming of the refugees.

• For further expansion and unity of factory shoras. Against dissolution of the shoras. For recognition of the shoras by the government. For independence and democracy of the shoras. Increase production by adding new work shifts and employing the unemployed. For a forty-hour workweek. Increase wages to keep up with the rate of inflation. Against firing members of political groups; all purges [of counterrevolutionaries and saboteurs] should be carried out through the workers' shoras. Abolish Article 33 of the labor code, which allows firings for no reason. Labor laws should be drawn up by the workers' shoras.

• Increase agricultural production; implement Section C of the land reform law, which calls for land of the big landowners to be divided among the peasants; land and ample resources for poor peasants.

- The right to self-determination for oppressed nationalities. Self-determination for Kurdistan. For an immediate end to the civil war imposed on the Kurdish people. For a military alliance with the oppressed nationalities against imperialism and the Iraqi military offensive.
- Equal rights for women; military training and arming of women.
- Freedom for anti-imperialist and working-class political prisoners.
- Mobilization and utilization of all resources toward victory in the war. For the expansion and unification of the shoras of workers, peasants, soldiers, and Pasdaran.
- For a workers' and peasants' government.

# NOTES

1. Jerusalem Day is the last Friday of the month of Ramadan. Since the revolutionary overthrow of the shah it has become an annual event in solidarity with the Palestinian revolution and the struggle against the Israeli government.

2. Khuzistan is an oil-rich province in southwest Iran with a large Arab population. It lies to the north of the Arab-Persian Gulf and borders Iraq.

3. The Pasdaran, or Revolutionary Guards, are a militia formed after the revolution under the Islamic Republic. As the bourgeois regime in Iran consolidated power and pushed back the advance of the revolution, the Pasdaran evolved increasingly into a volunteer component of the Iranian armed forces.

4. The Baseej-e Mustazafin (Mobilization of the Oppressed) was an organization to mobilize students and young peasants and workers as volunteers for the front. It was led by the Pasdaran.

5. The "army of twenty million" was a popular slogan for arming the population to fight the war.

6. November 4, 1980, was the first anniversary of the occupation of the U.S. embassy in Tehran. When the U.S. government invited the deposed shah to the United States in the fall of 1979, working people and revolutionary-minded youth in Iran saw the move as a major new step toward organizing a counterrevolution. When the

shah had fled the country twenty-six years earlier, it was recalled, the CIA had organized a coup through the U.S. embassy to return him and his brutal regime to power. On November 4, 1979, Tehran students occupied the embassy—popularly dubbed "the spy den"—as an expression of the popular determination to defend the revolution. Massive mobilizations took place in Iranian cities and villages.

7. Strike committees emerged in the factories prior to the general strike that began in the fall of 1978 and paralyzed the shah's regime during its final months. When industries reopened following the shah's overthrow in February 1979, workers organized committees called *shoras* that performed various functions of trade unions and fought for expanded workers' control in the factories.

8. Protection committees were units formed by workers in factories to defend production facilities against sabotage and counter-revolutionary bombing.

9. The Federation of Eastern Shoras encompassed some of the shoras in the factories in the eastern part of Tehran.

10. Komitehs were neighborhood organizations that sprang up during the revolutionary struggle against the shah's regime. Under the Islamic Republic popular participation eroded and they increasingly took on the character of police instruments.

11. Susangerd is a town in Khuzistan near the Iraqi border, located in an area with a predominantly Arab population.

12. The Friday Imam is the religious official who delivers a sermon prior to the mass prayer meetings held on Friday in the Islamic Republic. Such sermons often include an assessment of the political events of the week.

13. The Transitional Program was one of the founding documents of the Socialist Workers Party. Written by Leon Trotsky and adopted by the SWP following extensive discussion in 1938, it was later adopted as part of the program of the Fourth International, the world communist organization the SWP was then a part of. It is contained in *The Transitional Program for Socialist Revolution* (New York: Pathfinder, 1977).

14. Dhofar is a region in Oman, on the Arabian Peninsula south of Iran, where in 1975 the shah sent troops to help the monarchy there defeat an insurgent guerrilla movement.

15. In response to pressure from the peasants, the Islamic regime set up the Komitehaye Haft Nafare (Committees of Seven) to look into granting deeds to peasants who had already occupied land, and to implement a limited land reform. The committees came under criticism for allegedly transgressing Islamic laws safe-

guarding private property. Gradually their operations were greatly curtailed.

16. After a series of negotiations with Washington, the Iranian government released the embassy hostages in the summer of 1981. Exact terms of the agreement were never made available.

# In Defense of Socialism

**FOUR SPEECHES ON THE 30TH ANNIVERSARY OF THE CUBAN REVOLUTION**

### by Fidel Castro

Fidel Castro argues that not only is economic and social progress possible without the dog-eat-dog competition of capitalism but that socialism is the only way forward for humanity. Castro also discusses Cuba's role in advancing the struggle against apartheid in Africa. 142 pp., $12.95

# Cuba's Rectification Process

Two speeches by Fidel Castro reorienting the Cuban revolution toward the path championed by Che Guevara. In *New International* no. 6, $10.00

# 'Cuba Will Never Adopt Capitalist Methods'

### by Fidel Castro

Cuba's rectification process and the historic victory in Angola over apartheid's army. 30 pp., $2.50

# Building Socialism in Cuba

### FIDEL CASTRO SPEECHES, VOLUME 2

Speeches spanning more than two decades trace the fight of the revolutionary vanguard to deepen the proletarian course of the Cuban revolution. 367 pp., $19.95

*M*any of the articles that have appeared in the pages of
New International are also available in Spanish or French

# Nueva Internacional
*Una revista de política*
*y teoría marxistas*

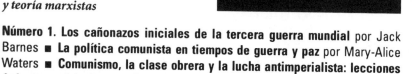

**Número 1. Los cañonazos iniciales de la tercera guerra mundial** por Jack Barnes ■ **La política comunista en tiempos de guerra y paz** por Mary-Alice Waters ■ **Comunismo, la clase obrera y la lucha antimperialista: lecciones de la guerra Irán-Iraq** por Samad Sharif ■ 290 págs. $10.00 ■ *Disponible en el verano de 1991.*

**Número 2. Che Guevara, Cuba y el camino al socialismo** ■ Artículos por Ernesto Che Guevara, Carlos Rafael Rodríguez, Carlos Tablada, Mary-Alice Waters, Steve Clark y Jack Barnes ■ *Disponible en el otoño de 1991.*

# Nouvelle Internationale
*Une revue de théorie*
*et de politique marxistes*

**Nº 1. Le communisme et la lutte pour le gouvernement révolutionnaire populaire,** articles de Mary-Alice Waters et Joseph Hansen ■ **Leur Trotsky et le nôtre,** par Jack Barnes ■ 256 pages, 10$

**Nº 2. La révolution à venir en Afrique du Sud,** par Jack Barnes ■ **La terre, la classe ouvrière et la lutte pour le pouvoir au Canada,** par Michel Dugré ■ 200 pages, 10$

**Nº 3. Le deuxième assassinat de Maurice Bishop,** par Steve Clark ■ **Le processus de rectification à Cuba,** discours de Fidel Castro ■ 230 pages, 10$

**Nº 4. Les premières salves de la troisième guerre mondiale,** par Jack Barnes ■ Cuba dénonce la guerre de Washington à l'ONU ■ 150 pages, 10$ ■ *Disponible à l'été de 1991.*

*Distributed by PATHFINDER, see page 2 for addresses*

# WORKERS AND PEASANTS IN IRAN
# AND IRAQ HAVE IDENTICAL INTERESTS

T HE FORCES of the Islamic Republic started their advance inside the Iraqi borders on July 13. According to various reports, these forces have advanced about twenty kilometers onto Iraqi soil, and fighting is continuing. This advance reflects a new stage in the war imposed by the Iraqi regime.

The recent advance has taken place after the continued counterrevolutionary aggression of [Iraqi president] Saddam Hussein, following Iran's great revolutionary victory in recapturing Khorramshahr.[1] In recent weeks, Iranian cities in the war zone—including Abadan, Ahwaz, Khorramabad, and others—have been savagely bombarded by the Iraqi regime's long-range cannons or by Iraqi aircraft, leaving hundreds killed or wounded. Furthermore, according to official reports, parts of Iran are still under Iraqi military control.

On July 14, the joint communiqué of the army and the Revolutionary Guards explained the aims of this advance, called Operation Ramadan: "This operation has started with the Twelfth Imam's blessings and directives, under the leadership of his worthy successor, Imam Khomeini. The aim is to complete the defense of the Islamic Republic, to prevent renewed aggression by Saddam and other American mercenaries, to protect the cities of the Islamic Republic from enemy fire, and achieve the goals that have been set. This operation is now proceeding intensely against the deceived enemy and Saddam's aggression."

In response to these advances, the imperialists have escalated their counterrevolutionary propaganda. All the positions on Op-

---

*This statement was adopted by the National Committee of the Workers Unity Party of Iran on July 23, 1982. The English translation, originally published in the October 4, 1982, issue of* Intercontinental Press, *has been checked against the Farsi original and revised.*

*ENDNOTES FOR THIS ARTICLE BEGIN ON PAGE 333.*

eration Ramadan announced so far by imperialist officials and their press have condemned the Islamic Republic. They indicate the imperialists' great apprehension over the recent advances.

The White House, despite its so-called neutrality in this war, has announced that "the United States, in the Iran-Iraq war, is willing to aid those countries in the region that see themselves threatened." Reports from the foreign press indicate that the United States is planning to stage new military maneuvers in the region.

Israeli prime minister [Menachem] Begin has announced, "If the Iranian forces are planning to advance toward Jerusalem, we will crush them midway." Officials of European governments, while making known their apprehension about Operation Ramadan, considered the advance made by the Iranian forces as a substantial threat to the economic interests of capitalist Europe in Iraq and the Middle East.

Radio Cologne has reported, "According to the finance ministry of the Federal Republic of Germany, the new Iranian operation is a serious threat to Germany's export market in the Middle East." The British newspaper *Financial Times* has declared: "The Iranian victory has changed the balance of forces in the region."

The *New York Times* has said, "Ayatollah Khomeini's Iran, in a messianic manner, has shouted for liberation from the foreign yoke and has plans for an expanded republic based on Islamic principles." And the American press, citing President Reagan, has said, "The aggression of the Iranian forces against Iraq can threaten the entire Persian Gulf area."

A recent United Nations Security Council resolution calls for establishing a cease-fire between Iran and Iraq, placing a so-called peacekeeping force in the war zones and opening negotiations between Iran and Iraq. This indicates that in addition to the world's imperialist governments, the Moscow bureaucracy is also worried about the continued victories against Saddam by the Iranian revolution.

Under these circumstances, imperialism's puppet governments in the region—such as those of Egypt, Saudi Arabia, and Jordan—continue to provide financial and military aid to the Iraqi regime. Hosni Mubarak, the Egyptian president, has asked for an emergency meeting of Arab leaders to discuss the Iran-Iraq war.

At the same time, leaders of counterrevolutionary pro-imperialist groups outside the country, such as Ali Amini and Shahpur Bakhtiar,[2] as well as the leadership of the People's Mujahedeen Organization—which is tending more and more in the direction of the imperialists' policies[3]—have all condemned the Iranian advance onto Iraqi soil.

AGAINST ALL THE statements, propaganda threats, and counterrevolutionary activities of the imperialists, of the region's reactionary regimes, of counterrevolutionary royalist and reactionary groups, and of reformist currents, revolutionary socialists declare their position on the recent advance of the forces of the Islamic Republic and the new stage of the war against Saddam's aggression to be the following:

1. The war imposed on Iran by the Iraqi regime is still the axis separating the ranks of revolution and counterrevolution in the region.

On one front of this war are the world's imperialist countries and the reactionary regimes of the region. They are trying to behead the Iranian revolution through Saddam's counterrevolutionary aggression.

On the other front are the dispossessed and oppressed masses of Iran: workers, peasants, and other toilers who, after the overthrow of the shah's regime, are struggling to completely eradicate the imperialist yoke and do away with imperialist exploitation, including exploitation by the capitalists and big landowners—the principal base of imperialism in Iran.

2. The recent advance of the Islamic Republic's forces onto Iraqi soil has taken place in defense of the revolution. It is a principled move that must be supported by all workers and peasants and their organizations, especially by the workers' shoras.

Continuation of the war on Iraqi soil does not change the character of this war. In order to defend its revolution, the proletariat, just as before, will fight the Iraqi regime's aggressive army on Iraqi soil, under the military leadership of the Islamic Republic. The extent of the advance inside Iraqi borders will be determined according to military criteria.

3. At this stage of the war, winning Iraqi toilers to the perspective of unity with the Iranian revolution has crucial importance in the struggle to eradicate the yoke of imperialism. In the present situation, victory in the war and the advance of the revolution are impossible without winning over the Iraqi toilers to the side of the Iranian revolution. Therefore, with the advance of the forces of the Islamic Republic—the bulk of them composed of volunteers from the anti-imperialist toiling masses, the Baseej-e Mustazafin—the proletariat will struggle for the rights of the Iraqi toilers in all areas.

Fulfillment of this fundamental task—winning over the Iraqi toilers—is crucial at this stage of the war. If for any reason the Iraqi workers and toilers see the Islamic Republic's forces inside Iraq as an army of foreign invaders, and thus mobilize and struggle against these forces, the proper political response will be to halt the advance inside Iraq and make the corresponding political decisions.

Objectively the war against Saddam's aggression has a class character: workers and peasants in Iran and Iraq have identical interests and are in one common front against the Iraqi Baathist regime.

4. The Saddam Hussein regime, which has been the most important instrument of imperialist intervention against the Iranian revolution in the recent period, is still a great danger for the struggles of the Iranian workers and toilers, and consequently for the Iraqi toilers as well. It must be overthrown.

The struggle to overthrow this regime is mainly up to the workers and peasants of Iraq. And it is also the right of the oppressed Iraqi people to choose their government freely. Nonetheless, entrance of the forces of the Islamic Republic into Iraq can be a powerful aid to the Iraqi workers and peasants in their revolutionary struggle to overthrow the yoke of Saddam and his imperialist supporters.

5. Since the Islamic Republic is a capitalist regime whose point of departure is not the interests of the toilers, it always creates obstacles to the defense of the revolution and its extension. Therefore, while struggling decisively against the aggression of Saddam's army under the military leadership of the Islamic Republic government, the proletariat continues to maintain its own political independence in this stage of the war.

It puts forward its own revolutionary program against the capitalist government and politicians.

The proletariat, just as before, condemns at every stage all the obstacles and sabotage created by the Islamic Republic against the defense of the revolution. By struggling for its own demands and those of its allies, the proletariat prepares for the establishment of a workers' and peasants' government.

This means that at this stage of the war as well, in order to strengthen the revolution's barricades against the Iraqi regime and imperialism and win over the Iraqi toilers to the perspective of unity with the Iranian revolution, the proletariat raises the necessity of deep-going revolutionary measures to eradicate the yoke of imperialism and its fundamental bases: the sabotaging capitalists and big landowners.

The proletariat emphasizes demands such as land reform; a state monopoly of foreign trade; workers' control of production; granting the rights of oppressed nationalities, including the oppressed Arab nationality, and ending the fratricide in Kurdistan; ending the limitations on the Baseej-e; and extending political liberties. The proletariat also demands the extension of workers' and peasants' shoras to all fields of the revolution.

# NOTES

1. Khorramshahr, the last major stronghold of the Iraqi forces that had occupied parts of western Iran since September 1980, was liberated by Iranian troops on May 24, 1982.

2. Ali Amini and Shahpur Bakhtiar were former prime ministers under the shah's regime.

3. Originating in the 1960s as an urban guerrilla movement against the shah, the People's Mujahedeen announced in June 1981 that it was "launching war" against the Islamic Republic. Thereafter it increasingly fell in step with the imperialist-orchestrated campaign against the Iranian revolution. During the Iran-Iraq war the organization used Iraqi territory to mount armed attacks against Iran.

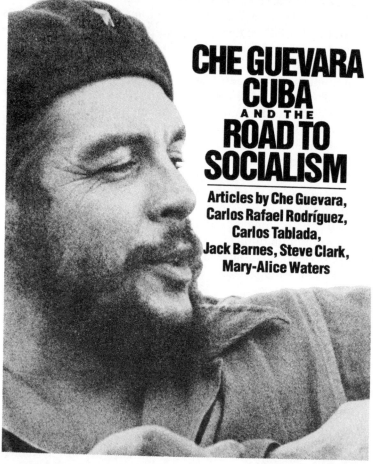

# New International

## A MAGAZINE OF MARXIST POLITICS AND THEORY

# CHE GUEVARA CUBA AND THE ROAD TO SOCIALISM

Articles by Che Guevara,
Carlos Rafael Rodríguez,
Carlos Tablada,
Jack Barnes, Steve Clark,
Mary-Alice Waters

*New International 8 $10.00*

**Their Trotsky and Ours: Communist Continuity Today** by
Jack Barnes ■ **Lenin and the Colonial Question** by Carlos
Rafael Rodríguez ■ **The 1916 Easter Rebellion in Ireland:
Two Views** by V.I. Lenin and Leon Trotsky

*New International 1 $8.00*

**The Working-Class Fight for Peace** by Brian Grogan ■ **The Aristocracy of Labor** by Steve Clark ■ **The Social Roots of Opportunism** by Gregory Zinoviev

*New International 2 $8.00*

 **Communism and the Fight for a Popular Revolutionary Government: 1848 to Today** by Mary-Alice Waters ■ **'A Nose for Power': Preparing the Nicaraguan Revolution** by Tomás Borge ■ **National Liberation and Socialism in the Americas** by Manuel Piñeiro

*New International 3 $8.00*

**The Crisis Facing Working Farmers** by Doug Jenness ■ **The Fight for a Workers' and Farmers' Government in the United States** by Jack Barnes ■ **Revolutionary Perspective and Leninist Continuity in the United States** Resolution of the Socialist Workers Party ■ **Land Reform and Farm Cooperatives in Cuba** Document and Speeches

*New International 4 $9.00*

**The Coming Revolution in South Africa** by Jack Barnes ■ **The Future Belongs to the Majority** Speech by Oliver Tambo ■ **Why Cuban Volunteers Are in Angola** Speeches by Fidel Castro

*New International 5 $9.00*

**The Second Assassination of Maurice Bishop** by Steve Clark ■ **Cuba's Rectification Process** Two Speeches by Fidel Castro ■ **Land, Labor, and the Canadian Revolution** by Michel Dugré ■ **The 50-Year Domestic Contra Operation** by Larry Seigle

*New International 6 $10.00*

DISTRIBUTED BY PATHFINDER, SEE PAGE 2 FOR ADDRESSES

# Join the Pathfinder
# Readers Club

*Pathfinder is the leading international publisher of books and pamphlets by revolutionary fighters whose struggles against imperialism, racism, exploitation, and oppression point the way forward for humanity.*

*Over 250 titles by Karl Marx, Frederick Engels, V.I. Lenin, Leon Trotsky, Rosa Luxemburg, Ernesto Che Guevara, Fidel Castro, Malcolm X, Farrell Dobbs, James P. Cannon, Joseph Hansen, George Novack, Evelyn Reed, Nelson Mandela, Thomas Sankara, Maurice Bishop, and others.*

*Joining the Pathfinder Readers Club makes it easier and less expensive to get the books you want to read and study.*

*For a U.S.$10 annual fee, members of the Readers Club will receive a 15 percent discount on all Pathfinder books and pamphlets at any Pathfinder bookstore around the world. You will also enjoy even higher discounts on special selected titles.*

*To join anywhere in the world, contact the Pathfinder bookstore nearest you or send U.S.$10 to Pathfinder, 410 West Street, New York, NY 10014.*

## PATHFINDER READERS CLUB